The Book of

PROVERBS

Titles from Kevin Swanson

Family Bible Study Guides

Genesis: A Family Bible Study Guide
Psalms I: A Family Bible Study Guide
Psalms II: A Family Bible Study Guide
Proverbs I: A Family Bible Study Guide
Proverbs II: A Family Bible Study Guide
Proverbs III: A Family Bible Study Guide

Christian Curriculum Project

Christian Classics Study Guide — Volume I
Great Christian Classics: Five Great Narratives of the Faith
Christian Classics Study Guide — Junior Level

The Second Mayflower
Upgrade: 10 Secrets to the Best Education for Your Child

Visionary Manhood (Mp3 / CD)
Vision for Generations (Mp3 / CD / DVD)
Reforming the Church in the 21ˢᵗ Century (CD)
Family Economics Conference Audio Series (Mp3 / CD)
Family Economics Conference Video Series (DVD)

The Book of

Proverbs

God's Book of Wisdom

BOOK III: PROVERBS 24–31

Kevin Swanson

Scripture quotations are taken from the
King James Version

Published by
Generations with Vision
10431 South Parker Road
Parker, Colorado, 80134
www.generationswithvision.com

For more information on this and
other titles from Generations with Vision,
visit www.generationswithvision.com or call 1-888-839-6132.

CONTENTS

INTRODUCTION   1

PROVERBS 24

The Evil of Fearing Evil   7

How to Build a Home   8

Wisdom for Men and Nations   10

Fools and Malevolent People   13

Major Priorities—Preserving Life
and Wisdom   18

God's Vengeance vs.
Our Vengeance   21

Evil Men and Revolutionaries   24

Righteous Judges   27

Honesty Under Duress   29

Creating a Household Economy   32

Maintaining Good Neighborly
Relationships   35

What a Slothful Home Looks Like   37

PROVERBS 25

Scientific Inquiry   39

In the Presence of Kings   41

Dealing with Conflict   44

A Word Fitly Spoken   46

Empty Promises and Persuasive
People   49

Too Much of a Good Thing   52

Three Analogies/Metaphors   54

Loving Your Enemy   58

Brawling and Backbiting   60

The Gospel to the Heathen Lands   62

When the Righteous Crumble   63

Narcissism and Hedonism   64

Controlling Your Temper   66

PROVERBS 26

Honor for a Fool   67

What Causes Calamity   69

Fools—Corporal Punishment   72

Fools—Apologetics with Atheists   73

Fools—Lousy Employees   76

Fools—Handling Truth Badly   77

Fools—Unworthy of Honor   79

Fools—Not Impacted by Truth   80

Fools—Can't Get Away
with Foolishness   81

Fools—Can't Stay Away from
Foolishness   83

What's Worse Than a Fool   84

The Slothful Man   85

Jumping into the Wrong Fight   88

Practical Jokes   90

Gossip and Contention   92

Thin-Coated Religion   94

The Salesman Out for Himself   95

What Goes Around,
Comes Around   97

Lies Hurt People   98

PROVERBS 27

Boasting and Praise   100

The Incredible Destructive
Capacity of Envy   102

True Friends and Grateful Hearts   104

Leaving Home   107

Friendship   109

The Reproach of a Rebellious Son   112

Foreseeing the Evil Day   113

Trusting Strangers 116

Cursing Your Friend and Plaguing
Your Family 118

The Power of Friendly Affirmation 121

Reaping and Sowing 122

The Horror of the Human Heart 124

How to Receive Praise 127

Fools vs. Children 128

Stewarding Your Flocks and Herds 129

God's Blessing for Faithful Sons 132

PROVERBS 28

Two Forms of Fear 134

Bureaucracies and Petty Tyrants 137

Losing the Antithesis 140

Rules and Relationships 142

What's Most Important 144

Seeking Wealth or Helping
the Poor? 146

Respecting God's Law 148

Destroying Christian Families 149

Wisdom Better than Riches 151

Righteous Men Produce
Good Countries 152

The Christian Life 154

Frightful Tyrants and
Foolish Tyrants 157

The End of the Violent and
Perverse Man 160

A Faithful Working Man 163

Bribes and Greed 166

Flattery and Robbing Parents 167

Trust in God and Humility 169

Happiness and Charity 172

When the Righteous Decrease 173

PROVERBS 29

The Chronic Rebel 175

Good Leaders and Bad Leaders 177

Uncommitted, Loose Lifestyles 179

Social Stability 180

The Snares of Flattery and Sin 182

Caring for the Poor 185

Scorn and Mockery 186

Contending with the Foolish 188

When the Wicked Turn Violent 189

Wise and Truthful Speech 191

The Problem of the Poor 193

The Rod and Reproof 196

Transgression Metastasis 198

Faithful Parenting 200

God's Law is Vision 201

Sullen Silence and
Garrulous Gabbers 203

Adopting a Son 205

Anger and Pride 207

The Domino Effect of Sin 210

Fearing Man and Fearing the State 211

Who's Abominable to Whom? 213

PROVERBS 30

The Character of a Wise Man 215

The Right Source of All Truth 218

Godliness with Contentment 220

Handling Business and Familial
Relationships 223

The Curse of a Fallen World 228

How God Views
Dishonoring Teens 229

Four Wonders 231

Four Disruptions to the
Social Order 235

Four Unassuming Wise Things 237

Four Smooth Operators 239

Bridle the Tongue 241

PROVERBS 31

A Mother Disciples Her Son 244

Leadership and Alcohol 246

The Business of True Statesmen 250

The Virtuous Woman 252

Economic Productivity 256

Charitable Endeavors 259

Overseeing the Needs of
Her Household 261

A Hopeful Outlook on Life 264

The Use of Her Tongue 265

A Competent Household Manager 268

Commendations for a
Virtuous Wife and Mother 270

The Fundamental Thing 271

INDEXES

Subject Index 277

Scripture Index 291

Topical Index 301

INTRODUCTION

When my wife and I set out to educate our children at home, we were confused by the hundreds of theories on the education of children that were presented at homeschool conventions. Parents who love their children really want to find the best *paideia*, or education, for their children, and we were no exception to that rule. So it was always with some frustration that we would attend the next seminar on yet another philosophy or technique of education. Eventually, we turned back to the Word of God.

Our first assumption, of course, is that God is very smart. Assuming that it is He Who is behind the marvelous design we call the "human being,"—and anyone that can create things like human beings has to be, well, *smart*—we turned to His Word. Thankfully, He didn't leave us without operating instructions. But, like most fathers who try to assemble a toy on a child's birthday and usually turn to the manufacturer's instructions as a last resort, most people do the same thing when trying to figure out how to operate a human being. So finally, I picked up the Word of God and looked up the word "education" in the concordance. Naturally, the Bible doesn't have much to say about things like schools and education. But I broadened my search to "knowledge," "understanding," and "wisdom," and found that God has actually dedicated an entire book of the Bible to the subject of transmitting knowledge, wisdom, and understanding to a child. This book—Proverbs—is Education/Knowledge/Wisdom 101, authored by God and conveyed by Solomon, who was endowed with supernatural wisdom by God Himself. This gives us both the method and content of a child's education. It is a textbook for young men (and young women), and provides the basic corpus of knowledge God requires of young people.

Now one of the things that takes many educators by surprise is that the book of Proverbs does not have a great deal to say about geography, geometry, or geology. So why would the Creator of the Universe—Who, as I mentioned, is very smart—neglect something as important as the Pythagorean Theorem in His textbook? I submit that it is because geometry is, in the grand scheme of things, not all that important. When it comes to the education of a child, it is faith and character that are primary in God's estimation. These are the warp and the woof of the *paideia* of a child if we are speaking of the Lord's nurture and admonition (Eph. 6:4). They constitute the foundation, the studs, and the drywall in the "construction of a child." And geometry, geography, and geology are only the wallpaper. To attempt to teach geometry apart from character is akin to trying to place wallpaper on walls that do not exist, and that would be a prime example of an "exercise in futility."

As you read this book, you will learn God's basic truths, addressing the classical philosophical divisions of epistemology, metaphysics, and ethics. You will grapple with the tensions of determinism and human responsibility. You will find an entire system of priorities for life's ethics and purposes. You will find the basic constituents of a biblical social system, as well as principles for sound economics, government, and general business management. The book gives insight into the proper views of theology, anthropology, and human psychology. Any education program will give you a categorical system by which you can understand life, history, truth, ethics, and reality. Some systems have a semblance of truth, but all will fundamentally be compromised if they do not begin with the book of Proverbs and the fear of God (Prov. 1:7).

Having taught in public and private schools, and seeing myself as an academic of sorts, I was at first uncomfortable with the book of Proverbs. A pastor once told me that there are those who teach the fear of God, faith, and character, and then there are those who teach reading, writing, and arithmetic; and according to his viewpoint, those who teach the book of Proverbs are not the same as those who teach chemistry and mathematics. But as time went on, I became convinced that Christians must not tolerate this dualism. This separation of the fear of God from the chemistry class has produced an ungodly, secular science and yielded the terrible destruction of science in our "brave new world." The separation of the fear of God from social studies and political science has undermined the Christian foundations of this country and created tyranny (Prov. 28:2; Neh. 5:15). I place the blame for the failure of the Christian faith in the West, the widespread apostasy, and the breakdown of our Christian institutions, at the feet of those who separate the knowledge of chemistry and political science from the fear of God. Christian teachers who teach chemistry should be less interested in their students learning chemistry as they are in their students *learning the fear of God through chemistry* (Prov. 1:7, 23:17). Thus, we do not separate discipleship from education, or the fear of God from "academic subjects." The same principle applies to Christian parents.

The book of Proverbs is presented by "Solomon the son of David, king of Israel... to give subtilty to the simple, to the young man knowledge and discretion" (Prov. 1:1–4). Therefore, every college in America—and certainly every Christian college—should require its students to memorize the book of Proverbs, because it is God's book on the education of every young person. It is God's theory on education, presenting both content and methodology in living color. If teaching colleges took up this theory, they would effectively be training future fathers and mothers to teach their children the lessons of life. Reading through the book of Proverbs, you can practically hear the writer's exhortations, warnings, and instructions filled with urgency, tenderness, severity, passion, and love. It may not fit in well with the professional teaching methodology you will learn in teaching colleges, but those theories have incorporated more from men like Dewey, Rousseau, and Plato than they have from the Christian God.

The Core Curriculum

As I considered these things, I became deeply convicted that my children were better educated in Saxon Math and the laws of grammar than they were in the book of Proverbs. They did not know the many lessons found in the book of Proverbs. So over the subsequent ten years, I set about the task of expositing, illustrating, and applying every verse in the book of Proverbs four times through. I assembled those lessons in this Family Bible Study Guide on the Proverbs with the hope that others might benefit from my efforts.

In our education program for our children, this book is the core, and sets the stage for all other academic subjects they pursue. It will prepare them well for any and all of their economic and "career" pursuits. But it will give them far more than this. It will prepare them for their own family discipleship program, for relationships within the church, and for a living, vital walk with God. By the time my children leave my home, I would like them to be familiar with every verse of this book.

God's Book on Life is for Everyone

Genesis is God's history book of the world, the book of Psalms is God's book on worship, the Gospels are God's autobiography of the Savior, and the book of Proverbs is God's book on life. Every child raised in a Christian family should be thoroughly versed in this book before leaving home. But also, when discipling any person into the Christian church for the first time, after teaching them the Gospel of Matthew and the book of Genesis, I would recommend a complete study of the book of Proverbs for the catechumen, or disciple. The Great Commission requires teaching others to observe and to practically apply every command of Christ to their lives. God's Book of Wisdom and life must never be neglected in this task.

Using this Study Manual

This Study Manual includes modern day applications and illustrations to help illuminate the meaning of the text. It also provides helpful family discussion questions to open up more shepherding opportunities for parents. Of all of the books of the Bible, the book of Proverbs will lead to the most family discussions on the application of God's truth to everyday situations and problems.

I recommend reading the Bible text in unison as a family before dad or mom reads the exposition and application questions. It is also a good idea to end each lesson with another reading of the text, in order that everybody will remember the lesson. Each proverb is packed with weighty considerations and is worthy of careful thought and meditation throughout the day.

You may also wish to memorize the verse together, as our family does. First, we repeat the verse three times together. Then, each person has an opportunity to say the verse, with Dad or Mom correcting as he goes. Each time a new family member recites the verse, the others should be encouraged to recite it silently in their minds. By the time everybody has recited the verse, everyone should be able to say it together in unison, without error. We have used this method of memorization since we first learned it from Pastor Henry Reyenga about five years ago, and it has worked marvelously for our family.

For the biblical text I have used the classic King James Version with only minor changes, replacing "thee" and "thou" with "you" and "your," and changing the older verb forms, for example, changing "seeketh" to "seek."

PART 212 ~ THE EVIL OF FEARING EVIL
Proverbs 24:1–2

Be not envious against evil men, neither desire to be with them.
For their heart studies destruction, and their lips talk of mischief.

This verse expands upon the lesson from Proverbs 23:17—do not desire the company of wicked men or envy their pleasures. When confronted by evil men, there are two temptations that assail us. On the one hand, we may become angry and fretful towards them. We may fear their evil machinations and think for a moment that they act out from under God's all-controlling hand. While opposing evil men and their wicked deeds is not a sin, becoming anxious and fearful is dangerous. There is a psychological reaction known in present day parlance as the "Stockholm Syndrome." In 1973, bank robbers in Stockholm, Sweden held a few people hostage for a period of time. Over the length of the ordeal, the hostages began to express adulation and positive support for their captors. In other words, their fear turned into worship. It is also interesting that this nation's top leaders and populace are far more supportive of the Muslim religion today than they were before the terrorists destroyed the twin towers in New York in 2001. Very often the ethical systems of those who have little integrity will collapse in the face of powerful, wicked men who are self-confident in their agenda.

Then, there is this second temptation in regards to evil men, and that is to join forces with them. The familiar quip, "If you can't beat them, join them" is taken to task in this proverb. The warning is emphatic—don't you dare join these men! In fact, don't even spend much time thinking about the accomplishments and the power of evil men. Don't give them too much credit, but recall that God is still the Judge of the earth. This is also the sentiment of Psalm 37.

"Fret not yourself because of evildoers, neither be envious against the workers of iniquity. For they shall soon be cut down like the grass and wither like the green herb."

Whether you are held hostage in a bank in Stockholm or shipped off to Siberia by some godless communist party, the message remains the same. Get a backbone! Stand up against evil! And whatever you do, don't join the side of the enemy though they are ten times stronger than any righteous coalition or cause. In the eternal perspective, their life's work will amount to nothing. All of their plans and projects will come to nothing. Bank robbers will end up in prison, and communist dictators will see their pitiful empires come to nothing. Incredibly, the great dictator of Cuba, Fidel Castro, recently admitted to a correspondent from *Atlantic Magazine* that Cuba's economic system "doesn't even work for us."[1] Think of all the hundreds of thousands of communists that joined Castro in this horrible experiment that persecuted the Christian church and destroyed a national economy! What a waste of a life for everybody who supported this fiasco! What a horrible legacy! How much better it would have been for them if their parents had taught them the wisdom of the Proverbs, especially this verse!

For related commentary, reference Proverbs 23:17.

Family Discussion Questions:

1. What's wrong with fearing evil?
2. What should our perspective be towards those who do evil?

PART 213 ~ HOW TO BUILD A HOME
Proverbs 24:3–4

Through wisdom is an house built: and by understanding it is established;
and by knowledge shall the chambers be filled with all precious and pleasant riches.

Wisdom, understanding, and knowledge are the three components of education. But what is the *goal* of an education?

1 Associated Press Online, September 8, 2010, Paul Haven, "Castro's Model Doesn't Work"

Ask the university presidents and the school principals about the goal of education and most would say that it is to prepare a child for a career or to prepare them to be good citizens of the state. You can immediately see a sharp difference between the socialist model for education and life and the order that God has established. God's educational program doesn't focus on preparing children for jobs, careers, and citizenship. What He wants are "houses." The biblical use of the word "house" conveys the idea of a family. But its essence goes deeper and includes the household economy with the members of the home functioning as a unit. At the basic level, the household is made up of a husband and wife—one flesh. Therefore, the household economy is a unit. If there are seven members of a household, there are seven people teaming up to bring in one income, functioning as one organization.

But a household is far more than income and the production of goods and services for the free market. The family is the seedbed for developing human relationships that are based on love, joy, peace, and longsuffering. Within the safety of a family, new generations and new families can grow. Healthy families form the basis of a healthy church. For if a man cannot rule his household well, he cannot rule in the house of God (1 Tim. 3:10). Also, the family home is typically where meaningful relationships are cultivated in regular times of hospitality.

According to this description of the "house," the only way to build upon a fruitful household vision is through wisdom, understanding, and knowledge. Foolish men will ruin their relationships, make rash decisions when it comes to marrying, and then watch their households fragment in divorce. They may be successful with their careers. They may even help to build a little piece of some big powerful empire. But in the end, their lives will be in vain because their families shriveled up and died.

So if we want our children building fruitful and blessed homes, we must give them this full-orbed education. We give them knowledge so they will know biblical principles, the nature of man, the laws of God, and the roles of husbands and wives. But they need understanding as well. They should also be able to discern error and recognize counter-worldviews. If the family is watching a movie, and somebody is taking God's name in vain, they should understand this as a violation of the third commandment. Should they happen to see a picture of a Proverbs 7 woman on a billboard, they should identify her as such. But even these two components aren't enough. If life is a journey, knowledge comprehends the destination, and understanding charts the course, it is wisdom that navigates the waters. Our children need to know how to resolve conflicts in a peaceable way, how to be joyful in trials, how to nurture a two-year-old, how to love a five-year-old, how to fear God in the midst of temptation, and how to rightly prioritize their daily schedules. They need to know how to stay out of debt, how to disagree in a winsome way, and how to change oil in a car so as not to waste God's resources. Every part of life requires the simultaneous application of these three elements for our children to build fruitful families of their own.

Family Discussion Questions:

1. What is the difference between knowledge, understanding, and wisdom? Give illustrations of each.

2. How do you build a home? Is our home a reflection of these things?

PART 214 ～ WISDOM FOR MEN AND NATIONS
Proverbs 24:5

A wise man is strong; yes, a man of knowledge increases strength.

Wisdom provides an edge in whatever you set your hand to do. For lack of wisdom, men fail in their endeavors. They may even lose their lives if they do something brash. Some men will accomplish more in life because they are wise. They will have healthier families, spiritually strong churches, and nations established by robust character. "Strength" implies a resistance to destruction. For example, a strong iron bar is not easily bent. Some churches will be strong as iron, while others will be squishy like balsa wood. Wise pastors and elders will construct strong churches, and wise fathers will build strong families. It stands to reason, then, that we should seek to build our families and churches upon the wisest doctrine, the wisest counsel, and men discipled in true wisdom. Wise men learn from their mistakes, and their strength increases throughout their lifetimes.

Despite their spiritual wisdom and strength, these men, their families, and their churches are never impervious to destruction. There are times when men gain a little strength and succumb to pride, setting themselves up for a dreadful fall. Allowing pride to gain a foothold is always a breach in wisdom. It doesn't matter how much strength is gained by an organization or an individual, there is always an enemy strong enough to overcome us, without God's constant protection.

Proverbs 24:6

For by wise counsel you shall make war: and in multitude of counselors there is safety.

Wisdom is important if you want to build families that will stand strong, businesses and farms that will produce well, and churches that will effectively shepherd God's people. But wisdom is also important for the civil magistrate. One of the most important purposes for the civil magistrate is to defend its people from "evildoers" that attack a nation from without. What, then, should our leaders consider before sending the nation to war? The following factors should be analyzed and weighed by wise men before the path to war is plotted.

1. A nation may not have the resources or the will to defend itself. In such a case, it may be more prudent to submit to the rule of a foreign power or a larger centralized government, than to risk losing the war and absorbing great losses to person

and property. You may remember that Jesus considered it wise for a king to count the cost before going to war. "Or what king, going to make war against another king, sits not down first, and consults whether he is able with ten thousand to meet him that comes against him with twenty thousand?" (Luke 14:31)

2. While Christians would generally consider the aggressor as the unrighteous party in a military conflict, things get a little more complicated in international relations. What might constitute an act of aggression? If a nation does not adequately control its anarchical elements, or if factions within the foreign government lend aid to terrorists as they attack your country, might these things be considered acts of aggression? What about unfavorable trade sanctions against your nation or steep increases in taxation on products that you ship into the country?

3. Sometimes war is the only way to resolve tensions within a nation. Although this is hardly a good reason to go to war, some leaders find that war can restore national purpose and a will to survive if the nation has sunk into hedonism, escapism, and other destructive patterns.

4. Often, relationships between nations disintegrate as sanctions between nations escalate towards aggression. When all-out war ensues, nobody really can remember who picked the fight. It could be that both nations were at fault, as it is with sibling rivalries and marital conflicts. Hence, attempts to make peace are probably worthwhile.

Hopefully, you can see now the complexity and importance of the question—shall we go to war? Men can fool themselves unless they are both honest and wise. These are the sorts of counselors who must make the important decisions in the highest offices of the land. Otherwise, nations resort to war too quickly, and many innocent lives are lost.

Now, the decision to go to war is one thing, but the wisdom required to win wars is quite another matter. If this is the case, what does it mean when wicked men win an occasional war? Some wicked men or unbelieving leaders have been known to receive good counsel on occasion; the kings of Egypt, Babylon, and Persia listened to the wise counsel of Joseph, Daniel, and Esther, for example. Yet, those in leadership who persist in wicked behavior usually meet an untimely end. God makes sure of it. This is the pattern for men like Nero, Hitler, Haman, and Ahab.

Family Discussion Questions:

1. How might wisdom build strength into a man's life? What is "strength"?

2. What is a just war? When would it be just and wise to enter into a war with another nation?

PART 215 ~ FOOLS AND MALEVOLENT PEOPLE
Proverbs 24:7

Wisdom is too high for a fool; he opens not his mouth in the gate.

Unfortunately, our modern democratic societies have not paid much attention to this nugget of wisdom. Rarely do you hear people drawn to one candidate or another because they are "wise," or that they have aligned themselves with the principles contained in God's Word. Merely holding membership with some certain political party or giving lip service to a particular political position does not imply that a person is wise. For example, he might profess to support life in the womb; yet, because he is fundamentally unprincipled and unwise in his leadership, this man may take the nation into unrighteous wars and endorse wicked scorched-earth methods in warfare, thereby proving himself a murderer. Merely subscribing to some political platform or some partisan issue does not constitute a wise man.

When it comes to leadership, wisdom is indispensable. An unwise leader, whatever political party he is aligned with, will drive a city or a state into the ground. It is also true that some fools will wreck things quicker than others. As some have said in our present day, "The Democrats will take us off the cliff at eighty miles per hour and the Republicans will take us at sixty-five miles per hour!" Nevertheless, there are still some fools that are so blatant in their foolishness that almost everybody can see the utter futility and stupidity of every one of their ideas. The fool does not last long in the position of power.

Proverbs 24:8

He that devises to do evil shall be called a mischievous person.

Some people are characterized by malevolence and wickedness. Their hearts and lives are committed to their sinful intentions. But how do you identify a man of evil character? On the outside, the man may appear to be an upstanding member of the community. He may be a doting father, a hard-working employee, or a deacon in his church. This was the case with Dennis Rader, a serial killer from Wichita, Kansas. For almost forty years, he lived a double life. At the time he was arrested, he was president of the counsel of Christ Lutheran Church, ELCA, in Wichita. Evidently, his family and church life was merely a cover-up for what he really wanted to do, and that was to murder people. Between each of his ten-plus murders, he was busy planning the next one. This man's entire life was centered on his commitment to break the law of God, specifically the sixth commandment.

A man's heart will dictate the direction of his life. If his heart commitment is to do wickedness—whether it is to commit adultery, murder another human being, or commit any other sin—then you can count on him continually planning his next foray into breaking God's laws.

Thus, it would behoove all of us to examine our own hearts. What is it that thrills your heart? Where does your heart run? What are your ultimate commitments? Those basic commitments will become evident to everybody at some point. Are you committed to Christ and His kingdom, or are you committed to going your own way and fulfilling your own sinful agenda?

Proverbs 24:9

The thought of foolishness is sin: and the scorner is an abomination to men.

How many different thoughts pop up in your mind in any given hour? Every second while you are awake, your mind is processing information, making plans, and formulating things to say to others. You may think twenty or thirty different thoughts inside of one minute, some of them overlapping each other. According to this verse, God cares about every thought that crosses your mind.

Of course, the mere observation of a sinful act or overhearing some suggestion that tempts you to sin does not necessarily constitute sin. When sensuous women display themselves on billboards or magazine covers, the accidental observation of these things is not sin. But what does the mind do with it? That is the deciding question. Jesus warns men not to look at women to lust after them in their hearts (Matt. 5). If the response of the mind to the temptation is, "Oh! There is a sensuous woman trying to tempt me to sin! That woman needs to get some clothes on and cover her shameful nakedness," then there is no problem. But if the mind pursues shameful thoughts about a woman—or "women" in general—by lustful thoughts, it is defrauding women who are made in the image of God. As this proverb plainly states it, "the foolish thought is sin." Every time we doubt the commandments of God in our minds, we echo the devil by saying, "Has God really said that?" and sin against God.

The scorner is an abomination to men. Nobody really likes the scorner or the proud rebel who will not submit himself to correction. The business manager doesn't want to hire him because he won't follow through on instructions. Police officers are put off by these teenage punks who serve mainly as a scourge to the community. After a while, nobody really wants to live in a community populated with these incorrigible youth.

Family Discussion Questions:

1. What makes a wise leader in the political sphere? What are some of today's destructive policies that a fool would support?

2. Describe a malevolent person.

3. What is the difference between temptation and a foolish thought?

4. What are foolish thoughts that you have thought in the last week or so?

Proverbs 24:10

If you faint in the day of adversity, your strength is small.

Most children today do not understand that life is filled with suffering and struggle. That could be because parents feel as if they must protect their children from all testing, trials, and even work. Somehow, people came to believe that childhood and "adolescent" years were supposed to be consumed with "fun and games." On the one hand, we do want to be careful not to subject our children to spiritual and emotional trials that would overwhelm them. Yet, on the other hand, the purpose of child training is to prepare them to joyfully accept the emotional, spiritual, and physical strains of life that are sure to come their way. As a young boy, David was tasked with feeding his father's sheep and defending them from lions and bears. Our sons should be no less prepared to face life-threatening circumstances of this sort.

Whether or not parents will try to delay the days of adversity for their children, in the final analysis there will be no avoiding these days. Eventually, the storms will come. As one songwriter put it, "Some days are diamonds and some days are stones." Thankfully, we do not face the lions and bears every day, but the days of adversity can never be avoided entirely. There are trying times that last a short while, but at other times it seems as if we are trudging through a swamp filled with mud and alligators for months and even years at a time. But we must realize that all of it comes by God's providential direction.

The hard truth is that when the hard times come, some will pass the tests and some will not. When a man or a woman collapses under the weight of trials, bad things happen. Emotional breakdown, broken families, divorces, fragmented churches, economic crises, and bankruptcies all play a part in the fallout when people buckle in the day of adversity.

So the proverb before us gives us the vaccine against such a dreadful outcome. What is needed is strength! Physical strength, yes, but the text speaks more of spiritual strength. Strong faith is needed to overcome the world. By faith, kingdoms were subdued, promises were obtained, and lions' mouths were stopped! (Heb. 11:33) For lack of faith, men fail to lead their families through the darkest valleys, the hardest attacks of the enemy, and the wildest seas. In the absence of faith, pastors will compromise their *teaching* of the Word of God and fail to speak the "hard" words. For lack of faith, love fails. It is precisely in our Christian marriages and churches, where true love should endure all things. "Increase our faith," is the heart cry of every Christian man or woman. Every trial is intended to strengthen our faith and prepare us for what lies ahead. Even as the man who works out in the gym every day is better prepared for the day he meets the bully in the streets, the Christian must work to strengthen his faith for the days of vicious attack that are sure to come. If you grow lax in your spiritual exercises and refuse to learn the lessons of faith that God teaches you when life is smooth sailing, don't be surprised if your ship takes a beating in rough waters!

Family Discussion Questions:

1. What happens when people fall in the day of adversity?

2. How might you grow in strength today, that you might be prepared for the challenges awaiting you in the future?

PART 216 ~ MAJOR PRIORITIES—PRESERVING LIFE AND WISDOM
Proverbs 24:11–12

If you forbear to deliver them that are drawn to death, and those that are ready to be slain;
if you say, behold, we knew it not; does not He that ponders the heart consider it? And He that keeps your soul, does not He know it? And shall not He render to every man according to his works?

We live in a sinful world, and until it is entirely redeemed in the final consummation, we must deal with the reality of evil. This has been the case since the fall of man. Before the worldwide flood, men succumbed to wholesale acts of unrestrained violence (Gen. 6:13), so after the flood, God provided a very important law that would preserve human society from disintegrating into the gross tyrannical and anarchical violence that characterized mankind prior to the worldwide deluge, "Whoso sheddeth man's blood, by man shall his blood be shed" (Gen. 9:6). This is the most basic civil law. When the civil magistrate fails to execute murderers, it fails at the most basic level to fulfill its role as a government over human society. As the minister of God, the civil magistrate is bound to use the sword (Rom. 13:1–4), and capital punishment is the just punishment for the crime of murder (Ex. 21:12–14; Num. 35:31; Deut. 19:9–13). The present text may indeed speak to kings, or kings in training, but does it have any other application? What happens in the case where governments fail to preserve life? And how might this text direct one who comes upon a violent crime in progress? One thing we know from Scripture is that a righteous man always defends innocent human life wherever and whenever it is threatened. Reuben delivered Joseph from almost certain death, and Jonathan protected David when Saul was out for his life.

God cares about every single life that He has created. Every drop of blood that falls on to the street, whether it results from murder or the negligent drunk driver, God takes special note of it. It is our responsibility to preserve that life. Cain asked, "Am I my brother's keeper?" The answer should have been obvious, "Of course you are!"

This obligation to preserve life is a major priority for every one of us. If life is being threatened in your immediate vicinity, you have an obligation to act. Drop everything else you are doing and immediately take action to prevent the loss of life. Perhaps the best example of this scenario is the Good Samaritan who rescued the traveler from almost certain death.

In our present society, most of us will probably confront these life-threatening conditions only a few times during our lives. A child is drowning in a pool, a toddler runs out into traffic, or a burglar takes a shot at a family member. Though such occurrences are rare, people do lose their lives through the systemic abuses of government fiats and tyrannical policies. For example, large corporations, hospitals, and clinics work in collusion with governments, media, and schools to murder hundreds of millions of babies in their mothers' wombs. What does a godly man do in such a murderous society? Some Christians have blocked clinics, others write letters to the editor of their local newspaper, and others work to elect righteous leaders who will advocate policies that will preserve human life. Probably the most effective thing to do in the short term is to convince individual mothers not to kill their children. The political, social, philosophical, and academic forces are extremely strong and deceitful, persuading millions of women to live their lives for themselves. But if you have a good relationship with a friend, relative, or coworker, you may be able to convince him or her to love the baby instead of killing it. Even under these conditions, Christians have a responsibility to do what they can to preserve human life. Different people will take different approaches in handling these things; some will be more involved politically, while others may spend more of their time with "Crisis Pregnancy Centers," working with the individual women. Wisdom will dictate the most effective way to fight these battles for each individual, given his own talents and experience.

Proverbs 24:13–14

My son, eat honey, because it is good; and the honeycomb, which is sweet to your taste;

so shall the knowledge of wisdom be unto your soul; when you have found it, then there shall be a reward, and your expectation shall not be cut off.

Wisdom is here compared to honey and the honeycomb, both of which are sweet and desirable to the taste. The only problem with honey is you can eat too much of it, and then it will cease to be fulfilling. Eat six cups of honey at one time, and you will understand the point. With some of God's blessings, such as wine or honey, there comes a point at which the blessing no longer satisfies. After the second and the third piece of chocolate cream pie, you might still be happy with the results and fully expect that the fourth will be just as satisfying. After the fourth helping, however, you might begin to feel a little sick. Thus, we must take these things in moderation and not place too high an expectation on how much they will satisfy the ultimate longings of our souls.

But none of this is true for wisdom. You cannot possibly over-indulge on wisdom! Study wisdom that you might improve your relationships, strengthen your family, and find ways to do all to the glory of God. Ultimate reward and fulfillment come with every minute lived by true wisdom. As self is purged from your actions and intentions, and as you live more for the service of God and others you will find true peace and lasting joy. May God help you to apply your hearts to wisdom.

Family Discussion Questions:

1. What is the first and most basic civil law which God revealed to men after the flood?

2. What sort of situations should you get involved with in order to preserve human life?

3. Do you find wisdom sweet to the taste? Have you ever been disappointed when you made a wise decision?

PART 217 ~ GOD'S VENGEANCE VS. OUR VENGEANCE
Proverbs 24:15–16

Lay not in wait, O wicked man, against the dwelling of the righteous; spoil not his resting place;
for a just man falls seven times, and rises up again; but the wicked shall fall into mischief.

This wise saying is directed towards the wicked man, even though it is unlikely he would be interested in the wisdom of this book. Nevertheless, there are wicked men who seem to be "out to get" the righteous. The world out there can be cruel, and believe it or not, righteous men like Joseph or Jesus are usually despised and abused by wicked men who run into them. So here is a "heads-up" for the wicked man who wants to pick on the good guys. More importantly, it is an encouragement to the poor righteous man that must endure the persecutions of the wicked.

When a wicked man uses the courts to persecute an innocent man, his intent is evil and destructive. He may proceed to take the good man's property or inflict permanent bodily harm. But two things happen in these assaults. The righteous man has what it takes to recover from every blow he receives. Whether it will come by a continual renewal of body and spirit, or by the final renewal at the resurrection, we know that the righteous man will always recover. Therefore, he has every reason to be thoroughly upbeat and optimistic in the course of his persecution. We certainly see this in the testimony of the martyrs who suffered greatly in the first centuries of the church. But the second thing that happens is that these persecutors themselves do not last very long. Studying the lives of the greatest persecutors of the Church—Nero, Domitian, Vespasian, James II, Hitler, and others—you will find that none of them lasted very long. They fell and never rose again. This is not the case for the just man. His legacy continues, though it may have been meager. will continue to grow, and it will reap eternal benefits!

Proverbs 24:17–18

Rejoice not when your enemy falls, and let not your heart be glad when he stumbles;
lest the LORD see it, and it displease Him, and He turn away His wrath from him.

Knowing how his son might react to the inevitable fall of some wicked tyrant (as pointed out in the previous verse), the wise father quickly corrects the fleshly response that might be gathering force in his son's mind. How easy it is to allow personal vengefulness to well up within us, rejoicing when we see an enemy take a tumble! But notice right away that there is a distinction between "your enemy" and "God's enemy." The wicked man is God's enemy, whereas our enemy is one who has set himself against us.

We might appropriately rejoice when we see enemies, like Nero or Mao Tse Tung, and their evil empires overwhelmed by the kingdom of Christ! But it is a different matter when we find ourselves in the torture chambers, receiving unrelenting blows from our persecutors. At times like these, we simply cannot take vengeance into our own hands. We stand with Christ in these situations and pray for those who despitefully use us. We should emulate the poor saint during the killing time in Scotland who was about to be burned to death for his faith in Christ. Turning to his executioner, he handed the man his boots, remarking that the man would make better use of them than he would in the flames!

Each act of mercy and kindness done for our persecutors will do one of two things: either the man will capitulate to the powerful message of love and kindness in the face of gross injustice, or he will harden his heart and suffer even more of the white-hot justice of almighty God. What is enjoined here is to restrain our impulses to personal vengeance, impulses which might shift God's displeasure from your persecutor to yourself. The lesson here is simple. God is a jealous God, jealous of His own right to mete out justice (as He sees fit). When wicked men take justice into their own hands and redefine it in their own terms, they violate His law and warrant His judgment. But we can do the same thing. We can usurp God's justice ourselves by taking personal satisfaction in the suffering of some wicked man. Again, the problem is that this man has not violated *our* laws (even if he were to violate our person or property). He has violated God's laws! Be very careful that you do not take the place of God, even as you sustain injustices inflicted upon you at the hands of wicked men.

Family Discussion Questions:

1. What two things happen when wicked men start beating up righteous men?

2. What is the difference between awareness of God's vengeance on the wicked and taking personal vengeance against our enemies?

3. How would you react if evil men were to torture you for your faith?

PART 218 ~ EVIL MEN AND REVOLUTIONARIES
Proverbs 24:19–20

Fret not yourself because of evil men, neither be envious at the wicked; for there shall be no reward to the evil man; the candle of the wicked shall be put out.

You can laugh when the wicked fall, or you can fret over their success in the acquisition of power. Either way, you give way to faithlessness. Wicked men assume that God is disconnected with His world (Ps. 94:6–7). For you to doubt God's existence or His justice is to give into the same unbelief! He is the Judge over all things and we can rest assured that He will reward evil reprobates according to their works.

What applies to the evil tyrant applies just as much to an evil neighbor, co-worker, or businessman who has defrauded you in some way or another. How many hours are consumed with worrying about a co-worker setting you up for failure, or some neighbor who insists on cutting down your trees and poisoning your animals? What is this, but doubting the administrative capability of God over His universe and every individual person in it? Unless these evil persons humble themselves and seek forgiveness of God and their neighbors, they will suffer great deprivation in this life and the life to come. Instead of fretting over their sins, we would better use our time by pitying their souls and crying out for mercy for these hardened hearts that will fuel the fires of hell forever if they never repent.

For related commentary, reference Proverbs 23:17 and 24:1.

Proverbs 24:21–22

*My son, fear the LORD and the king; and meddle not with them that
 are given to change;*
*for their calamity shall rise suddenly; and who knows the ruin of them
 both?*

This passage speaks with tremendous force to the present
revolutionary states that have governed much of the world
since the French Revolution. In the 2008 presidential
elections, the most powerful man in the world was elected
on the campaign promise of one word: "Change!" Nobody
cared what sort of change Barack Obama would bring,
but the word meant everything to people indoctrinated in
revolutionary democracy. Typically, a "conservative" party
will try to retain some respect for written constitutions and
systems of law encoded by previous generations, moderating
the "change." But once the revolutionaries capture the schools
and universities, the possibility of retaining stable, prosperous
nations dissolves into revolutionary chaos. Thus, while
economies break down by a rejection of the sound economic
principles contained in the book of Proverbs, the political
states also break down because they reject the all-important
lesson contained in this verse.

For a time in the 1980s, Marxists would kidnap young sons
of African chiefs and take them to China for indoctrination
in revolutionary governance. Upon returning to Africa, they
were tasked first with killing their own fathers. This was
intended to cut off all ties to the "old ways of life" and replace
them with the new revolutionary systems.

Thus, man tries to save himself by "change." If he can bring
about constant revolutionary change to his society, perhaps
this will save him from his predicament (as he defines it on his
own terms). Of course, this is futile and only takes a society
into a cyclone of repeated bloody revolutions—a frightening
prospect! Every country that has adopted this revolutionary
culture has come to a quick end.

As this proverb asserts in no uncertain terms, nobody is safe in such a revolutionary environment. The head of the French Revolution, Maximilien Robespierre, eventually lost his own head at the guillotine. The great Marxist revolutionary, Leon Trotsky, was assassinated in his home in Mexico at the hands of a Russian secret agent.

This does not obviate all change. It is just that we do not support change solely for the sake of change. What we are after in all of our efforts is better conformance to the laws of God. But one of those laws involves an honor for our fathers and the systems they have given to us. It is not for us to throw away all that our fathers have given to us. Even in politics, righteous men will respect the constitutions laid down by the founding fathers of the country. While there are some wild-eyed "Christian" revolutionaries who would like to throw out the nation's Constitution and replace it with the "Bible," this would negate the honor that is due to those who went before us and constitute revolutionary change. We have to work from the established structures of governments and culture that we have inherited from our forefathers; and then we must work to bring them into better conformance with the laws of God. In the words of the inspired text, we are to fear Yahweh *and* the King (which might include the king's constitutions and systems of law).

As we have opportunity, we ought to bring our political systems (and our theological systems) into better alignment with the truth of God's Word. But we do so in a careful and lawful manner. Oftentimes, the spirit of dishonor is strong in the youthful generation, and this clouds their interpretation and application of God's Word. This particularly marks the present generation, as the youth prefer revolution to reformation in theology and culture. These are men who are constantly given to "reinventing the wheel." They cut themselves off from all theological and cultural roots, and in the end they destroy sound theology and good, solid cultural systems. Usually, these revolutionaries have revolted against their own fathers first, rejecting everything good their fathers stood for in music, dress, culture, morals, and theology. In our current culture, young men everywhere are moving rapidly from one theological perspective to another. There may or may not be anything credible and good in their new-found theology, but that is not what draws these men to these positions. Their fundamental basis for change is a hatred for their own fathers, and you can be sure this will never produce any good.

Family Discussion Questions:
1. Have you ever fretted over a neighbor that has done you wrong, or a coworker that was out to get you fired? Why did you fret over those circumstances? In retrospect, what should you have done?
2. What is the difference between somebody given to revolutionary change and somebody who looks to make positive changes?
3. What happens to countries that embrace a revolutionary approach to society?

PART 219 ~ RIGHTEOUS JUDGES
Proverbs 24:23

These things also belong to the wise. It is not good to have respect of persons in judgment.

Our lives will rarely intersect with "judgments" within the civil realm. Unless a person's profession is directly related to the judicial system, passing judgment will not be an everyday occurrence for most people.

Family life does not usually include the sort of judgment we find in the context of this verse, but it does involve relationships. There will be times when we offend each other and must pursue reconciliation and forgiveness. The Bible uses the word "chastisement" rather than "judgement" when referring to familial discipline. There will be times when parents must chastise their children for behaving unkindly or lying (or any other sin, as determined by God's law). The chastisement they choose to employ upon each child is based upon the parent-child relationship, as well as the child's temperament. A father may also prefer to give a gift to one child over another child. There is no biblical law preventing this sort of thing (within the context of the family). When children demand absolutely equal treatment in the home, they give in to the sin of Joseph's brothers.

However, when we find ourselves in a court of law, we enter into an altogether different situation. The law is unbending and unforgiving; all must be treated equally under the law and there cannot be any partiality shown to one person or class of persons.

A judge may be able to forgive an acquaintance for running over his daughter with a car while in a drunken state. But should he be sitting in the seat of judgment the next day, he has no right to forgive a man who has killed another human being in an act of gross negligence (Ex. 21:29). Before God, that judge cannot pass a lighter sentence than that required by God's law. His right and responsibility to make judgments are established by God Himself. When the judge passes a judgment therefore, he must act as a proper representative or minister of God, for he exercises God's vengeance on the evil doer (Rom. 13:4–7).

In most court trials today, a judge will recuse himself from the trial if he has any knowledge of the defendant or the witnesses who will testify in the trial. Even unbelieving judges know that they must adjudicate fairly and consistently in order to maintain stable societies. But as Christians, we know that the law is unchanging because God is the absolute standard of justice and He does not change. Granted, it takes thoughtful effort to properly understand the facts of the case and apply the law to the situation at hand. But the standard of the law does not change. If a man committed a murder with hate in his heart, lying in wait (which implies malice and forethought), it is murder pure and simple. The man must face execution. To sentence one man to capital punishment for murder and not to do so for another is arbitrary and capricious. A civil society cannot survive when the standard for justice constantly changes with the whims of each election and instatement of a new legislature. This is one reason why judges are typically appointed for a lifetime in this country. Nevertheless, our civil judges in Western countries seem to have given up on their commitment to the laws of God and to their Constitutions—they seem to be adopting more revolutionary changes every few years.

Family Discussion Questions:

1. How does judgment differ from other experiences and relationships in our lives?

2. If a judge is finds himself presiding over the case where somebody killed his own daughter in gross negligence, what should he do? What if there is no other judge available to take the case?

3. Who is the ultimate determinant of justice for the courts and legislatures?

Part 220 ~ Honesty Under Duress
Proverbs 24:24–25

He that says to the wicked, "You are righteous"; him shall the people curse, nations shall abhor him;
but to them that rebuke him shall be delight, and a good blessing shall come upon them.

When the wicked gain a little power, not many will have the courage to stand up against them! No better example of this is found in recent history than Germany's Third Reich. To this day, most Christians (including Lutherans) have a hard time comprehending the deafening silence of the Lutheran Church in the midst of the atrocities committed by the national socialists. Only a few religious leaders spoke out against it.

When four thousand pastors and priests united to endorse Joseph Stalin as their honorary president at the Congress of Christians in Romania, one man stood against them. Richard Wurmbrand writes, "My wife and I were present at this congress. My wife sat near me and told me: 'Richard stand up and wash away this shame from the face of Christ! They are spitting in His face.' I said to my wife, ' If I do so, you lose your husband.' She said, 'I do not wish to have a coward as a husband.'"[2] Wurmbrand then rose to declare Christ's kingly rights over the communist regimes—and he paid dearly for it. Yet, seventy-five years after this auspicious convention, one man remains a hero, and the fawning supporters of those mass-murderers, Stalin and Ceaucescu, are either ignored or despised by the masses.

To this day, many nations abhor all those pastors and priests that rushed out to support Adolf Hitler and Joseph Stalin. Ironically, most of these nations would quickly promote their own wicked men to power and blindly reenact the same mistakes made by Germany, Russia, and Romania in the 20th century. No doubt, there will be more opportunities for righteous men to stand against great tyrannies in the years to come!

Truly, there is nothing more admirable or courageous than a man who is willing to speak clear, strong words of rebuke before a tyrant, especially when nobody else is willing to speak the truth. Occasionally, somebody will break the silence and point out the true evil character of some tyrant. He may lose his head for it, as in the case of John the Baptist, but posterity will never forget a man of this kind of forthright courage. The examples of honorable men are rare and refreshing treasures in the annals of human history.

Proverbs 24:26

Every man shall kiss his lips that gives a right answer.

Using the American idiom, we call these men "straight shooters." Generally, people like straight shooters. They do not make a practice of pulling the wool over people's eyes and they refuse to resort to flattery. Sure, there are those who prefer to play games, but our personal and business relationships cannot progress where people are not dealing in the truth. Businesses succeed and relationships develop depth when men and women deal in the truth. They don't sugar-coat the bad news but they won't overstate the case, either.

But not all cultures would agree with this Proverb. Refusing to give a straight answer to an honest question, they will "beat around the bush." They won't tell you that they dislike you or that they disagree with something you are doing or something you have said. Instead, they will resort to speaking poorly of you behind your back or give you the cold shoulder. These cultures even consider it impolite to deal with issues head-on. Of course, these cultural inclinations run headlong against the lesson in this proverb. By this strong reticence to deal with the truth, these people create an environment for mistrust, bitterness, and long strings of broken relationships. They learn to hate the faithful witnesses who point out their sin and call for repentance. But unless they embrace the straight-shooting preacher who brings the bad news and the good news of Christ's atonement for their sin, they will never enter the kingdom of God.

The only solid relationships in the world will be based on friends that are able to look each other in the eye and talk straight to the important issues in each other's lives. These are good, close friendships. The idea of men greeting each other with a kiss is odd in a day where only a lustful, *eros* expression of love governs all forms of intimacy. But as Christians, we must begin to build back human relationships in the church, relationships that are formed upon what the New Testament refers to as *phileo* love and *agape* love. In a world where relationships have grown transient and stark cold, Christians must be examples to the world of brothers who truly love each other. Where nobody wants to speak the hard words to a friend and certify the friendship with a true kiss of loyalty and *phileo* love, *we* must work to build churches where this a common practice.

Family Discussion Questions:

1. Why do we find courageous men who stand up alone against evil to be the most impressive men who have ever lived?

2. What is it to be a "straight shooter?" What is the difference between being rude and being a "straight shooter?"

PART 221 〜 CREATING A HOUSEHOLD ECONOMY
Proverbs 24:27

Prepare your work without, and make it fit for yourself in the field; and afterwards build your house.

This is one of those rare jewels of wisdom for every young man who is between the ages of twelve and twenty-eight. It establishes an order of priorities for his life's responsibilities. But for most of the last century, young men and women have lost any sense of responsibilities and priorities. Before they are able to provide a household economy sufficient to sustain themselves, they engage in frivolous and sometimes fornicating relationships with each other. It is not unusual for many little boys and girls as young as eleven and twelve years old to engage in these "dating relationships." The problem, of course, is that they are just children. Even at eighteen or nineteen years old, they are incapable of providing an income for themselves. Their parents raised them to play and to fill their "adolescent years" with fun and games, and so most little boys will not grow up until they are well into their 30s! Meanwhile, birth control pills and abortion are the only ways to keep fourteen-year-old "Sally" from having to deal with her own children. That would force her to grow up, and she is too busy having fun! All of these things have become very destructive to our entire socioeconomic system. This life of adolescence, leisure, self-centered existentialism, fun and games, dating, abortion, birth control, teen culture, and the refusal to mentor young men into life's real responsibilities is destroying our society. When a social system starts to fail, there are those who will not participate in that society—they will build their own. There are those who take life and the future seriously. They are raising their sons and daughters according to the principles contained in the Bible, especially the book of Proverbs.

In 1958, one popular song asked the question about marriage between two teenagers. (It should be noted that until the 1960s, a Christian-influenced culture frowned upon pre-marital fornication.)

"She was only seventeen and he was one year more.
She loved him with all her heart, and he the girl adored.
But all their friends believed they were too young to know
  the score,
'Cause she was only seventeen and he was one year more.
Are they old enough to know if love will last a life?
Isn't he too young to be a husband, her a wife?
Within the past I bet it's happened more than once before,
When someone else was seventeen and another one year
  more
Do we have the right to question love that seems so strong?
As long as God has no objection, there can be no wrong."

Again, the popular culture typically ignores the basic principles of God's Word, this time in relation to the marriage of a man and woman. Honor of parents in the selection of a future mate, avoiding equal yoking (where a believer marries an unbeliever), and proper provisions for a household economy are all important considerations as a couple looks to marriage. It seems that the only thing that matters to the teenage world of the 1950s was "romantic love."

It is true that young men approaching adulthood begin to notice young ladies in a different light, and they might even consider one particular lady for marriage. This is natural. But what is it that lies in the way of an eighteen-year-old young person getting married? The dating and fornication game is out of the question. If a young man will work towards an intimate relationship with a young lady, he must be prepared to marry her. There is certainly no sin in an eighteen-year-old young man getting married. But what might prohibit him from getting married is the *absence of a family economy.* A man cannot build a home for his future wife until he has fields to plow. For thousands of years, young people understood this basic principle. Almanzo Wilder was Farmer Boy in the Laura Ingalls Wilder stories about life in the 1800s. Before he married Laura Ingalls, he established an income base on plowing his fields and gleaning a harvest or two. Then he built his cabin and brought Laura home with him.[3]

Wisdom passages like this one discourage living beyond your means. Instead of running headlong into debt, this text encourages young men to produce income before they think about building a comfortable home for a wife and family. From as early as twelve years of age, our sons should work towards developing income-producing businesses and skill sets. It may take five or six years before they have sufficient income to build a twelve-by-twelve foot building to provide a little space to cook food and rest at night. But this proverb puts first things first, laying out Life's Very Basic Lessons for every single young man who has ever lived. May God help us to revive this important responsibility in the hearts of our young boys, especially in this age that has life virtually expunged one of life's most rudimentary lessons!

Family Discussion Questions:

1. What must a young man do before he establishes a home?

2. How has the world affected us, in these areas of self-centered existentialism, irresponsibility, dating for fun, perpetual adolescence, etc.?

---

3 Laura Ingalls Wilder, *These Happy Golden Years,* (Harper Collins)

PART 222 ~ MAINTAINING GOOD NEIGHBORLY RELATIONSHIPS
Proverbs 24:28–29

Be not a witness against your neighbor without cause; and deceive not with your lips.

Say not, I will do so to him as he has done to me; I will render to the man according to his work.

Many texts in this Book of Wisdom address the area of human relationships. You may also recall that the last six of the Ten Commandments are concerned with how we treat others. By nature, we are self-centered and we couldn't care less about others. Even when men do seemingly "good" things for their neighbors, they are consumed with self-interest and self-reward while they do them.

This lesson comes almost directly from the ninth commandment. If you do not have solid evidence proving that your neighbor has committed some crime or offense, then you have no business speaking against him in any context. While the text speaks mainly to court trials, it may also apply to relationships within the family, business, or church. Have you ever drawn the wrong conclusions about somebody's behavior or motivations, and later discovered that you had slighted him in your words or thoughts? Maybe you acted on too little evidence. Or if you countenance an unloving, ungracious, and bitter spirit towards others, your heart may quickly—and wrongly—interpret evidence. Should you catch your heart in such a state, be careful not to draw any conclusions whatsoever about others. You are not qualified to make judgments. You are incapable of interpreting the evidence in such a condition. When it comes to the condemnation of others, you must not rely on a "gut feeling" or guesswork. Even before confronting a brother who may have sinned, you need to make a careful and honest assessment of the data first. Determine whether it is a major sin worth bringing up to him or if you may be holding him to a higher standard than you would impose upon yourself. Only after passing the muster of these tests should you lovingly confront your brother.

One of the worst mistakes that people make in human relationships is trying to keep everything on a *quid pro quo* basis. Marriages, especially, will not survive long in such a system. Where husbands and wives repay wrong for wrong, insult for insult, or hateful accusation for hateful accusation in their arguments, those relationships will start to sink. When neighbors are taking neighbors to court over the slightest irritation, societies break down into ugly tyrannies that undermine freedom and destroy economies.

God's laws bring God's vengeance on only the more severe crimes. For example, in cases of gross negligence when somebody loses his life, the responsible party will face the death penalty. But the civil magistrate should refuse to take up every petty case of dogs barking at night, or neighbors who fail to water their lawns (though they may negatively impact property values in the neighborhood). Those who live their lives with *quid pro quo*, tit-for-tat systems are taking the place of God. They think that *they* are the perfect arbiters of justice. They can weigh their own behavior and the behavior of others in the balances of perfect justice and mete out the proper sentence every time. Not only is this foolishness, but it is just another attempt to displace God as the sovereign Judge of the universe.

Family Discussion Questions:

1. In what ways might we misinterpret the evidence concerning our neighbor's faults? How have you fallen into this trap?

2. Does the Bible advocate *quid pro quo*? What about the law requiring an "eye for an eye" and a "life for a life?"

3. Why is *quid pro quo* such a lousy system for conducting our family relationships?

PART 223 ~ WHAT A SLOTHFUL HOME LOOKS LIKE
Proverbs 24:30–34

I went by the field of the slothful, and by the vineyard of the man void
of understanding;
And, lo, it was all grown over with thorns, and nettles had covered the
face thereof, and the stone wall thereof was broken down.
Then I saw, and considered it well; I looked upon it, and received
instruction.
Yet a little sleep, a little slumber, a little folding of the hands to sleep;
So shall your poverty come as one that travels; and your want as an
armed man.

Wisdom starts with the revelation of God's wisdom found in His Word. But another component of wisdom is obtained by *observation*. The wise father doesn't drive past a home set in brambles and overgrown weeds and ignore the meaning of it. Rather, he considers carefully the world around him and interprets the data that he obtains by observation. When surveying the world around us, it is easy to miss the lessons it contains, but all of the scenes before us shout messages that, interpreted properly, yield good wisdom. It is for us to listen carefully for the messages, study the scenes, and interpret them in light of the Word of God.

Solomon here identifies the slothful man by his surroundings. To build a house takes a great deal of work, but to maintain a house takes less effort. However, over the years, this man lets things go and fails to keep up his investments There are those who receive a property by inheritance (or by debt), yet they fail to take care of it. Year after year, people driving by the home notice the peeling paint, the rotting fence posts, and the dying shrubbery and grass. This kind of deterioration doesn't happen overnight. And it takes even longer for a stone wall to disintegrate. But given enough time, as the winds blow and the storms beat on the improvements, they begin to disintegrate. Sloth grows over a man as ivy grows over fences. After ten or twenty years, his neighbors cannot help but conclude, "Now there lives a lazy man!"

Just as most people never know when the thief will break in to rob their home—he almost never sends a note ahead to announce his intentions—slothful people almost never see poverty coming. Quietly, slowly, and unexpectedly, it creeps up on them. It takes a while to use up the capital of previous generations and then spend your way into debt (which has happened in the present era of easy access to credit). Now slothfulness is almost a universal problem for our young men, 70% of whom are not "grown up" and ready to lead a household by 30 years of age (up from 30% in 1970). Since Proverbs deals with this temptation repeatedly throughout the book, it is safe to assume the temptation has always been real and present for young men in our sinful world. Therefore, it would be prudent to go after every instance of slothfulness. The problem with a little slothfulness is that it will morph into more slothfulness. A little extra sleep on Saturday turns into a little extra sleep on Sunday, Monday, and Tuesday. An occasional binge will, over time, turn into a habit, and habits will determine the character of a man. Once the character trait of slothfulness is ingrained in the man, it is extremely difficult to root it out of him.

Family Discussion Questions:

1. What does a slothful home look like? What does our home look like?

2. What are the first signs of slothfulness? Why is it important to address these first signs?

PART 224 ~ SCIENTIFIC INQUIRY
Proverbs 25:1–3

These are also proverbs of Solomon, which the men of Hezekiah king of Judah copied out.

It is the glory of God to conceal a thing; but the honour of kings is to search out a matter.

The heaven for height, and the earth for depth, and the heart of kings is unsearchable.

Our world is complex and interesting. Even the brightest scientific minds do not know the basic nature of light, whether it is a wave or a particle. There are a few of the deepest thinkers in the world who will attempt to plumb the depths of human behavior in their literary works and psychological treatises, but for the most part, they can only give us theories.

While great minds seek the cure for cancer and governments invest billions of dollars on the project, the solution remains elusive. Still, that is no reason to give up the quest for it. The complexities of the universe give cause to glory in the God who created such a world! To search out deep mysteries in the fields of chemistry, biology, astronomy, physics, and psychology is an honorable enterprise. Usually, great discoveries only come with dogged persistence in the quest.

Christians who have a firm grasp on their worldview will always do the best science. For there is no better framework in which to discover God's world and practice good science than within a Christian view of the world. As people who believe in God, we know for sure that this is a real world which may be studied objectively. We also believe that the world functions in an orderly fashion. Though God may choose to perform miracles that short-circuit the natural cause and effect relationships from time to time, these are highly unusual occurrences. The world functions in normal cause and effect patterns because God is in control of every atom in His universe and He will see to it that it is orderly. This is the worldview that has produced the greatest poets, botanists, doctors, physicists, and agriculturalists. This is the worldview substantially embraced by scientists of the highest caliber who paved the way for the industrial revolution, men like Isaac Newton, Robert Boyle, Louis Pasteur, James Clark Maxwell, Michael Faraday, Lord Kelvin, Gregor Mendel, James Joule, and Johann Kepler. The devolution of science only occurred because of the philosophical shift made by atheistic scientists like Charles Darwin, John Dewey, Sigmund Freud, and Linus Pauling.

Think of a grandfather who arranges an elaborate treasure hunt in the backyard for his grandchildren. Before the children clamor out of the house into the yard to commence the search for treasures, they must first believe that "Grandpa" exists! They must also assume that Grandpa is good and not some malevolent ogre who is out to disappoint them. Well, God's world contains hidden treasures for you to discover. Even the bush outside the window may hold the secret to the cure for cancer. That bush is no meaningless accident in a chance universe, as the naturalist evolutionists would lead us to believe. All of this should inspire a sense of wonder in the hearts of God-fearing men and women, a wonder hundreds of times greater than what you find in the university laboratories directed by godless professors! As we teach lessons concerning the natural world around us, if we have failed to inspire wonder before this creation and the Creator who put it there, we have failed in our teaching. May God help us to see the beauty, the complexities, the majesty, and order in the heavens and earth, as well as in the heart of God's most complex creature—man!

God is incomprehensible and His creation is unimaginably complex! To think that man could ever comprehend the universe and its many intricacies is pure hubris. In fact, the increase of true knowledge means an increase in humility. We can know a few things, but at best, our understanding of theology and science is only a guess or an approximation of the truth. As we stand on the ledge of a theological or scientific system of thought, we should lift up our eyes and see the great expanse of what we do not know! When we teach our children a few things about the world or about theology, we take them up a ladder to the top of the "well of knowledge." As they climb up the well, often they look down at the others who have not learned these things and they will feel a surge of pride. But the lesson is not complete until we have slid back the covering of the well, and shown them the infinitude of what they do not know.

Family Discussion Questions:

1. Why can men who have faith in God be good scientists? How do their basic beliefs (presuppositions) help them?

2. Why are scientific, theological, and psychological investigations honorable tasks?

3. What was the difference between scientists like Newton, Boyle, Pasteur, Maxwell, and Joule as opposed to scientists like Darwin and Freud?

PART 225 ~ IN THE PRESENCE OF KINGS
Proverbs 25:4–5

Take away the dross from the silver, and there shall come forth a vessel for the finer.
Take away the wicked from before the king, and his throne shall be established in righteousness.

Important men do not make every decision by themselves; they rely on others to do the research for them and to recommend certain conclusions. This is the nature of political leadership. When Supreme Court Justices or Circuit Court Judges bring down their decisions, we are told that most of their work is the product of clerks, interns, and assistants. Thus, you can see how important it is that they hire the right people to assist them. Too often, it is the arrogant revolutionaries, unprincipled and dishonorable people who are drawn to holding a political office today. Modern democracies are filled with men who compete for power and seek to aggrandize themselves and the state at the expense of the peoples' freedom and well-being.

But when a righteous man is elected to power, he should be very careful whom he appoints to assist him in his duties. He should not go after the most obsequious, fawning power mongers. Very often these are the men or women who appear the most motivated and supportive of the leader. But here the father cautions his son concerning this criterion for involvement in political office. Righteousness is what produces stable societies and legitimizes governments and it takes righteous men to enforce God's righteous laws in the civil magistrate. Lamentably, Rehoboam did not listen to his father and he appointed young men of questionable wisdom and character to office. They gave him unwise counsel which resulted in the disintegration of the nation of Israel.

Proverbs 25:6–7

Put not forth yourself in the presence of the king, and stand not in the
place of great men;
for better it is that it be said to you, Come up hither; than that you
should be put lower in the presence of the prince whom your eyes
have seen.

The Lord Jesus gave a similar lesson in Luke 14:8–10, drawing the principle out in the eleventh verse, "For whosoever exalts himself shall be abased; and he that humbles himself shall be exalted." This runs exactly opposite to the inclinations of modern men. Everywhere you look, people are bucking for power. Life in the world is a Nietzschean power grab and the fellow with the most power and money holds the winning position. Sports stars look for their names on the sports page. Successful businessmen glory in the recognition of their achievements in the business section. Entertainment stars are pleased when their names appear in the entertainment news, whether or not the report is favorable. Meantime, the mayor of some small city thrills in his popularity, hoping this will yield him a senate seat and perhaps even a gubernatorial position later in his career.

Women, almost universally, set their value by the positions they gain in politics or the corporate world. From the time they are small girls, they prepare themselves to enter the rat race and prove themselves the biggest rat on the wheel. Hence, women and men increasingly see themselves as competitors rather than complementing team members with distinct roles in the home. If a woman does not achieve money and power, her life is considered worthless by the feminists. Yet God considers a meek and quiet spirit of even more value than a woman's net income (1 Pet. 3:4). Actually, He is repulsed by women who are grappling for power and usurping authority from men (1 Tim. 2:11–12). Both Marxist egalitarians and free market capitalists usually take great offense with these injunctions from Peter and Paul. That is because both Marxists and free market capitalists are materialists and usually measure human success and happiness by money. But we should not be surprised that God uses a different metric (Is. 55:8–9). He is looking for love, joy, peace, meekness, and faith.

The followers of Christ are content to fly "under the radar." This is their default mode of operation. If they are noted and congratulated from time to time, so be it. But this is not what motivates them. They do not need to check their internet accounts for recognition and approval from their 475 contacts. They don't toot their own horns and they don't need to play political games in the work place to gain the favor of the employers. Rarely, if ever, do they request a raise in pay or a promotion. Generally, the laws of economics and the free market will force a settlement upon just compensation for the work a man does. However, this is not always the case in the world of big corporate politics. In accord with what is known as "the Peter Principle," every employee rises to his level of incompetence. When a man plays the game of corporate politics and wins a promotion to a position that he cannot handle, he becomes obsolete "dead wood" in the organization.

On the next economic downturn, his name turns up at the top of the list for layoffs.

The moral of the story for the rest of us, is to put our hand to the plow and work faithfully to the glory of God. As Joseph was faithful in the fields, in Potiphar's house, and in the prison, we too are called to faithful diligence wherever God puts us. Indeed, it is God who grants us favor in the eyes of our managers and writes the promotions. It is for us to be faithful.

Family Discussion Questions:

1. Why is it important for the president to choose only the men of the highest character to work under him?

2. What is wrong with men and women competing with each other for power and position?

3. If we as Christians are not motivated by power, what should be the motivating factor in our lives?

4. Who is the One who promotes us and rewards us in an ultimate sense?

PART 226 ∼ DEALING WITH CONFLICT
Proverbs 25:8–10

Go not forth hastily to strive, lest you know not what to do in the end thereof, when your neighbor has put you to shame.
Debate your cause with your neighbor himself, and discover not a secret to another;
lest he that hears it put you to shame, and your infamy turn not away.

Not a day goes by when we do not have opportunity to disagree with somebody. As someone has remarked, "You can't water every plant with your blood." In the many battlefronts of life, it is unwise to view every single hill as something worth defending and dying for. Therefore, wisdom recommends that you consider carefully before you enter into a conflict with somebody. Before arguing with the taxman concerning the legitimacy of his taxing authority, consider the possibility of losing the case. Or before you take a neighbor to a small claims court over some questionable injustice, it would be better to speak to him face to face first. Otherwise, you may lose both the case and the good favor of your neighbor forever. Taking a neighbor to court almost always permanently destroys the relationship. If you have ever had a neighbor who was hostile toward your family, you know how the contention can make life miserable for everybody. It can result in long term stress and become a thorn in the side for decades.

In any disagreement, you need to remember this simple rule: the less said, the better. Never forget that any words of slander or gossip spoken against another are pure poison and they will come back to bite you. Nobody appreciates a slanderer, and your reputation will be tainted if others are privy to what you have done.

Of course, it takes courage to face a neighbor or a brother with a disagreement. But this is a hundred times better than nursing a disagreement for months on end and then resorting to gossip or the small claims court. It would be better to overlook the fault entirely, because 90% of all disagreements can negatively affect a relationship for a period of time. If, however, you cannot overlook the fault, then you will need to apply the delicate art of loving confrontation. Do not resort to letter-writing or even phone calls. You need to speak to your neighbor face to face about the matter. First, admit whatever fault you bear in the conflict and ask for his forgiveness. Hopefully, this will clear the air for you to bring your grievance to his attention.

Family Discussion Questions:

1. Do we as a family enter into too many conflicts with each other or with others outside the home? What is a proper balance between avoiding conflict and dealing with issues? Under what conditions might it be proper to enter into a conflict and face somebody with a disagreement?

2. Why is it so tempting to talk about disagreements with others and give way to gossip?

3. What is the best way to approach people if you have to confront them with their sin?

PART 227 ~ A WORD FITLY SPOKEN
Proverbs 25:11–13

A word fitly spoken is like apples of gold in pictures of silver.
As an earring of gold, and an ornament of fine gold, so is a wise reprover upon an obedient ear.
As the cold of snow in the time of harvest, so is a faithful messenger to them that send him; for he refreshes the soul of his masters.

This passage introduces the first of several series of analogies, all brought out in sets of three. The first set of analogies speaks of things that are beautiful, precious, refreshing, and blessed. First, we have the apples of gold set in a carved silver frame. These are both precious metals and a pure silver setting would have been beautiful enough. But placing a solid gold apple within the silver framework, increases the value from $1,500 to $300,000. This is the beauty and precious value of a word fitly spoken. The right words spoken at the right time are exceedingly valuable to those who hear them. A sermon, an exhortation, a compliment, a warning, or an encouragement really can profoundly affect someone's life!

The word fitly spoken comes from the right heart motivation, a heart consumed by love and faith. It is a word that meets the need of the day. It is a word that is carefully adjusted to the right force, the right emotion, and the right content. An adjective is selected for its appropriateness and the verb is taken for its gentle persuasion. All of it must reflect the truth. No slander or pandering is allowed. At times, it could be a word of correction that directs itself to a particular sin that entangles a brother (verse 12).

A word fitly spoken may take six hours to prepare. It may even take a number of weeks of careful consideration. But how much better are ten words spoken upon thoughtful reflection than thousands of words aimlessly cast about in casual conversation! If you think about it, most of the talk you hear around you is of little value. Not many conversationalists are carefully assessing their every word for edifying content before speaking. In the age of electronic communication, conversations fill up with more of the trite, the inane, and the meaningless. If relationships are not quickly damaged by what is said, they often become stagnant because there is little heart behind what is being communicated. Before sending a card to a loved one, take a few extra moments to speak from your heart to his. Five extra minutes of thought could make all the difference in your relationship.

The second analogy speaks of a fine work of intricate ornamentation made out of gold. The work itself is of great value, and the material from which it is made only increases its value. In other words, there are two complementing characteristics that together produce an ornament of great value. If it were made out of plastic, the trinket may be worth $120. If it were just a chunk of gold, the piece would be worth $1,200. But the processing of the gold and the added work of the artisan adds substantially to the value of it. Even then, the weight of gold alone takes the tiny piece of jewelry to $1,200, but the intricate design places the value at $5,000. And so it is with a wise reprover and an obedient ear. Reproving a young man who is unwilling to listen is a frustration and a waste of time. But if you can reprove a young man who is open to hear that reproof, you have an opportunity of tremendous value that will result in great advancement for the kingdom of God.

Finally, there is this analogy of moisture soaking into the thirsty soil. Without moisture, the soil will not receive the nutrients that are needed to grow plants for the harvest. This is the blessing of the winter snow. The analogy introduces another picture. At the time this proverb was written, there were no refrigerators cooling the water in the late fall. Yet the mountains may have collected some cold snow which, upon melting, flowed down into the valleys and provided cool water for the thirsty reapers in the fields. There is nothing so refreshing as a cold glass of water for hard working men who have been bailing hay in the fields all afternoon. The proverb speaks of a faithful employee. Loyalty is hard to come by in the present age of corporations. In fact, since 1920, these businesses have resorted to what is known as "collective bargaining" or labor unions in order to stay in business. Employer-employee loyalty became so tenuous in these large corporations that the workers would use the force of the mob to obtain their rights. This continually fosters an environment of discontent, slothfulness, and ingratitude among the work force. In contrast to these attitudes, this proverb presents the willing worker whose heart is committed to the vision of his master. His enthusiasm is as fresh on Monday morning as it is on Friday afternoon as he wraps up his work week. His positive attitude and willingness to apply himself to his tasks is as refreshing as a cold glass of water on a hot August day.

Where there is true faith in action, Christians will be the most faithful and loyal of employees. Throughout his epistles, the Apostle Paul is always encouraging servants with these same words (Eph. 6:5–6; Col. 3:23–25; 1 Tim. 6:1–2). Joseph is the archetypal faithful man in Potiphar's household as well as in the prison. Some may accuse us of being sycophants (or "brown-nosing"), but working with diligence and grace, doing everything with all our heart as unto the Lord, is never wrong. To resort to dishonest flattery or to submit to an employer who would have us break a contract with a customer or undermine our integrity in similar ways is definitively wrong. Yet a man who is out for his employer's success will find ways to advance the cause of the business without breaking God's law and thereby bringing God's curse upon the company.

Family Discussion Questions:

1. Can you think of a word fitly spoken, a sermon, or a brief encouragement that really helped you?
2. What does it take to deliver a "word fitly spoken?"

3. Should you even try to reprove a young man who doesn't want to listen to you?

4. What, if anything, is wrong with labor unions?

5. What does a faithful employee look like?

PART 228 ~ EMPTY PROMISES AND PERSUASIVE PEOPLE
Proverbs 25:14

Whoever boasts himself of a false gift is like clouds and wind without rain.

There are those who love to speak of their brave plans for what they hope to accomplish and how they will bless God's people. Sometimes, church leaders set up in the minds of their people certain expectations of how they will shepherd the congregation and then fail to deliver on those expectations. Or some visionary father talks of how much he "plans to love" his children and how he hopes to run his household. He may even status the relationship with an occasional "I love you." Yet he never quite delivers on "the vision." Failure to deliver on expectations sets others up for cruel disappointments. Merely telling another person that they are loved does not mean that anything is being done for that person *in* love. Relationships require the sacrifice of time, money, spiritual leadership, and thoughtful consideration.

Expectations are communicated in different ways, and we ought to be aware of the sort of expectations we have cultivated in those around us. Sometimes when people get married, they sell themselves as somebody who they are not, thus creating bright expectations of a wonderful relationship. Once married, the spouse wakes up with a different person altogether. For this reason, biblical law requires a stiff penalty for the wife who marries a husband under false pretenses concerning her virginity (Deut. 22:17–20). In the New Testament, Ananias and Sapphira died because they acted disingenuously when they presented themselves as more generous than they really were. You can see that God is serious about this matter. Honesty is essential in human relationships. It would be best to speak far less about what you have done or what you plan to do and just be faithful in good works every single day.

Proverbs 25:15

By long forbearing is a prince persuaded, and a soft tongue breaks the bone.

Persuasion does not come by loud and long arguments. Overwhelming a man with irrefutable logic, a hundred lines of reasoning, and sarcastic responses to his feeble thrusts will do little to convince him of the truth. How many times must we remind ourselves of this essential fact? For a man convinced against his will is of the same opinion still! In the old fable, the gentle sun persuaded the man to remove his coat while the east wind could not get it off in spite of how hard it blew.

Instead of winning the argument, we need to "win the person." Our actions speak louder than our words. If there is any substance to our theological or political persuasions, then our lives should reflect that. Patience is the key, especially when you are dealing with fundamental issues. It is one thing to convince someone that it is raining outside. It might be a little more difficult to convince a friend that one flavor of ice cream is better than another. But it is quite another thing altogether to convince a legislator who aborted her child that abortion is evil and ought to be legislated against. Or it may be equally as difficult to convince somebody who believes in baptismal regeneration to see baptism as more of a means of grace. Only by the Spirit's work will people come to truly face the real import of their sins and understand the fundamental truths of Scripture. Resorting to the force of anger, browbeating, and debates usually only destroy relationships. Instead, the man of God should always look for opportunity to answer straightforward and sincere questions. He is, of course, never ashamed to testify of his own faith in Christ and His resurrection, and he shows tender interest in those who are facing severe trials, serious disease, or the loss of a loved one. In the long run, this will bear more influence upon the unbeliever than dumping a thousand recorded tapes on him explaining the folly of evolution or the evils of communism.

Nevertheless, there is still a place for "hard words" and severe warnings. These are usually more effective when we speak to those who already agree with us. For example, the hard words of Christ against the Pharisees in Matthew 23 were spoken in the presence of Jesus' disciples. He warned them concerning Pharisaical doctrines which also happened to bear the strongest sway on the minds of the people of the day. The scribes and Pharisees made up a political and theological powerhouse, and Christ opposed them in no uncertain terms.

To convince a prince or a governor of some political position can have great effect on the lives of numerous people! For example, when William Wilberforce persuaded the English parliament to do away with the slave trade, he made an indelible mark on human history. But it took a full eighteen years before he made any substantial progress. The Slave Trade Act received full royal assent on March 25, 1807. It wasn't until 1833 that England abolished slavery altogether. By long forbearing is a prince persuaded.

Family Discussion Questions:

1. How do you set expectations? Give several examples. Have we set any expectations that we have failed to meet?

2. What is the difference between "winning the argument" and "winning the person?"

3. How are people convinced of the most important theological matters?

4. Give historical examples of men who worked very hard in government to achieve good results.

Part 229 ~ Too Much of a Good Thing
Proverbs 25:16

Have you found honey? Eat so much as is sufficient for you, lest you be
filled therewith, and vomit it.

Now the Book of Wisdom warns about too much of a good
thing. God created bread, but He also created honey. To the
credit of His goodness, He didn't have to create honey, but
He did, and we ought to receive it with gratefulness. Yet,
in His wisdom He provides more bread than honey, more
grain than bees. So, it is appropriate to have a little honey
with the bread and not the other way around! When there
is more icing than cake and more cake than potatoes on the
dinner plate, we begin to lose a godly sense of balance. God
intends for all things to be received in moderation and in
thanksgiving. When men fail to take these good things in
moderation, several things happen. They give way to idolatry
by fixating on those things that appease the flesh, and they
suffer the consequences of their immoderate behavior. They
vomit. Their teeth rot. Health problems multiply. One recent
study based on a sampling of a million people concluded that
extreme obesity shortens the average lifespan by eight to ten
years.[4]

This principle may be broadened to apply to all forms of
human comfort. The cushy life of the modern avoids all that
smacks of strenuous labor. We can sit in homes or business
environments set at seventy-two degrees Fahrenheit (give or
take a degree), consume a steady stream of delicacies, and
take three showers a day. Consequently, wealthier nations are
beset by a constant train of colds, flus, and a host of other
diseases—remedied by a steady stream of drugs, all of which
have their own side effects. After a time of experiencing this
lifestyle, some will figure out that the body was not made
for such a sedentary, Epicurean type of lifestyle. To live a
happy and productive life requires some amount of strenuous

4 http://articles.cnn.com/2009-03-18/health/healthmag.obesity.lifespan_1_bmis-
mortality-risk-body-mass-index?_s=PM:HEALTH

activity balanced with a moderate dose of creature comforts here and there.

Therefore, we must apply the principle of Proverbs 25:16 to anything that is good. Too much work on the job, for example, can ruin a man's family life. Too much entertainment, too many novels, and too many movies may disconnect a person from reality, resulting in "getting lost in the metaphor." It may have been a good story, but by losing himself in the story, he loses the meaning of the metaphor and fails to engage the spiritual battles taking place in the real world.

Proverbs 25:17

Withdraw your foot from your neighbor's house; lest he be weary of you, and so hate you.

The wise father makes another application similar to that in the previous verse. As in the case of honey, too much of a good thing is counter-productive. Spending too much time with a neighbor or a brother in the church may destroy relationships.

To some of us who are trying to renew relationships in a cold institutionalized world, it seems impossible that any person could ever spend too much time with somebody else! Yet relationships require careful wisdom and attention. Loving a person includes limiting the time spent with him. Our goal is always their edification. We want them to grow spiritually and to be encouraged in faith and love. Of course, fellowship is basic to Christian community (Acts 2:46–47), but there is a point at which people are no longer edified in the fellowship. Too much talk can lead to sinful gossip and arguments over issues of little consequence. After you have said everything you need to say, you should remind them of your love for them and leave. There is other work to do and other people to disciple. There are also other important priorities in your life that demand your time.

Self-centeredness is the largest contributor to the breakdown of human relationships in families and churches. This self-oriented love creates dependence, subjection, and constraint in the relationship. Nobody likes to feel like a caged bird, and this is what happens when self dominates on one side or the other. Eventually, self-oriented love turns into hatred and when relationships sour, it must be a foregone conclusion that there was too much "self" involved on one side or the other. Nevertheless, the solution is not the abandonment of human relationships altogether—an approach too easily taken by many today. Instead, we must humbly return to the "drawing board," assess our own mistakes, and re-engage the relationships once again with less self and more Christ! When we begin afresh, there must be more serving and less leaching off our neighbor.

Family Discussion Questions:

1. What happens if you eat too much honey?

2. What happens if you get too much fellowship with brothers and sisters in the church?

3. What is the goal of our fellowship with others?

4. What is a major contributor to the breakdown of human relationships?

PART 230 ~ THREE ANALOGIES/METAPHORS
Proverbs 25:18

A man that bears false witness against his neighbor is a maul, and a sword, and a sharp arrow.

This proverb initiates a second set of three more analogies in this chapter. In fact, this verse contains three metaphors, all of which refer to common weapons used at that time—a maul, a sword, and an arrow. When men bear false witness in a court trial, they undermine the foundation of a society. False testimony not only affects the defendant, it will influence the lives of many other people around him. It is <u>akin</u> to setting off bombs in the courthouse and bringing the building down. Hence, it should be clear that governments cannot tolerate false witnesses in the court. In the Old Testament, God in His wisdom provided a system of laws for Israel's civil state. There He recommends capital punishment for the man who lies in a capital murder trial. It is *that* serious. Do you think a witness would measure his words carefully if he were to testify in such an important trial?

From this lesson you can see that there is no truth in the old children's rhyme, "Sticks and stones may break my bones, but words will never hurt me." Your words can be dangerous and there are occasions where you will be held accountable for the words that you speak. If you are ever called upon to witness in a court of law, be very careful in what you say.

Proverbs 25:19

Confidence in an unfaithful man in time of trouble is like a broken tooth, and a foot out of joint.

The most basic functions of life include eating and walking. Without these abilities, you will be severely handicapped. You might be able to ignore a few other maladies in the body, but a broken tooth and a sprained foot are significant disabilities. These analogies apply perfectly to the unreliable employee or team member. Just as the body needs all parts to function in coordination to get things done in life, a family economy or corporation needs all members of the team functioning to get the work done. When one member of the team refuses to get his work done on time and "drops the ball" in an important task, the whole group becomes well aware of it. The problem is heightened when the group finds itself in a life-threatening emergency. Suppose a fire chief tasked one of the men with bringing the oxygen to a house fire. If the fireman failed to follow through, the victims caught in the flames could die because of the fatal oversight. The fire chief may have reminded the man on multiple occasions to load the oxygen tanks in the truck, but his inability to follow directions, his unwillingness to submit to supervisors, his careless attitude towards human life, or his characteristic lack of diligence will be evident for all to see during a time of crisis. Once his coworkers begin to see the man's true character, they will remove him from the team. This is because the man was like a sprained foot and a broken tooth—he was of no use to them.

When our young sons are still in the home, they should prove themselves to be faithful workers, obedient to their fathers, and diligent about their labors. Learning to be faithful in small things at home and looking out for the interests of your father's economy will grant you success elsewhere.

⁹/₂₅ Proverbs 25:20

As he that takes away a garment in cold weather, and as vinegar upon <u>*nitre,*</u> *so is he that sings songs to an heavy heart.*

These analogies speak of sources of irritation. It is both inconvenient and irritating to any poor soul to lose his coat in sub-zero weather. Likewise, the combination of vinegar with nitre (probably what we would call "baking soda") creates a violent reaction.

Music will not always cheer people. It can, in fact, do just the opposite. On one occasion, a group of carolers sang "Joy to the World" to a man who had lost both his wife and daughter in the same year. When they had finished the song, he told them there was no joy for him. The music was just what he *didn't* need. He felt worse after hearing the joyful song. Obviously, the man was in the depths of despondency. Until he could cling to some hope, or to a promise of the resurrection of Jesus Christ, no music would rouse his depressed spirits. Therefore, sometimes men must hear the sermon and believe the message before they can respond in joyous praise.

You must not be an idiot about your friendships or you will lose them. Wisdom is an essential component for cultivating relationships and properly meeting the needs of others. Indeed, many a friendship has been ruined by an unwise, ill-timed comment or a lousy joke. So to preserve your friendships, you need to be *sensitive* to the heart condition and needs of others. Learn to ask questions that might give you a glimpse into their spirit. Is your friend discouraged? Depressed? Confused? Before you can minister to him, you should get a good sense of what he needs. Also, be careful not to presume on your friend's good graces. If he has had a hard day and he is stressing out, it may not be the best time to open the conversation with a comical insult. If he takes it in the worst light, he will think you are slighting him and you will have distanced yourself from your friend. When reuniting with a friend (even after only a week's absence), reaffirm the relationship immediately with true, sincere affection. Proceed to discover his frame of mind and then converse freely to the edification of both of you.

Because friendships do require wisdom, it may be wise to limit the number of close friendships you cultivate at one time. Of course, this depends a great deal on the personalities involved. Choose your friends wisely and be careful to maintain the friendships well. While you should be cordial to new people that move into your neighborhood or church, and do your best to make them feel comfortable and welcome, you do not have to turn them into close friends in the space of a couple weeks. The Bible instructs us to both love the stranger and love the brother. But we love them in different ways. Over time, some strangers will turn into close friends and brothers, but it is always wisdom that directs this process.

Family Discussion Questions:

1. What kind of damage does a person do when he lies in a court trial?

2. How do you know you will be a faithful man and do the right thing in time of crisis? How can you prepare now so as not to be a sprained foot when you are called upon to help someone?

3. Are you sensitive about the needs of others? Or do you run roughshod over their feelings by saying whatever comes to mind? How might you become more sensitive to people's needs?

⁹⁄₂₅ PART 231 ~ LOVING YOUR ENEMY
Proverbs 25:21–22

If your enemy be hungry, give him bread to eat; and if he be thirsty, give him water to drink;
for you shall heap coals of fire upon his head, and the LORD shall reward you.

What is taught in this verse is confirmed by our Lord in the Gospels: "Love your enemy... Bless them that curse you... Do good to them that spitefully use you." In fact, the Apostle Paul repeats this proverb almost word for word in Romans 12:20. Contrary to prevailing opinions, there really is no contradiction between Old and New Testaments when it comes to God's ethical expectations.

Why does Yahweh want us to look after the well-being of our enemies? Ask the ironsmith about the purpose of those coals of fire and you will find that he uses them to both harden and soften steel! How your actions of kindness will be used is the business of the Great Ironsmith who works in the hearts of men. Suffice it to say that your actions are immensely powerful and penetrating. Just as white coals of fire harden the steel or melt it, so your kind deeds will either harden or soften your enemy. But if it hardens him in his commitment to treat you with wicked injustice, then he will only add up for himself "wrath against the day of wrath" (Rom. 2:5). You must hold to the certainty that every person and every single action will one day be called into judgment. Though evil men may mistreat you and continue in their unkind behavior, you must rest assured that God will take care of every injustice. To the same degree that His justice is served on the evildoer, He will reward you for patiently enduring these persecutions.

Yet, there is also the possibility that our kind deeds will melt the cruel heart of the persecutor. We should be hopeful in this as well. From the Centurion at the crucifixion of our Savior to the Apostle Paul and thousands of other persecutors, there are numerous records of hearts marvelously changed by the power of God and by the hot, hot coals of fire poured over them by peaceful and loving saints.

Nothing is wasted. No good deed goes unrecognized by the all-seeing eye of Heaven. If you ever have an opportunity to do good to a neighbor, a coworker, a fellow church-member, or anyone who insists on persecuting you, take full advantage of it! Be on the lookout for how you can meet his needs. Be creative in your kindness. Be persistent. You have no idea whether your good deeds will harden him or soften him—that is in God's hands. All you know is that God will be glorified in whatever happens and that person may repent of his sins and come to a saving knowledge of Christ. That would be glorious!

Family Discussion Questions:

1. What are the two purposes of coals of fire for those who work with metal? When you treat your enemy with kindness, how will those deeds affect his life?

2. Do we have any enemies? How do we treat them?

Three More Analogies

PART 232 ～ BRAWLING AND BACKBITING
Proverbs 25:23–24

The north wind drives away rain; so does an angry countenance a
*   backbiting tongue.*
It is better to dwell in the corner of the housetop, than with a brawling
*   woman and in a wide house.*

Now for the third set of analogies in this chapter. The first in
the sequence is a little difficult to understand because of the
imprecision of the Hebrew idiom, but it is usually best to take
it in its simplest sense. When the wind starts blowing hard,
you sense that a rain storm or snow storm is on its way—
wind and rain come together. Similarly, gossip and bitterness
follow on each others' heels. Gossip creates the environmental
conditions necessary for mistrust, bitterness, and fractured
relationships.

Sometimes, you walk into a room and sense tension in the
area. People are walking on eggshells as they inter-relate with
one other. There is a general air of mistrust or discomfort in
relationships. These are signals you pick up from the characters
in the room! It is what this translation of the Bible refers to
as the "countenance." Human beings have an amazing ability
to pick up messages from body language without a single
word being spoken. Naturally, there are many different causes
that produce these porcupine-like relationships, but gossip
is a big one. Wherever people will talk freely about others
behind their backs, they will create the atmosphere for weak,
distrusting, ineffectual relationships. *You must avoid talking*
about others behind their backs at all costs, especially if a word of
it is negative! It doesn't matter if you are talking about people
in a different state or country; when you speak of somebody
else in a deprecating way, people readily assume that this is
how everybody is treated in this relational context. Gossip
contaminates relationships and is as disconcerting as garbage
dumped into a swimming pool.

Although verse 24 is not directly connected to the analogy in verse 23, our attention remains directed towards the sins of the tongue. Gossip destroys relationships and an argumentative woman can turn a home into a terribly uncomfortable place to live. In fact, it would be better to be consigned to some 400-square-foot shack than to live in a 20,000-square-foot mansion with one of these contentious women. They know how to make life miserable for anybody who comes into contact with them. They are discontent, ungrateful, and impossible to please.

One of the most risky activities in which young students participate today is an activity known as "forensic debate." It is especially popular among home schooled and private schooled students. A woman trained in competitive debate who tries to bring that training into her marriage is in for some serious problems. While there is a place for arguing a certain set of facts in a court trial or in a legislative committee hearing, family life is far different from the business of courts, legislatures, and empires. Families are made up of covenant human relationships. Consensus in a marriage is not based on "the weight of the evidence" or the rhetorical ability of competitive debaters. Communication in a marriage should be marked more by humble submission and sacrificial love in the decision-making process. In fact, a married couple should not have to employ "Robert's Rules of Order" and parliamentary procedure to come to consensus on matters of disagreement. Therefore, wisdom dictates that husbands and wives avoid most if not all arguments for the sake of peace. The interpretation of the facts will be biased by love on the part of the husband and humble submission on the part of the wife.

For related commentary, reference Proverbs 21:9 and 19.

Family Discussion Questions:

1. What things put a damper on relationships?

2. Describe an argumentative woman. Why are people uncomfortable around this woman?

3. What is so dangerous about young people learning debate techniques? What is the difference between communication in a court trial and family discussions around the dinner table?

PART 233 ∽ THE GOSPEL TO THE HEATHEN LANDS
Proverbs 25:25

As cold waters to a thirsty soul, so is good news from a far country.

The prophet Isaiah remarked, "How beautiful upon the mountains are the feet of him that brings good tidings, that publishes peace; that brings good tidings of good, that publishes salvation; that says unto Zion, Thy God reigns!" (Is. 52:7). Referring to this same verse in his epistle to the Romans, the Apostle Paul says the same thing of those who preach the Gospel to those as far away as Rome was from Jerusalem (Rom. 10:15). Believe it or not, there are still some people in the far flung corners of the world who have never heard the good news of the resurrection of Jesus Christ and His blessed reign of peace over the globe! Granted, there are many in the Western world that have heard the message a thousand times and choose rather to take the Lord's name in vain than to serve Him in fear and love. The message of the Gospel offers no relief to them because they are hardened to it. Yet, to many who have never heard the Gospel, it comes as a cold glass of water to a thirsty soul in a very dry land.

This verse illustrates the tremendous fulfillment found in missionary work. But first you must be convinced that you have the good news—indeed, the best news of all! You must also realize that many others around the world have never heard this good news and would so love to receive it. Do not be discouraged if people around you do not appreciate the good news of the Gospel. There will always be those who are awaiting the good news and it is your job to find them. They may be people in your own family, your own church, your own neighborhood, or just on the other side of town.

Family Discussion Questions:

1. In what parts of the world today are there people who have never heard the good news of God's salvation?

2. How can we support the spread of the Gospel in other parts of the world?

3. Are there some folks in our city or state who have never heard the Gospel of Christ?

PART 234 ~ WHEN THE RIGHTEOUS CRUMBLE
Proverbs 25:26

A righteous man falling down before the wicked is as a troubled fountain, and a corrupt spring.

Following the analogies of the driving rain and the refreshing glass of cold water is the third analogy concerning the troubled fountain and corrupt spring.

Recently, a nationwide news program conducted an interview with one of the most important evangelical Christian pastors in America. The newsman asked him what he thought about homosexuality. The pastor wavered. He quivered. He said he thought it might be a sin, but then he said, "Hey, we're all sinners. I don't want to bash anybody with this." On a separate occasion, another evangelical pastor told a major secular news source that homosexual marriage was no real concern of his. He dismissed these socially degrading sins, telling the media that, "Some people are a little overweight and there are others who get headaches and need to take an aspirin to alleviate it. Everybody has problems. Why should we condemn homosexuals getting married?" With the tremendous social acceptance of these sorts of sins in the present age, it is hard to find men willing to stand for righteousness. Of course, the news media would never countenance a strong Christian testimony in the present day. They would far rather find a righteous man who would cower before these powerful media centers and make a spectacle of him!

In the 1980s, a national news personality interviewed one of the most important evangelical Christians on the topic of abortion. As the well-known Christian leader took a position against abortion, he also made exceptions for children conceived in rape and incest. The liberal, pro-abortion interviewer asked him about the consistency of his position. "If it is wrong to take a human life in the womb," he asked, "why should the child suffer for the misdeeds of his parents?" The leader had to concede that his position was inconsistent. Such responses come across as supremely weak and cast a terrible light upon Christian evangelicals. By refusing to stand on principle in the face of these powerful media moguls, these evangelicals undermine the cause of righteousness. Their compromise poisons the testimony of righteousness that we need to bear amongst a wicked and adulterous generation! A righteous man who waffles in the presence of the wicked media is truly a corrupt spring and a troubled fountain.

Family Discussion Questions:

1. Why is it important that the righteous do not dissolve their testimony of righteousness by compromise?

2. How resolute and courageous would you be if you had to condemn a popular sin in the face of powerful people who support that sin?

PART 235 ~ NARCISSISM AND HEDONISM
Proverbs 25:27

It is not good to eat much honey; so for men to search their own glory is not glory.

Two things are condemned by this verse: narcissism (selfish vain conceit) and hedonism (pleasure-seeking). The two are related, for both are thought to be shortcuts to happiness. When men seek their own happiness, they look for shortcuts to the Town of Happiness. Most men will instinctively seek after happiness through their taste buds and the accolades of others. Whereas the exciting thrills that come by the praise of men are intensely attractive to the average person, they always deliver far less than they promise. The same goes for food, wine, honey, and chocolate cream pie. All these things appear to present the shortest distance to happiness, but none can deliver it. Whatever fulfillment they grant is insubstantial and fleeting.

Specifically condemned here is what we call "fishing for compliments." Ask yourself why you are so eager to talk of your own exploits or share your accomplishments with others. Why do you tell people about the large fish you caught, or one of your successful business ventures, or even the men that you disciple? Or why would anyone want their name etched into the foundation blocks of some charitable institution? Whether or not somebody wants to give us a little credit for what we have done, this should be of little interest to us. We agree with the words of Christ in the New Testament: "Therefore when you do your alms, do not sound a trumpet before you, as the hypocrites do in the synagogues and in the streets, that they may have glory of men. Verily I say unto you, They have their reward" (Matt. 6:2).

The sooner children learn this lesson, the better. You may receive a little fame in your life, and you may enjoy a little honey on your toast in the morning. But don't become fixated on these things, as if they are more important than everything else in life. Take the lesson from wise Solomon who had it all. Your only fulfillment in life comes when you give God all the glory due His name. There are more important things to seek in life than your own glory. If you are privileged to receive some reward from men, use it only to get more disciples for Christ, to feed more widows, and to give God more glory. Invest everything in that which has eternal value!

For related commentary, reference Proverbs 25:16.

Family Discussion Questions:

1. Define narcissism and hedonism.

2. Why is it so tempting to seek pleasure in sweets or human accolades?

3. Where should our pleasures come from? Where do we find true fulfillment in life?

PART 236 ~ CONTROLLING YOUR TEMPER
Proverbs 25:28

He that has no rule over his own spirit is like a city that is broken down, and without walls.

To properly understand this proverb, you have to put yourself in a small village during this time in ancient Israel. There were hundreds of marauding tribes that would invade these little settlements, kill the men, and kidnap the women and children for slaves. The only defense available to the inhabitants against these attacks was a city or a castle in the vicinity. With their high walls, these fortresses could protect the people from devastating attacks. Where there were no walls, the little villages would be susceptible to catastrophic loss.

The very same thing can be said for the man who is unable to control his emotions. In the same way that the poor villagers had no way to defend themselves against the ever-present threat of attack, this man remains in a constant state of danger. At every moment, he is just a hairs breadth away from ruining his business, his marriage, and other relationships in his life. The angry man is especially at risk. In one brief moment of rage, he throws a rock at a friend, hits him in the head, and kills him. According to biblical law, a righteous court has no other alternative but to put the man to death. Hours before he killed his friend, if someone had asked the fellow of any intention to murder, he would have vehemently denied it. The forethought for such an act probably wouldn't take more than a mere five seconds! But he would regret those five seconds for the rest of his life, whether he lived out his days in a prison cell or received just retribution at the gallows. This world is filled with millions of heartbreaking stories of men and women who abused their children or killed their friends in a fit of passion. Usually, people try to reduce their culpability by calling it a mental breakdown. "Something snapped," they say, "and that person did the horrible deed." This may be true, but there was an underlying problem that was never addressed and it eventually contributed to the foul deed. The perpetrator failed to get control of his spirit. In these cases, except in the clear case of an accident, the Bible requires eye for eye and life for life.

Many, if not all, children are born with a temper. It is true that some are worse than others, considering the order of magnitude, but all must be trained to control their tempers. Without patient and caring parents applying themselves to this task for month after month and years upon years, there would be far more murder and mayhem in the world. With each successive generation, it seems that we find less wise and consistent parenting. Millions of parents rely on drugs to control the spirit of these boys and girls because they cannot imagine the children ever achieving any meaningful control over their spirits. This being the case, we may find more broken down walls and destruction in families and economies in the years to come.

Family Discussion Questions:

1. What is so risky about not controlling your temper?

2. Are we gaining any ground in controlling our tempers in this family?

3. If feelings of hopelessness and depression were to get out of control, might these also lead to catastrophe? How do we train our children to respond to feelings of sadness or hopelessness?

Part 237 ~ Honor for a Fool
Proverbs 26:1

As snow in summer, and as rain in harvest, so honor is not seemly for a fool.

Elsewhere in Scripture, you will find certain warnings regarding inappropriate or "unseemly" behavior. This is the principle behind the prohibition of seed mixing or plowing fields by yoking an ox and donkey (Deut. 22:10–11). Sometimes people want to do strange things such as dress a pig in a beautiful gown or stretch the human neck to outlandish proportions. Since 1930, an organization called "Ripley's Believe it or Not" has chronicled the strange things that people do, much of which is too gross to talk about in civilized company. God expects us to use His creation according to the designed purpose for which He created it. You need wisdom to know how to use God's creation in the right way. Although children will do foolish things like dress a pig in a gown, hopefully, by the time they have reached adulthood they have learned the wise and proper use of God's creatures. We must learn the purposes for which things were created and how to treat all things and all people in an appropriate fashion.

The present text supplies a good example of this sort of wisdom. It is inappropriate to lavish honor on a fool. Frost and snow in summer would ruin a good crop and rain in the harvest is not helpful to the farmer. So to honor some proud fool who rejects the living God would be both inappropriate and destructive (Ps. 14:1). Over the last century or so, we have witnessed a fair amount of honor lavished upon atheistic scientists such as Linus Pauling, Charles Darwin, and Sigmund Freud. Given another hundred years or so, the world may come to fully understand the true extent of their errors (even in their so-called scientific discoveries). The unabashed, enthusiastic endorsement of these fools on the part of the reigning scientific establishment may prove to be far more destructive than any of us could imagine.

How much honor is bestowed upon the great actors and actresses in motion pictures, many of whom have never done anything heroic in their lives but have degraded themselves to the extent of divorcing their spouses and consuming inordinate amounts of illicit drugs? The same can be said for many sports figures and popular music stars. The present age is unusual in the history of the world. Prior to 1920, there were no mega-stars with drug problems and dysfunctional families raking in $50 million per year. There were no big star-producing machines that would turn a marginally-talented, egotistical actor or singer into an overnight success. There were no special effects, no cosmetic surgeons, and no hi-tech sound editing intended to make the stars look and sound bigger and better than they really were. A society that refuses to judge a person's character on the basis of biblical revelation will end up lavishing way too much honor on worthless characters.

Family Discussion Questions:

1. What are examples of using God's creation contrary to its intended design?

2. What is wrong with giving honor to a fool? Describe a "fool" biblically.

PART 238 ~ WHAT CAUSES CALAMITY
Proverbs 26:2

As the bird by wandering, as the swallow by flying, so the curse causeless shall not come.

The prototypical Greek tragedy tells the story of Oedipus who is destined to murder his own father, though he has no desire or intention of doing so. He is a victim of "the Fates." From this worldview perspective then, nobody has any control over what happens to him. Therefore, nobody is responsible for his actions, and that includes the guy who robs banks for living.

Why do people do bad things? And why do bad things happen? There are only a few possible answers to this:

1. Bad things just happen. There is no ultimate reason why bad things happen.

2. Some impersonal power beyond us causes these things to happen and there is nothing we can do about it.

3. Every evil thing that happens can be traced back to two "personal" causes—God and man.

Suppose that a child is wounded when a bomb drops on his house during time of war. The poor child loses both legs and lies recovering in the hospital. What do we credit as the cause of this horrible calamity? I suppose you could blame the bomb, or the airplane, or the man flying the airplane. But the pilot did not intend to hurt the child and he would not have been flying the airplane if his country hadn't decided to enter the war. What, then, were the contributing events that undermined the relations between countries? Undoubtedly, there were a hundred contributing factors. I hope you can see how complicated it is to try and identify the true and ultimate cause that brought about this terrible tragedy on a little child. Who do you blame, then? What is the ultimate cause? The Greeks would tell you that it is impersonal fate. From the beginning of the universe, they say, the Fates determined that the child would lose his legs, and there is nothing that anyone could do about it. Others will tell you that the universe is just a matter of random, chaotic events, and there is no cause for these tragedies. If this is the case, we could not consider this a tragedy at all!

Have you ever seen a hummingbird fly here and there, jerking from one flower to another? He follows no map. Before he set out on his morning rounds, he did not pause to make a list of flowers he would visit. His whole itinerary seems quite random. But is the poor child in the hospital a victim of random chance? Of course not! In a biblical view of reality (metaphysics), we acknowledge that there is a cause in everything that happens. God is behind it all. He is the cause in every event that has ever happened on this globe. "I form the light, and create darkness; I make peace, and create evil; I the LORD do all these things" (Is. 45:7).

Of course, God's hand is present when every sparrow falls and when every hurricane beats on the shores of Australia and Indonesia. But why is there evil in the world? Why is there death and pain? The answer to this is simple. When Adam ate the forbidden fruit in the garden, he brought pain and death into the world (Rom. 5:12). So why does the little boy suffer from war wounds in the hospital? The simple answer is that Adam sinned. According to Romans 5, we are all equally culpable for Adam's sin because he was our representative. Therefore, we conclude that man is the cause of sin, which brought the curse of death into the world. Adam is the source of this sin. But there are also national governments that sin when they declare war unjustly against other nations. There are unjust dealings between nations when they impose trade sanctions on each other. The hatred of racism stimulates some wars. Whatever may have caused the war, little children will suffer in these wars because of the sin of mankind (traced all the way back to Adam) and because of their nation's sins. Like it or not, that is the way that God created the world. There is a corporal culpability for the sins of a nation. When God judged Judah, even godly men like Daniel, Shadrach, Meshach, and Abednego were impacted by the exile. They were part of the nation, and they bore part of the curse upon that nation and its sins. We suffer because Adam sinned. We suffer because our nations sin. We suffer because we sin. Can you see how the Christian worldview takes a far different view of reality than did the Greek tragedies?

Family Discussion Questions:

1. What are the causes that bring about the bad things that happen to us?

2. Why do godly men sometimes suffer with the wicked?

3. Who brought sin into the world at the beginning?

4. How does our explanation for calamities differ from the Greeks or the humanists?

5. What are we doing when we gripe and complain over our own trials and sufferings?

PART 239 ~ FOOLS—CORPORAL PUNISHMENT
Proverbs 26:3

A whip for the horse, a bridle for the ass, and a rod for the fool's back.

The Bible does not forbid what we call "corporal punishment." While it places clear limits on its application , it does require some use of the rod for children. Since children have a problem with foolishness, Proverbs 22:15 recommends the use of the rod for taking care of that problem. But what happens to the young man who never learns wisdom at all? He refuses to work. Worse yet, he steals from his employers. According to biblical law, this man should be sentenced to restitution for his crimes. Our present systems would rather take the "more liberal approach" in dealing with these problems, so they put him in a cell with other convicts who teach him to be a life-long criminal. The state provides a warm bed, clean clothes, hot meals, health care, and suitable entertainment for him in the prison at an average cost of $45,000 per year (charged to the taxpayers). In a biblical system, the man must work to restore up to five times the value of what he stole. These just, biblical courts' would even permit him to live with his wife and children. During the daytime hours, he would be required to work. If he still refused to work, one of two things would happen. Seeing that the man refuses to abide by the instructions of the judge, the court may sentence him to execution (Deut. 17:8–13). There is, however, one last-ditch alternative for salvaging the incorrigible rogue, and that is the rod. His employer may encourage him to work by the application of the rod. The Bible limits all corporal punishment to no more than forty stripes (Deut. 25:3).

Obviously, all of this is in lieu of a heart change on the part of the fool. In order for social systems to function, there must be some law and order in the land. Hence, every social system will use prisons, restitution, work camps, or execution to keep their nations from degrading into economic and social anarchy. It would be ideal to function without beatings, prisons, and executions, but the social systems in this fallen world could never survive without them. Of course, the most effectual change of all is the heart change that comes by the witnessing of the Gospel and the work of the Spirit of God.

Family Discussion Questions:

1. What happens in our present system to the rebellious young man who refuses to work? What happens to him in a biblical system?

2. How does a system of restitution differ from the modern prison system?

3. How do you change the heart of a fool?

PART 240 ~ FOOLS—APOLOGETICS WITH ATHEISTS
Proverbs 26:4–5

Answer not a fool according to his folly, lest you also be like unto him. Answer a fool according to his folly, lest he be wise in his own conceit.

Here is some highly useful advice for those who live amongst fools. Following the "Christianized" medieval period in Europe, a new age of skepticism, agnosticism, and outright atheism flourished. And since the 1700s, most people in Western nations refuse to begin their thinking with Proverbs 1:7. They do not fear God, and they challenge God to prove His own existence before they will believe in Him. C.S. Lewis was tracking this emerging agnosticism when he wrote, "For modern man, man is the judge and God is in the dock. The trial may end in God's acquittal, but the point is man is on the bench and God is in the dock."[5] The modern fool does not assume the existence of God as his basic foundation for knowledge. The fool has said in his heart, "There is no God," and there are plenty of fools about today.

This Proverb informs our conversations with fools. First, we do not answer the fool according to his folly. We must not

5 C.S. Lewis, "God in the Dock" from God in the Dock: Essays on Theology and Ethics

seriously consider any assumption that God does not exist. The key word here is "seriously." If we were to do this, we would jettison the most important and basic presupposition of all our understanding. The fool believes in his own ability to interpret data and make decisions about important matters such as God's existence, his own existence, and so on. Before he would believe in God's existence, he assumes the integrity of his own mind. What wisdom is telling us here is to avoid playing the game that Lewis described. Do not take the game seriously. The fool thinks he is sitting like a judge at the bench and God is trying to argue His own existence before the fool. You must not succumb to the temptation to play defense attorney for God. If God is who He says He is in His Word, how would He prove His existence? Should He show you His driver's license? Then again, who would issue a driver's license to God and how would you prove that guy's existence? Should the fool ask God to do a few miracles? Would that be enough to prove the case? In the parable of Lazarus and the Rich Man, Abraham speaks to the Rich Man in Hades and tells him, Abraham saith unto him, They have Moses and the prophets; let them hear them. And he said, Nay, father Abraham; but if one went unto them from the dead, they will repent. And he said unto him, If they hear not Moses and the prophets, neither will they be persuaded, though one rose from the dead" (Luke 16:29–31). The hearts of fools are in such rebellion towards God, and their minds have been so blinded by sin, that they can never be trusted to think rationally concerning these things. While proud men demand all the proof in the world to substantiate His existence, God needs no defense attorneys. This is an example of *not* answering a fool according to his folly.

But then we are *told* to answer the fool according to his folly, lest he be self-confident in his own foolishness. Usually, atheists and agnostics are very certain in their rebellion. They consider themselves the supreme rationalists and laugh in the face of Christians who believe in a God they cannot see! We hear them taunt Christians all the time with their arguments,

"Why don't you believe in the great spaghetti monster in the sky?" Occasionally, Christians might enter into a discussion with the fool to remind him of the incoherencies in his own thinking. Although we will not seriously consider the truthfulness of the fool's way of thinking, we certainly can point out the weaknesses of it. We should ask him how he can assume ethical absolutes if there is no God over all to establish those absolutes. We should ask him how cosmic dust could ever live for a purpose if, indeed, everything is only matter in motion. Without a Creator and without a purpose communicated to us by God, how can we ever find any ultimate purpose for life at all? How can we retain human responsibility for our actions if everything that happens in this world is linked to indeterminate or determinate causes? These are called "ultimate questions." By asking these ultimate questions, we point out that the fool's worldview is insufficient to answer them.

Consider that everybody lives in some sort of house of knowledge, and some houses are better-built than others. When we answer the fool according to his folly, we enter his house of knowledge and begin to kick the pillars around. As we ask our pointed questions, huge pieces of the building start falling around us and it quickly becomes obvious that his house of knowledge is intolerably flimsy. Then, we invite him into *our* house of knowledge. We don't feel any obligation to defend any one proposition. Our house of knowledge holds together very well because we can explain our basis for ethics, purpose, logic, and truth. We show him that our God predestines the free actions of men, thus retaining human responsibility and order and purpose for the universe. We have answers—he doesn't. However, at the end of the conversation, we may not have convinced him of our way of thinking. You have to remember that the fool has a fundamental bias against God. As the old saying goes, "A man convinced against his will is of the same opinion still." The important thing is that we have dislodged the fool a bit in his self-confidence.

Family Discussion Questions:

1. Does God need a defense attorney? What evidence would it take to convince a fool that God exists?

2. How do you challenge the fool in his folly? What sorts of questions might you ask Richard Dawkins or any other well-known atheists if you were sitting next to him on an airplane?

3. What is the goal of apologetics when interacting with foolish men and women (according to these verses)?

PART 241 ~ FOOLS—LOUSY EMPLOYEES
Proverbs 26:6

He that sends a message by the hand of a fool cuts off the feet, and drinks damage.

Before you read these proverbs, you should remember several important contextual points. First, the proverbs were directed towards the son of a king who would have servants working for him. Anyone who works in leadership and management today must communicate constantly through e-mail, faxes, and phone calls, but none of this was available to kings in 960 B.C. when these proverbs were written. There were no airplanes or trucks to carry the mail. All messages were hand-carried by dependable servants who wouldn't wander from the task.

To hire a fool as an employee is akin to sawing off your foot with a hacksaw. It would be agonizingly painful. Like poison in the body, a fool will eventually corrupt the organization. Of all the decisions made by leaders in business organizations, the hiring decisions are the most important. Therefore, a proper analysis of a man's character is critical before introducing the man to the organization.

But who is this fool that is so unreliable? As mentioned above, he is a man who either denies God's existence or challenges it. But there is more to say about the fool. So far we have learned that the fool is not teachable and he is utterly entrenched in his own folly (Prov. 10:8, 17:12). He despises instruction (Prov. 15:5). He is completely confident in his own knowledge (Prov. 12:15). He trusts in his own heart (Prov. 28:26). He cannot think that he could ever make a mistake (Prov. 17:10). He cannot control his tongue, but pours out foolishness (Prov. 12:23). He flaunts his own folly (Prov. 13:16). He destroys himself and his relationships by the words he speaks (Prov. 18:7). In sum, the foolish man is dull, stubborn, obstinate, boorish, and stupid. You would never want to hire such a fellow for your business. Be aware that fools may show up anywhere and everywhere, including church leadership, government, and the business world.

Children will always flirt with foolishness when they are young. Given years of neglectful parenting, that foolishness will be solidly entrenched in their lives. Sadly, this is not an uncommon condition in our day. Generally, children are unreliable messengers and helpers until they are trained to faithfully follow through on the instructions they are given. Therefore, it is important for parents to patiently work with them until they have learned to complete a task and do it with excellence.

Family Discussion Questions:

1. What makes an employee dependable? Would you be a dependable employee?

2. How might parents train a child to follow through on his tasks?

PART 242 ~ FOOLS—HANDLING TRUTH BADLY
Proverbs 26:7

The legs of the lame are not equal; so is a parable in the mouth of fools.

A parable is a story used to illustrate truths that cannot be explained very well through a set of logical propositions that are systematically presented in outline form. The parable gives insight. It cracks the door of knowledge a little. It shines a little light on extremely complex and difficult issues that the minds of men will never completely comprehend. Our understanding of the kingdom of Christ and the efficacy of His redemptive work relies heavily on the parables of the New Testament. But when fools begin to teach these things, beware! There is a reason why there are so many pseudo-Christian cults and hundreds of contradicting explanations for the simple Gospel of Christ! Ever since the coming of Christ in the 1ˢᵗ century, a good many fools have had access to the biblical accounts and they have not handled them well. Instead of carefully contemplating the deep truths contained in a parable, they jump to quick conclusions as to its meaning. The fool is far too confident in his own wisdom. He turns the parable to say what he wants it to say. If it doesn't comport with his preconceived system of truth, he'll twist it some more until it fits. His over-reaching confidence in his own abilities to rightly interpret Scripture and comprehend truth is actually fatal error. Such heart attitudes have produced innumerable deceptions and heterodoxies in the history of religion.

To those of us who wish to get the truth out, is it sufficient to hand out Bibles? Do we assume that all who receive the parables will handle them rightly? It is the teaching of the Word of God and the work of the Spirit of God that brings about true conversion. Above all other means, the Apostles emphasized the teaching and preaching of the Word as the primary means by which men were saved (Rom. 1:9, 10:14; 1 Cor. 2:14, 9:18, 15:14; Gal. 2:7; 1 Tim. 3:16, 4:13, 5:17; 2 Tim. 4:2; 1 Pet. 1:12, 25, 4:6). But churches must be careful not to hand the mysteries of the kingdom over to a fool. The Apostle Paul warned Timothy not to give the eldership or the diaconate over to the novice (1 Tim. 3:6, 9). What the parable really said and the fool's interpretation of the parable may be two different things. The incongruity of his thinking comes across like a crippled person hobbling along with one leg six inches shorter than the other.

Family Discussion Questions:

1. Why are there so many cults in the world?

2. Could we misinterpret the Word of God ourselves, or are we immune to such mistakes? How might we avoid starting another cult based on a bad interpretation of God's revelation?

PART 243 ~ FOOLS—UNWORTHY OF HONOR
Proverbs 26:8

As he that binds a stone in a sling, so is he that gives honor to a fool.

The sling is used to hurl stones in hunting or warfare. Of course, David knew how to use a sling, and we assume Solomon was versed in its function as well. If some foolish soul were to tie the stone up securely in the sling, the stone would not be properly released at the critical moment. Such foolish actions would probably result in serious injury to the fellow handling the sling. There really are people in the world lacking basic, common sense. Take the genius who jams a rod into the muzzle end of the gun for example; he advances a bullet into the chamber and pulls the trigger. Of course, the resultant explosion in the barrel will do catastrophic damage to the man holding the gun. This is the sort of analogy used for the fellow who gives honor to a fool. When you honor a fool it undermines your own credibility. Initially, others may not be aware of the fact that the man you honor is a fool, but when others discover the true character of the fool whom you honored, they will think less of you.

Many of the Nazi officers who fawned over Adolph Hitler saw their reputations ruined after World War II. Some were imprisoned. Many left the country in shame and spent their remaining years in South America. Sadly, they chose to honor the wrong man, a godless, Nietzschean megalomaniac who sought to build a utopia without Christ. When will men learn that all these socialist schemes will end in ruin? Be careful how much honor you bestow on arrogant university professors, entertainers, politicians, and pastors. The honor should be commensurate with the position the man retains and his character. And no man must ever receive more honor and glory than the King over the whole earth—the living, resurrected Christ of God. This is why Christians will worship Jesus Christ daily and gather weekly on the day that we celebrate His resurrection from the dead.

Family Discussion Questions:

1. Why is it important not to give too much honor to certain people?

2. Why do you think people gave Adolph Hitler so much honor?

PART 244 ~ FOOLS—NOT IMPACTED BY TRUTH
Proverbs 26:9

As a thorn goes up into the hand of a drunkard, so is a parable in the mouths of fools.

On a Sunday morning, the pastor preached his heart out to the congregation, drawing an impacting message from one of the Psalms. Truth was set against error. The rebellion of sin was described in its true colors. By the end of the sermon, God's redemption salvaged the sinner from complete ruin and many hearts rose in unison to praise God for His goodness to men. However, several young men in the congregation yawned through the whole message. Occasionally, the preacher's impassioned cries awakened them from their slumbers and daydreams, but only for a brief moment. They heard a few of the words, but those words didn't mean anything to them. They had no impact. These men were not struck to the heart and they didn't fall down on their faces and worship God (1 Cor. 14:24–25). They didn't get it. Here the Proverb draws the comparison to the drunkard who falls on a nail that punctures his hand. He doesn't even say, "Ouch!" As the alcohol dulls his brain to any physical sensations, even a nail pounded through his hand would hardly get a reaction out of him. So is the fool who comes into contact with the deep truths of divine revelation. As Paul explains it, these truths are foolishness to the natural man, for "they are spiritually discerned" (1 Cor. 2:14).

How does one explain the phenomenon of sight to a blind man? The believer may scream into the faces of the fools who reject the truths of God's existence, His justice, and His great redemption. Earnestly, he warns them to flee the wrath to come! He speaks of a hell where there will be gnashing of teeth and where the fire is never quenched. The fool gives him a blank stare and tries to change the subject to some professional football game. How, then, does the believer witness to a dead man? There is no use in screaming. If you believe that the dead can come to life (Eph. 2:1–2) then you will poke a man with the truth on occasion to see if he will say, "Ouch!" If he fails to respond, then wait a little while and poke him again. Listen for "Ouch!" Without the Spirit's internal work, there will be no life in the corpse and no response to the Word preached.

Family Discussion Questions:

1. Why are fools impervious to the most impassioned warnings and exhortations from the Word of God?

2. How does a dead man react when you poke him with a sharp stick? How do believers witness to dead men?

PART 245 ~ FOOLS—CAN'T GET AWAY WITH FOOLISHNESS
Proverbs 26:10

The great God that formed all things both rewards the fool, and rewards transgressors.

Some people have suggested that the famous evolutionist Charles Darwin was a deist of sorts. He could have been satisfied with a distant god who created a formless mass of matter and energy, but Darwin didn't want the God whose hands formed creation. By the 19th century, many Europeans and Americans agreed with him. Intuitively, people understand that a god who did not form every creature and every valley with his own hands would distance himself from his universe. Sure, he may have tossed a few planets in a solar system deep in the recesses of the Milky Way Galaxy, but then he forgot where he put them! According to these deistic thinkers, the various species of life forms develop without divine intervention, by chance evolutionary processes. The idea that God's hand is providentially active in every birth and in every catastrophe is reprehensible to the naturalistic evolutionist. If God's hand is involved in the tiny details of every creature's life, then of course He is interested in the actions of that creature. Indeed, that is what Jesus meant when He told His disciples that the heavenly Father is vitally interested in every sparrow that falls to the ground (Matt. 10:29). While the sparrow is amoral and unable to sin against God, that is not the way it is for human beings. Men are moral creatures and they know they are moral because they talk about morals all the time. If, therefore, the actions of men are moral and God is vitally interested in their actions even more than those of the sparrow, then there will be a good many rebel sinners in serious trouble. And this is exactly what Charles Darwin wanted to avoid. So the entire scheme of evolution served as a "scientific" apologetic for deism. Assuming that God was uninvolved in the evolution of the creatures, then man must have appeared on the scene by random cause-and-effect processes.

In this verse we read that the great God formed all things and He did it by the Word of His power (Ps. 33:9; Heb. 1:3). His hands carefully formed every creature just as a potter deliberately, carefully works a piece of clay into something beautiful. There are no accidents in God's world. Therefore, we can be sure that nothing and nobody will escape His all-seeing eyes. Our ethical accountability is directly tied to God's absolute sovereign, providential hand on history. If you remove God's hands from history, you will create a world where He is less involved in the ethical doings of His creatures. This is precisely what Charles Darwin and other philosophers and scientists have been doing for the last two hundred years. Though fools and transgressors may "get away" with foolishness and injustice, there is a God who will bring every single action into account (Eccl. 12:4; Matt. 12:36).

PART 246 ~ FOOLS—CAN'T STAY AWAY FROM FOOLISHNESS
Proverbs 26:11
As a dog returns to his vomit, so a fool returns to his folly.

It is practically impossible to train dogs not to do doggish things, such as licking up their own vomit. Likewise, until the heart of the fool is changed so that he becomes something more than a fool, he will continue to act the part of the fool.

Dogs may walk on their hind legs for a hundred yards or so and there will be fools who will cease from their folly for a short period of time. You can baptize a fool and put him in a church for a couple of years. He may have escaped the pollutions of the world for a time and traversed the way of righteousness (2 Pet. 2:19–20). He may have installed Internet filters on his computer and submitted to an accountability system. But if his heart is awash in foolishness, then he will return to his vomit and embrace his online pornography with renewed enthusiasm. Or as the poet Rudyard Kipling described it, "The burnt Fool's bandaged finger goes wobbling back to the Fire."

Family Discussion Questions:

1. What does God's creating the world have to do with fools not getting away with their foolishness?

2. Why did Charles Darwin come up with a theory that did not include God in the creation and the formation of His creatures?

3. How do you explain the fellow who goes to church and tries to be good for awhile but always falls back into foolishness and sin?

PART 247 ~ WHAT'S WORSE THAN A FOOL
Proverbs 26:12

Do you see a man wise in his own conceit? there is more hope of a fool than of him.

From these words you can see that there is something worse than being a fool. It is bad enough to be unreliable, unteachable, dull, stubborn, obstinate, boorish, and stupid. But it is quite another thing to be a fool with a PhD. Of course, not every man with a PhD from a university is a fool, but there are a good many on the planet who are brilliant fools. As the Apostle Paul says, "There is a knowledge that puffs up," (1 Cor. 8:1) and there is a fair amount of this pride that accumulates in the universities.

The man who is wise in his own conceit is entrenched in his foolishness because he has developed a complex system of arguments that appear, on the surface, to be "smart." He has been to the university. He is a scientist who can "prove" his deism. He can use really big words to defend his commitment to atheism. Of course, there are fatal flaws in his system of knowledge but they are buried under layers of big words and fat hubris.

So the worst thing that can happen is to send an arrogant teenager, who refuses to his parents, to learn more revolutionary ideas at college. That experiment has been tried with men like Karl Marx, Friedrich Nietszche, Fidel Castro, Vladimer Lenin, Mao Tse Tung, and Pol Pot. All of these men formed their revolutionary ideas at the university as they connected with other revolutionary radicals. All of them were committed atheists who formulated ideas that brought about much destruction and misery to the modern nation-states. In total, these men were responsible for the murder of at least

250 million people. Even the mass-murderer Kim Il Sung of North Korea left his devoted Christian family for communist ideals during his high school years, thanks to associations with campus radicals. These are fools who become wise in their own conceit and they are dangerous men who embrace a materialistic, atheistic worldview, and institutionalize that worldview throughout many of the modern nations. The universities, at least in this country, are more godless than ever before. Hence, in future years, there will be plenty of opportunities to foment even more radicals and more arrogant atheists in the seedbed of these universities. The most arrogant man of all is the one who dethrones God in his mind, defends his action by intellectual arguments, and then institutionalizes this idea in the schools and nations.

Family Discussion Questions:

1. What is worse than being a fool?

2. Why is it important to be humble and honoring towards your parents before you go to college?

PART 248 ~ THE SLOTHFUL MAN
Proverbs 26:13–16

The slothful man says, There is a lion in the way; a lion is in the streets.
As the door turns upon his hinges, so does the slothful upon his bed.
The slothful hides his hand in his bosom; it grieves him to bring it
   again to his mouth.
The sluggard is wiser in his own conceit than seven men that can render
   a reason.

At this point, it should be clear that slothfulness is one of the major sins which has plagued every culture in every era of history. But how do we sniff out the problem of slothfulness in our own homes? This passage gives four descriptions of the slothful man.

1. First, real or merely perceived problems intimidate the slothful man from getting his work done. He procrastinates because he is intimidated by obstacles and difficulties. There is no "can-do" attitude with this guy. For children, they meet the lion in the streets in their lessons. Almost without exception, our children find him in their mathematics classes. Inevitably, every child will meet the lion in the textbook. As parents go over the child's lessons, they discover work left unfinished and many problems missed on the test. Upon interrogation, it is clear that the child has effectively "given up" on the class. He is discouraged and disheartened. He has no further interest in pursuing his studies in mathematics. Does this sound familiar? The parent must now point out the lion. If there is a lion in the way, the farmer must take out his .400 bore rifle and shoot the lion in the head, and then proceed to plow his fields. We do not want to shelter our children from all challenges. They must learn to overcome their obstacles. This is a very necessary part of training. For when our children grow up, they will face obstacles all the time. Challenges are part of life, hardwired into the system from the fall of man in the garden. Whether it be technical glitches, bugs in a computer program, natural disasters, broken appliances, difficult business relationships, rejection, conflicts, flat tires, or illness, life is filled to the brim with difficult challenges that must be overcome. But the slothful man simply cannot handle them.

2. Secondly, the slothful man likes his sleep. Now this is not to say that all men do not *need* sleep, but the slothful man loves his bed and it is difficult to get him out of it. When Monday morning approaches and he knows he must rise and work, he ignores the alarm clock, rolls over, and goes back to sleep. He has less motivation to get up and address the challenges of the day than to stay where he is in bed. He is supremely unmotivated.

3. Thirdly, even the most menial efforts require an inordinate amount of will power and effort from this man. Most people would have no trouble feeding themselves but as time progresses, this man begins to find that menial things like

filling the car with gas, taking out the trash, or making his bed are tiresome and odious chores. It may come to the point where he has trouble opening the fridge door and grabbing a carton of milk for his boxed cereal in the morning. His position has rapidly deteriorated. At first it was the lions in the street. He began avoiding the serious obstacles in life. Instead of learning to enjoy life's assorted challenges, he becomes habitually intimidated by them. He resists any contact with them. This is how he comes to find all work and all menial effort utterly intolerable.

4. Finally, the sin of slothfulness is a weed with a root system that runs deep and wide into that soil. It is very difficult to root it out. Once it is entrenched in a man's life, it cannot be coaxed out of him very easily. He has every excuse for why he cannot work. In fact, he has an entire library of excuses to give anyone who pursues the problem. If one excuse doesn't work, he'll try a different one. As you can see, this is a desperately horrible condition. If the sin of slothfulness is rampant in your life, you would do well to pray to God to deliver you from it!

Family Discussion Questions:

1. How do you handle challenges? Do you procrastinate, take long breaks, and complain about obstacles before you? What are your lions and how do you overcome them?

2. Have we become slothful as a family when it comes to preparing food? Do we resort quickly to processed foods and boxed meals so we can get on with more entertainment?

3. Do you exhibit any slothfulness in your sleep patterns? What is a sufficient amount of sleep for the average person? What about you?

PART 249 ~ JUMPING INTO THE WRONG FIGHT
Proverbs 26:17

He that passes by and meddles with strife belonging not to him, is like one that takes a dog by the ears.

Now here is a picture that is hard to forget. Have you ever taken a pit bull by the ears, and held him up in front of your face? It's definitely not a recommend activity. This could be the stupidest thing a person could do, unless he was planning to have his face chewed off. Such is the illustration used for getting involved in somebody else's fight. You need to leave the dog alone.

There are manifold applications of this very important principle. Sometimes, national leaders will move towards what is known as "isolationism" in their foreign policy. Prudent leaders refuse to meddle in conflicts between other nations where power-mongering leads to war on an international level. In the modern age, the most powerful nations in the world were formed in Europe. But power fed off of a constant state of war in which nations like England, France, and Spain acted as the primary contenders. By the 1700s, war between the European nations was a matter of routine. But with the establishment of the American Republic in the 1780s, President George Washington warned about "entangling alliances" with foreign nations in his final speech to the American people. Then, President John Adams strongly resisted the urgings of Alexander Hamilton to participate in these European wars. Continuing this isolationistic attitude in the early 1820s, President James Monroe issued the famed "Monroe Doctrine." This document formed American foreign policy for several generations. Generally, the document resisted involvement in foreign wars, stating that, "In the wars of the European powers, in matters relating to themselves, we have never taken any part, nor does it comport with our policy to do so. It is only when our rights are invaded, or seriously menaced, that we resent injuries, or make preparation for our defense." However, all of this changed in 1898, as America gave way to the temptation to empire building in its war with Spain over control of the Philippines. Subsequent participation in foreign wars has led to the sacrifice of hundreds of thousands of American lives.

There is a definite duty to protect our families and our nations from aggressors who aim to kill or reduce us to subjection. But this is far different from taking sides in a war where either side is fighting over control of some foreign colony. Both sides may be power-mongers looking for more political control over more economic interests.

Some strife *does* belong to you. That is, there are some situations in which you need to be involved in the act of peacemaking. When you are in conflict with brothers and sisters within the covenant relationships of the family or church, it may be important for you to act as a peacemaker. But filling this role takes some maturity and wisdom. Often, people who try to act as peacemakers contract the same sins that ooze out of pores of the other players in the fight. They take on the pride, anger, or bitterness found in the contenders and the conflict just metastasizes. That is why Paul encourages only the "spiritual" to restore the wayward (Gal. 6:1).

In the present climate of frequent contention within and between churches, it is even more important to choose your associations carefully. Some communities become utterly toxic by conflict rooted in pride and bitterness. Considering the history of the conflicts and the characters involved, you soon realize that there is nothing you can do to resolve these deep-seated contentions. The best thing you can do is take a wide berth around this community of folks and establish healthier relationships elsewhere. If you choose to fellowship with "Contention Community Church" on an ongoing basis, you would find your family profoundly influenced by the bitterness and the pride in those associations over five to ten years. If you find yourself living in proximity to the "Hatfields and McCoys," families in long-standing feuds, keep them at arm's length. You do not have to be ugly towards them. But neither should you spend any concerted time with them. If one party wants to gain your confidence to take their side in the matter, do your best to change the subject. However, if one party is overwhelmed by their *own* sin and guilt before God and needs your counsel, then be sure to show them the forgiveness and grace of Christ. This is the only possibility for healing in these conflicts.

Family Discussion Questions:

1. Why is isolationism generally a good policy ? Is this country likely to get involved in some world conflict today?

2. What should you do if you find yourself living between two neighbors who hate each other?

PART 250 ~ PRACTICAL JOKES
Proverbs 26:18

As a mad man who casts firebrands, arrows, and death, so is the man that deceives his neighbor, and says, Am not I in sport?

In comparison to all previous centuries in world history, leisure and sports contribute far more to the life of the modern person. Those things that are done "in sport," are of little consequence, but they can be entertaining and sometimes help us to laugh a little. When young people want to turn life into fun and games, they resist serious, meaningful conversations that might truly edify and build relationships.

If you have read the Bible through, you probably noticed that the Scriptures have very little to say about fun and sports (Gen. 26:8; Judg. 16:27; Prov. 10:23). When these things are mentioned, there is usually a cautionary note attached. Gravity and sobriety are important traits for the young men and women growing into adulthood (Tit. 2:4–6). This is not to say that Christianity doesn't involve joy, but we must retain a sober and honest analysis of the dangers that are around us. Nobody appreciates the comedian in the foxhole who fails to protect his buddies in the battle. Granted, children are not old enough to be aware of the serious spiritual battles going on, and they will play their games. At some point, however, children must grow into mature adults.

There is yet an even more serious concern that arises here in the present text. When everything is reduced to joking, verbal cuffing, insults, and meaningless talk, people begin to lose track of what is real and what is pretense in the relationship. The steady stream of informal and unmannerly banter will eventually break down the fabric of relationships. If the conversation isn't serious, people figure out pretty quickly that the relationship isn't worth much either. Also a true friend might receive a "friendly" insult at face value, and take serious offense by it. The important questions to ask in the matters of teasing and practical jokes are:

1. How will this edify my brother, and how will this improve our relationship?

2. Is this joking and teasing causing our family to be less sober and equipped in spiritual battle, or better able to the handle the battle with the right spirit of courage, joy, and optimism?

3. Does my brother understand that I am joking and will he "get" the joke in a reasonable time frame so that our relationship will not be ruined and he will not act unwisely on a untruth?

For example, if you tell your brother that there is money to be made in some worthless endeavor, and he puts time and money into developing a business around that endeavor, you are misleading him. It may have been a joke at the beginning. But your humor is malicious and destructive to your brother's interests. The proverb describes the man given to this malicious joking as dangerous. He is like the mad man running around the house swinging maces and tossing coals from the fire onto the wood floors. Given enough opportunities, this man will burn the house down!

Family Discussion Questions:

1. What is our family's position on practical jokes? At what point does it get "out of hand?"

2. Are we a sober-minded family? Are we joyful? Do we joke around too much?

3. Is there a pretense about our relationships? Do people know when you are serious? When is it appropriate to speak more formally and seriously to one another?

PART 251 ~ GOSSIP AND CONTENTION
Proverbs 26:20–21

Where no wood is, there the fire goes out; so where there is no talebearer, the strife ceases.
As coals are to burning coals, and wood to fire; so is a contentious man to kindle strife.

Strife is an inevitability of life where there are sinners involved. But wise men can and will learn to contain it. Should contention be allowed to burn out of control, it will ruin churches, businesses, and families. Therefore, it is essential that fathers and leaders be always on their guard for strife wherever it breaks out. Every city understands the potential devastation of fire and they will keep fire trucks and firemen on the ready for when fire breaks out here or there. It is not a question of if, but a question of when it happens. As long as there are at least two people in relationship with each other, conflict will ensue.

Peacemakers will do their best to quench the conflicts when they arise but there are two sources of fuel that only exasperate the problem of conflict—gossip and contention. If a town of 30,000 people had to deal with a fire every month or two, the fire station could keep it under control. But if one pyromaniac with 200 gallons of gasoline walked around the town and lit ten fires every day, the town would be utterly devastated within just a few months. Somebody would have to stop this madman if that community was to survive the year! In a similar sense, a church or small community simply cannot survive with a contentious person and a spirit of gossip in the mix. From the outset of any church gathering, wise leaders will be very careful to warn their congregations against the sin of gossip. Men and women must be extremely careful not to vent their discontentment or speak negatively of others behind their backs. The survival of the community depends on it.

Proverbs 26:22

The words of a talebearer are as wounds, and they go down into the innermost parts of the belly.

Words can wound, and these wounds can go deep. Occasionally, a family catches wind of criticism leveled against them, perhaps regarding something about their choice of immodest clothing or how they discipline their children. Almost without exception, they will take serious offense to the criticism. They might even internalize the hurt for years, and never fully recover from it. Even in the best of scenarios, peacemakers will work hard to resolve the conflict and make things right between the parties involved. But these wounds do not go away immediately. Sometimes scar tissue forms and the relationships are strained for decades, until finally the church fellowship breaks apart. Ideally, the truth of Christ's forgiveness should be so overwhelming to men and women of true faith that it will heal the deepest wounds. But in reality, there is little true faith in Jesus' precious forgiveness with many folks. So we must be especially careful not to initiate the wounds that will never heal, whether with neighbors, co-workers, or with people who visit our church communities.

Family Discussion Questions:

1. What are the two sources of fuel that feed contention in a community?

2. What sorts of things might we say that could hurt another family in the church?

PART 252 ~ THIN-COATED RELIGION
Proverbs 26:23

Burning lips and a wicked heart are like a potsherd covered with silver dross.

How many times do men broadcast their love for Jesus with a "fish" symbol on their business card and then proceed to trade in a dishonorable way? In this country, people are particularly wary around those who "wear their faith on their sleeve." We are hardly surprised anymore to learn that the weepy television evangelist with his gushy words about Jesus is picking up prostitutes in his off hours or skimming a little extra out of the church offerings. We practically expect the big pop music stars who sing fervently about their love for Christ to announce their next illegitimate divorce or their endorsements of homosexuality.

It is important to knock the watermelon to assess its integrity. Or you may scrape the surface of the silver vase a bit to make sure there is something besides a thin coat of silver plating over it. Be careful not to assess the character of a man by mere appearances. In assessing the character of Jesse's sons, God advised Samuel to look upon the heart. "But the LORD said unto Samuel, Look not on his countenance, or on the height of his stature; because I have refused him; for the LORD sees not as man sees; for man looks on the outward appearance, but the LORD looks on the heart" (1 Sam. 16:7).

When you base your assessments on superficial conditions, you betray your own superficiality. Superficial people attract other superficial people. Thus, it is usually wise not to over-commit yourself to an acquaintance, a business partner, a musical genre, or a spiritual leader until you have followed them for awhile. Test the quality of the faith they profess. How would they hold up under temptation to compromise? Do they handle power and money without corrupting themselves? As you assess their behavior over the long run, you will begin to determine the true nature of the heart.

Family Discussion Questions:
1. What are the signs of superficiality?
2. How do we avoid superficiality ourselves?

PART 253 ~ THE SALESMAN OUT FOR HIMSELF
Proverbs 26:24–26

*He that hates, dissembles with his lips, and lays up deceit within him;
when he speaks fair, believe him not; for there are seven abominations
in his heart.
Whose hatred is covered by deceit, his wickedness shall be shown before
the whole congregation.*

Wisdom discerns the heart. Without a proper discernment, it is impossible to interact wisely with the people around us. Sadly, we live in a dangerous world, because it is filled with wickedness and hardened malevolence. If you do business with that world, or even with a false brother, you will find men there who are out to destroy you. They will take advantage of you at every opportunity. To sell you on some cheap time-share condominium, they will wine and dine you. Before you have had a chance to compare values in the marketplace, they will force you into an impulsive decision that could bankrupt your family. These people will do anything for a $15,000 commission. There are seven abominations in their hearts! We don't often think of these people as "hating" their customers, but if they are not after the best interests of their neighbor, and if they are committed to their own profit at all costs, then it is fair to say that they really do hate their neighbor.

In a smaller community, the deceptive salesman's true intentions and false dealings would eventually destroy his reputation. But in the present day, he gets lost in the big cities and moves from one dishonest company to the next.

It is very difficult to judge a man by the content of his words. Be especially careful with smooth talkers. If you have been taken by a shyster, you know how persuasive these men can be. They can appear to be out for your good. They know how to get on your good side, and manipulate the conversation a hundred different ways. If you cannot make a judgment call concerning his motivations, at the least give yourself some time to consult with wise counselors if you are about to make a momentous financial decision. If you ask for time to make the decision, and he appears angry, impatient, and hurt, or he tries to shame you for "walking away from a really good deal," then you must conclude that the man is out for no good. If the deal appears "too good to be true," that is probably the case.

Human nature is not to be trusted. Without checks and balances in the marketplace and good records of a man's dealings and reputation, you should be very cautious as you proceed in any business arrangement. If he has proven himself to be a hateful, deceitful man in his transactions, then stay away from him altogether—unless he comes to repentance at the cross of Christ. To think that you can reform the man yourself is foolishness. Over the long haul, the honest will survive in the free market. Those who are out for dishonest gain will lose their wealth, their honor, and their businesses.

Family Discussion Questions:

1. How do you prevent a situation where you are taken advantage of by an unprincipled salesman?

2. What relationship should you maintain with a man who has proven himself to be untrustworthy in his business dealings?

PART 254 ~ WHAT GOES AROUND, COMES AROUND
Proverbs 26:27
Whoso digs a pit shall fall therein; and he that rolls a stone, it will return upon him.

Digging a pit or rolling a stone refers to setting traps for others. This sort of thing can happen on the macro or micro scale. On the macro scale, we find the French revolutionaries in the 1780s preparing the guillotine for their political enemies. Towards the end of the bloodbath in Paris, leaders like Robespierre were beheaded with the same machine they designed for others. Haman is another obvious example of one who set a trap for the people of God, but in the end he swung from the gallows he had made for Mordecai and the other Jews.

In the masterful novel *Jean de Florette*, Marcel Pagnol tells the story of a man who secretly stops up a year-round spring on a piece of property and then deceives his neighbor into selling that property. As the story proceeds, over successive years the dissembler suffers untold loss himself by unrequited love, suicide, material loss, guilt, and sickening regret. Although it is doubtful the author of the novel was a Christian in the true sense of the word, there are a few sagacious men in the world who understand the unmitigated truth of this proverb. If you dig a pit, you will fall into it, eventually. Of course, all of this assumes that there is a God who will make sure that the stone will roll back on the man who intended for it to crush others. Some may think that they can get away with their false dealings because they are not convinced that God is sovereign enough to take care of these details. But the God who is in charge of every tiny sparrow that falls from the sky will make sure every stone will roll in the right direction throughout the course of history.

It would be good, therefore, for young men to avoid defrauding young women in romantic relationships that are not consummated in marriage. If they victimize others in this game, they should certainly expect themselves to fall prey to the same cruel dealings in later years. Sadly, many divorces come about because of the games played in the dating scene years earlier. What goes around comes around.

Now, this does not eliminate the possibility for repentance. One can always return to the pit and fill it up again. You can open up the spring that you filled with concrete and return the money that you stole from your neighbor. When the swindling tax collector encountered the Lord Jesus Christ, he committed himself to repaying those from whom he had taken dishonest gain (Luke 19:1–10). If, by God's truth, you are made aware of your own malevolent dealings towards others, do what you can to restore what you have taken from them. At the very least, ask their forgiveness and ask God's forgiveness for the foul deed.

Family Discussion Questions:

1. Can you think of other examples in history or in your experience that confirm the age-old principle: "What goes around comes around?"

2. Are you aware of any dishonest dealings towards others that should be made right? Does God always provide opportunity for repentance?

PART 255 ~ LIES HURT PEOPLE
Proverbs 26:28

A lying tongue hates those that are afflicted by it; and a flattering mouth works ruin.

Sometimes, it can be difficult to define a "lie." But one thing we do know is that lying brings affliction upon those who are misled by those lies. Flattery works ruin on those who come to believe what they heard. Ultimately, it is God's truth that gives us the standard by which we ought to speak and live.

To the extent that men speak concerning philosophy, history, or science without giving due credit to the revealed truth of God's Word, they will mislead others, and people will suffer by their deceit.

But an important precursor to lying is hatred. If you hate a person, you have a motive fore misleading them. This is fundamental to all lying. To avoid lying, then, you should double-check your motivations before you say anything to a single person or before you speak to a crowd. If you do not love the people to whom you are speaking, you will probably bend the truth, present yourself in better light than you deserve, and defraud your audience with your message. Ask yourself if you love the people to whom you are speaking. Do you want the very best for them? Or is there a little spite in your heart towards them? If you do not feel compassion towards the people with whom you converse, then you may neglect to mention the grace of God in salvation. Or you may flatter them with man-glorifying messages that neglect to call men and women to repentance. Too often, teachers who desire popularity and money for their ministries will say the things that everybody wants to hear. They sell millions of books to a populace who want their ears tickled. In truth, however, these teachers are more interested in their profits than they are in seeing people come to the knowledge of the truth. Paul speaks of those unruly and vain deceivers, "Whose mouths must be stopped, who subvert whole houses, teaching things which they ought not, for filthy lucre's sake" (Tit. 1:11; also 2 Tim. 4:3–4). If they subvert entire families with their books and tapes, it becomes clear that their love of money drove the lie and that lie will lead millions towards the path of destruction.

Family Discussion Questions:

1. How do lies hurt people?

2. How might somebody write a best-selling book that flatters the people who read it, but in the end would bring about their ruin? Why would it be a best seller?

PART 256 ～ BOASTING AND PRAISE
Proverbs 27:1

Boast not yourself of tomorrow: for you do not know what a day may bring forth.

Here is yet another reminder of our inability to predestine the future. Effectively, James says the same thing in his epistle:

"Go to now, you that say, Today or tomorrow we will go into such a city, and continue there a year, and buy and sell, and get gain: whereas you know not what shall be on the morrow. For what is your life? It is even a vapor that appears for a little time, and then vanishes away. For that you ought to say, If the Lord will, we shall live, and do this, or that" (Jam. 4:13–15).

The most powerful person on earth has no control over the future. He may or may not wake up alive in the morning. So this is an important reminder for men that think they have control over empires and whole financial institutions worth billions of dollars. In previous eras, Christians used to use the acronym "DV" (short for *Deo volente*) when they communicated their plans to others. The Latin phrase is translated "God willing." When people use phrases like this, they humbly acknowledge God's ultimate control over every detail of their lives. Though men may pretend they can command the future and follow through on some planned event, they are lying to themselves and to others. Only God knows the future because He has determined the future (Is. 46:11). This is basic to a Christian view of reality. Therefore, Christians should use phrases like "God willing," or "if the Lord is willing," as frequently as the average person says "hello" and "goodbye."

Proverbs 27:2

Let another man praise you, and not your own mouth; a stranger, and not your own lips.

One of the most common temptations for people is to seek recognition from others. When we're not fishing for compliments from others, we are complimenting ourselves. It is extremely difficult to overcome these temptations. The problem, of course, is pride. The business of trying to be a god is wearisome because from the outset nobody is worshiping you the way you think they should. So you will wear yourself out trying to get others to give you credit for this or that. The better thing is to give God the glory. Spend your time collecting glory for the true and living God, instead of collecting kudos for yourself.

There are no limits to human ambition and no end to popularity contests in the world. Political campaigns encourage men to "sell themselves" to the populace. In the corporate world, employees often feel the need to "toot their own horn" if they want to be recognized and remunerated fairly. There are even professing Christian "worship leaders" today who hire publicity agents and image consultants. Recently, a young professing Christian won the Miss America beauty contest—a competition largely based upon physical appearance and "swimming suit" modeling. Would Peter or Paul have recommended a "modest, meek, and quiet spirit" contest for the young ladies in Asia minor? In such a contest, the most humble person would most likely forfeit the prize to somebody else!

It doesn't matter what the world thinks of you, what matters most is what God thinks of you. Even if men compliment you, don't let it go to your head. Their compliments do not mean much, and typically, the praise of men is fleeting. Corporate executives lose their jobs. Politicians are voted out of office. Miss America contestants grow old and wrinkled within a few decades and nobody cares about them much anymore.

But what is the difference between reporting on your accomplishments to an electorate or a manager, and complimenting yourself? All of us will put our names on reports, books, patents, and business brochures. Everybody engages in marketing their own products or services on one level or another. It is better to market a business than a person. It is also better to speak as objectively as possible about yourself, without drawing subjective conclusions. You may report to your employer that you made 10,000 widgets without pointing out that you did a "better job" than other employees in your division. That is something for him to find out on his own. A humble political candidate might speak of his own political positions and his voting record without casting aspersions on his competition. He doesn't have to outline the seven areas in which his own character outshines that of his opponents in the race. He can insist on his commitment to balancing the budget (as long as that is the truth) without calling his opponent a "spend thrift." He would let others do the comparisons and draw conclusions about who is the better man in the race.

Family Discussion Questions:

1. Why should you be careful about announcing your plans for tomorrow? How do you announce your plans to others? Do you ever say, "God willing?"

2. Should Christians participate in beauty contests? Why or why not?

3. How might you speak of your "strong points" and your "weak points" in an interview? How would a Christian leader run a political campaign?

PART 257 ~ THE INCREDIBLE DESTRUCTIVE CAPACITY OF ENVY
Proverbs 27:3–4

A stone is heavy, and the sand weighty; but a fool's wrath is heavier than them both.
Wrath is cruel, and anger is outrageous; but who is able to stand before envy?

Uncontrollable anger is a problem. Because a fool hates to receive correction, things can get out of control when he gets angry. A wise man might heed a word of correction, should he get angry, and this might moderate his indignation somewhat. But a fool isn't known for listening to correction. That is why he is called a "fool"! So when he loses control of his temper, nobody and nothing will rein him in. The message from this proverb is simply this: when a fool gets angry, you had better get out of his way. Nothing will stay his wrath. The best example of this type of fool in Scripture is Abigail's husband, Nabal, whose name literally meant "fool." He set his household up for disaster by picking a fight with David and his forces (1 Sam. 25). If he had listened to the wise counsel of his wife, he might have made a wise decision himself and averted a costly military conflict. But he was an angry fool. Thankfully, Abigail saved the family by interceding with David herself. Interestingly in this story, David's anger was pacified by Abigail's counsel, while Nabal's was not. Here you can see the difference between a wise leader and a fool: one listens to counsel and the other does not.

But there is something worse than uncontrolled anger and that is the dastardly sin of envy. There is a marked difference between these two sins. Anger, on the one hand, does have a destructive capacity. But it does not always *intend* to destroy. Envy, on the other hand, has one goal in mind, and that is to destroy another person, his property, and happiness. Envy will not be satisfied until everything in its sight is laid waste. Envy is a blind, destructive rage. It is the sin that incites the masses in socialist revolutions, labor strikes, and liberal redistribution programs. With the forced redistribution of wealth, the institutionalized thievery and violence produced by revolutionary forces, comes destruction to social and economic systems. After one hundred years of Soviet rule, the Russians have little to show but huge alcoholism problems, imploding birth rates, the highest abortion rate in the world, a powerful criminal element, an unmotivated populace, and severe economic strains. Only remnants of the Christian faith were left in the Orthodox church, and by the early part of the 20th century it was powerless to fight the spirit of envy and atheism that virtually destroyed Russia and its surrounding states. Who can stand before envy?

Be careful never to flaunt your success or your wealth. The spirit of envy is very much alive in the hearts of men and it is far worse than covetousness. When someone covets what you have, he only wants to possess it. Maybe he will steal it from you. But envy sets out to destroy everything you own. Once a man is inflamed with the spirit of envy, nothing will stop him until he has burned down your house, destroyed your reputation, and tangled you up in a hundred lawsuits.

Family Discussion Questions:

1. What does the name "Nabal" mean?

2. How do you know you have an angry fool on your hands?

3. Describe the difference between anger and envy.

4. What are the sorts of things that envy might do to your family or to entire nations?

PART 258 ~ TRUE FRIENDS AND GRATEFUL HEARTS
Proverbs 27:5–6

Open rebuke is better than secret love. Faithful are the wounds of a friend; but the kisses of an enemy are deceitful.

Friendships are not true friendships until they have been through the wild rapids of conflict, honest confrontation, forgiveness, and restoration. This is a necessary process in forming a friendship, in the true sense of the word. Rebuking or correcting somebody is not easy, especially if you hope to retain a friendship in the end. But true lasting friendships will probably not form unless there is a little wounding here and there. When this happens, be very careful that you do not allow your pride to resist the wounding. If your heart resists and you begin to grow bitter, you will fail the test and lose another friend. But if you receive the wound, embrace your friend, and allow the relationship to be repaired, you will have a better friendship for it. These are the kinds of friendships that will stand in good stead through the many storms of life that are sure to come.

Love is willing to take a risk for a friend, but would it risk losing the friendship? Herein lies the real test of friendship. True love is more interested in the well-being of the friend than the friendship itself! This "secret love" referred to in verse five is a love that appreciates the other, but is unwilling to do anything strenuous for the best interests of the other. Even worse than secret love, however, are the "kisses of an enemy." Judas serves as the infamous example of this. It is easy to create shallow friendships and to give twenty hugs on a Sunday morning at church, but would we be willing to give our lives for these people (John 15:13; 1 John 3:16)? Today, many professing believers will shake hands or hug a brother, but they leave the brother in the lurch over every tiny doctrinal disagreement or conflict. These are not true friendships.

We live in a sinful world, and it is difficult for one sinful person to live with another sinful person. But if we care about each other enough to point out each other's sins, and if we are humble enough to confess our sins to one another, we will live fruitful lives in this sin-cursed world.

Proverbs 27:7

The full soul loathes an honeycomb: but to the hungry soul every bitter thing is sweet.

Now here is a simple little piece of wisdom especially directed towards the discontented, spoiled sort of person. Foreigners that visit America from third world countries are always shocked to discover a discontented, complaining spirit among the masses. Young teens appear dour, sullen, and unfulfilled. They have plenty to eat. They have every electronic gadget available on the market. They keep their weeks filled with a constant stream of entertaining pastimes. They are filled. It is as though their stomachs, esophagi, and mouths are crammed up with Chocolate Cream Pie. But the blessings have turned into a curse for them—they have experienced whatever material delights are available to them, and there is nothing more.

How does a parent look on the spoiled child who has a zero sense of gratitude? Would he want to lavish more gifts on the child? To do this would only harden the child in his foul ingratitude and further putrefy the parent-child relationship. Our Father in heaven understands this well. If He should withhold some good gift from His children, it is only for their good, that they might better learn the lesson of gratitude. In light of this, you should understand His irritation with His children in the wilderness (Ps. 95:8–11; Heb. 3:7–10). They failed to learn the lessons of contentment, faith, and gratitude. Throughout the journey in the wilderness they faced periods of hunger, thirst, pain, and difficulty. But they had the cloud, the fire, the manna, and the quail. Somehow, they expected a life without testing and trial. But this is only a form of rebellion. We will experience the life that God wants us to experience, and chances are it will be filled with difficulty, economic shortages, temptation, and even hunger. But God wants us to learn the lessons of faith and gratitude along the way.

When a family gives way to grumpiness and discontentedness, it might be a good idea to fast for awhile. Suffer deprivation on an extended camping trip or go without desserts for six months. Limit the rations a little. Sooner or later, everybody will learn this great lesson that "to the hungry soul every bitter thing is sweet."

Family Discussion Questions:

1. How do you receive a wound from a friend without losing the friendship?

2. How can we become more faithful, more genuine friends?

3. What does a spoiled child look like?

4. Are we a contented family, or is there a fair amount of grumpiness around here? How might we learn to be a little more contented?

PART 259 ~ LEAVING HOME
Proverbs 27:8

As a bird that wanders from her nest, so is a man that wanders from his place.

Some proverbs are easier than others to understand, and this is the case here. There is a profundity in this proverb that requires some serious reflection.

First of all, this verse speaks to the importance of roots. The average American moves 11.7 times in his lifetime.[6] Compare this to bygone eras where families stayed in the same village for hundreds and hundreds of years. Few Americans today know where their own grandparents were buried! Most do not consider this a problem. In fact, they would rather not stay too long in an area where they would have to form relationships and deal with conflict. It is always easier to start over every couple of years with new relationships, new employment, and a new climate. Sometimes men seek a paradise, and they think they leave their problems behind them when they move to a new area. They may believe that success comes by a change of environment rather than a change in their own hearts and lives.

More and more, the modern metro man or woman calls no city or country home. They are willing to pull up stakes at the drop of a hat, to seek citizenship in yet another country. Transportation and communication systems have enabled much of this mobility, but the age-old biblical truths remain. The absence of roots is a curse. For killing his brother, Cain was made a vagabond in the earth. This is also one of the most severe curses listed in Deuteronomy 28 (v. 64).

6 http://www.census.gov/population/www/pop-profile/geomob.html

Yet this does not prohibit all transience. Persecutions and tyranny often result in a dispersion of citizens (especially Christians). Also, God calls missionaries to give up their citizenship in one country in order to plant churches somewhere else. But these are not the reasons why the average American moves 11.7 times in his lifetime. In general, rootless lives produce shallow covenant relationships, weak discipleship, and long term decline for the kingdom of God.

This text speaks to another application peculiarly important to the present day. When a man goes on a business trip without his family, he removes himself from the familiar furniture of his family relationships. Be it even a week or two, he will quickly develop a sense of anonymity in his new surroundings. For a time, he has no accountability systems in place. If he wanders into bars, night clubs, or other places of disrepute, he may very well make choices he will live to regret. Long-term separation from the home may also result in divorce. In the age of the Internet, a man hardly needs to leave home to wander from his nest. The wandering man is more likely to surf the Internet and enter unfamiliar territory where snares are laid for him. As he wanders from website to website, clicking on this link and that link, he can find himself far away from home in no time at all!

Family Discussion Questions:

1. Do you know where your grandparents or great grandparents are buried?

2. How might we avoid unnecessary transience?

3. Do we enjoy anonymity, or do we like to be with the people we have known for many years?

PART 260 ~ FRIENDSHIP
Proverbs 27:9

Ointment and perfume rejoice the heart; so does the sweetness of a man's friend by hearty counsel.

The smell of a cologne or perfume can change your moods. It is a funny phenomenon which affects just about everybody. When a husband gets a whiff of his wife's perfume, his heart skips a beat and he rejoices in her presence. We must assume that God created the olfactory system in such a way that smells can be either pleasant or disgusting. He also designed certain plant oils to give forth a wildly pleasant odor for men and women.

Do you have a friend who cares about you, enough to look you in the eye and give you a little heart-felt counsel? You know that he loves you and wants the very best for you. It may not be easy for him to say what he says. Perhaps he took an hour out of his busy schedule to write you an encouraging letter laced with wise counsel. To know that your friend cares for you is a great comfort to the heart. In the fast-paced world of the modern person, conversations between friends can be superficial and inane. Electronic communication is usually limited to self-oriented updates and unimportant "chit-chat." Even when acquaintances interact in the foyer of the church on Sunday, the exchange is no more than a disinterested, "Hey, how's it going?" and "Pretty good. See you next week." But when a friend sits down with you and shares his heart, bears your burdens, counsels you through a difficult sin issue, that's when you know that you are not alone in the universe. It is sweet to have a true friend in a lonely age where so many wander in an endless electronic wilderness.

Proverbs 27:10

Your own friend, and your father's friend, forsake not; neither go into your brother's house in the day of your calamity; for better is a neighbor that is near than a brother far off.

When a man wanders from his own home and severs his roots, he loses friendship. Before deciding to take a better job with better compensation, it would be wise to assess the value of friendships lost (or gained) in the decision process. For when a man leaves the town in which he was raised, more often than not, he forsakes his father's friends and his own friends. He fails to consider the benefits of friendship such as moral accountability, opportunities for mentorship, contacts for trade, and a hand in the day of calamity. This is the thrust of the second half of the verse. Friendships are most helpful in the hard times, unless, of course, the government is your friend. In the 21st century the socialist state programs like unemployment insurance, socialist healthcare, Social Security, and the Federal Emergency Management Administrations have come to your aid in the day of your calamity. So you probably won't need your father's friends, unless these socialist programs fail! During the Great Depression of the 1930s, Americans pulled through largely by neighbors helping neighbors. What the future holds for people who have no friends—but have a whole lot of confidence in the socialist state—is anybody's guess.

"Better is a neighbor that is near than a brother far off." As it turns out, well-cultivated, long-term friendships are of more value than familial relationships. This principle is manifest in the brotherhood of the church wherever the hearts of brothers are warmed to one another. When John speaks of the brother in need, he says, "But whoever has this world's goods, and sees his brother have need, and shuts up his bowels of compassion from him, how dwells the love of God in him?" (1 John 3:17). If there is any friendship left anywhere in the world, you would think that you would find it in a church. The unity we have in Christ should produce much stronger bonds of friendship

than that which exists in family relationships. Should a man cruelly abandon his wife, and her brothers and father refuse to provide for the woman, it is right that she should find aid from her brothers and sisters in the church (if she is a true believer and living amongst true believers). Sadly, many single mothers have no meaningful church relationships and in their distress they seek out the civil government for their sustenance.

Over a lifetime, you will have opportunity to cultivate a fixed number of friendships. Those who disrupt their friendships by transience or by unresolved conflicts will soon find themselves living lonely lives. Disrupting friendships is a dangerous thing to do, because it usually results in increasingly shallow relationships as life goes on. God only gives us so many friendships in a lifetime. May each of us be careful not to waste any of these precious friendships!

Family Discussion Questions:

1. Of all the communication that we engage in, how much of it is heart-felt, edifying counsel for our friends? Can we say that we have edified others at the end of our church fellowship on Sunday?

2. Give several reasons why it is important to retain old friends that you have known for twenty, thirty, or fifty years.

3. Who will we turn to if the economy turns very bad in this country? Do we have friends who would help our family if the going gets really tough?

Part 261 ~ The Reproach of a Rebellious Son
Proverbs 27:11

My son, be wise, and make my heart glad, that I may answer him that reproaches me.

Leaders in the state and church understand the force of this statement. Not every social system considers wise children an important value. The family is an afterthought to many utopian Socialists. But not so for Christians! A biblical social order rests upon 1 Timothy 3, "A bishop then must be . . . one who rules his own house well, having *his* children in submission with all reverence" (vv. 1, 4–5). Before ruling in church or state, a leader must prove his leadership by shepherding his own family well. In the last generation, rebellion and apostasy among children of leaders became the accepted norm. The best candidates for president or vice president of the United States—people who took a public stand for righteousness— had lesbians for daughters and children with children born out of wedlock. Sadly, the legacies of Presidents Ronald Reagan and George W. Bush was to have their own children characteristically take public stands against their father's more "conservative" policies on homosexual marriages and socialist medicine. Nothing undermines a father's reputation and standing more than his own children.

But having this damage done to a father in the ministry can be even worse. Theoretically, men in the ministry are responsible for teaching others about Scriptural principles found in Ephesians 6:4 and Deuteronomy 6:7. When they fail to emulate these principles themselves, they hardly serve as a good example for those whom they claim to lead. Over the prior two centuries, many missionary and pastor families undermined their own ministries by turning their children over to boarding schools or immature, foolish peer groups for misdirected discipleship. Even so, in spite of every neglectful omission on a parent's part, any child who abandoned the best of his parent's faith and teaching will bear the burden of his own dishonor and reproach. That young person's rebellion undermines a father's reputation, teaching, and kingdom work. It gives every detractor reason to discredit the man's ministry. There is hardly any greater shame that a young man could ever bring upon his father, the church, and the kingdom of God. When the homeschooled twelve-year-old son of an elder in an evangelical church in Colorado admitted to shooting his parents to death, unbelieving "bloggers" had a heyday pointing out the hypocrisy and the "vacuity" of the Christian faith.

Hopefully, you can hear the desperation in a father's voice as he cries out to his son, "My son, be wise, and make my heart glad, that I may answer him that reproaches me." Everywhere around us, family relationships are broken down and generational vision fails. But what can we say about ourselves? Will the righteousness, peace, and joy of the kingdom of God resonate through the generations in our own family? A father's reputation relies a good deal on a wise and honoring son. This is the true measure of the contribution of each family to the kingdom of God: will we have wise sons and daughters?

Family Discussion Questions:

1. How might a son ruin the reputation of his father (whether or not this father serves as a leader in church or state)?

2. Whose fault is it when a son rebels against his father and mother?

PART 262 ~ FORESEEING THE EVIL DAY
Proverbs 27:12

A prudent man foresees the evil, and hides himself; but the simple pass on, and are punished.

If a Class Five hurricane with 200 mph winds was moving at 120 mph towards New Orleans, just 240 miles off the coast, it wouldn't take a prophet to predict devastation being only hours away! It is possible to foresee an evil event—not infallibly, of course. At any point, God could divert a storm, but that would be an extreme exception. It is a miracle when God chooses to interrupt the natural course of events.

But what shall we say about a generation that killed eighty million children between 1960 and 2010? During the 1960s, that generation fomented a teen rebellion unlike anything we have seen in any society in thousands of years. On the one hand, they institutionalized child hatred by the plague of abortion and the birth control pill with its abortifacient qualities. Through their cultural revolution, they solidified the vision for a multi-generational rebellion that would sever the hearts of children from their fathers. Now, add to this a bankrupt nation with household debt as a percentage of the Gross Domestic Product doubling from 1970 to 2010 (42% to 84%).[7] Add to that the breakdown of the character of the nation, with 70% of young men failing to "grow up" by thirty years of age, up from 30% in 1970. What will the nation do with the baby boom generation playing golf and the thirty-somethings are playing computer games? Calculate into this equation a bankrupt social Security System that spent itself into the red by $42 billion for the first time in 2011, which also happened to be the first year the baby boom generation retired. In the mind of the prudent, all of this makes for "the perfect storm," a socioeconomic maelstrom that may very well produce some sort of international repercussions. Europe will reach its retirement peak by 2025, and China by 2040. In 2008, the American people elected a candidate for president who proved himself to be the most pro-infanticide candidate ever to run for the office. Now, many of us are asking, "What will the future hold? What will happen when a parent-dishonoring, death-oriented culture faces a bankrupt social security system? What will happen to eighty million retiring baby boomers that imploded their birth rate and aborted eighty million in their own generation?" Only one word comes to mind—euthanasia, the killing of the elderly.

7 http://www.calculatedriskblog.com/2010/04/household-debt-as-percent-of-gdp.html

What then does a prudent man do in such a situation? Can he foresee the evil that is to come? Those who read this lesson after the year 2030 A.D. will have seen the brunt of this particular socioeconomic hurricane. For the rest of us, it would be good to take proper precautions for the future. We might stop relying on social security programs, and stop killing our children. We should count children a blessing. Then we build our own hospitals and medical care systems in our church communities. It would make sense to restructure family relationships and tighter, relational communities. We prepare for an economic downturn by refusing to worship material things, and by willingly and gladly adjusting to a lower standard of living. That is the sort of thing a prudent man would do.

That a man should seek to protect himself and his family from almost certain economic collapse and social breakdown should be obvious. But these are all temporal matters. There is more at stake than a man's pocket book or a bankrupt medical system that would try to hasten his death to save a few dollars. The real prudent man can see beyond death into the throne room of Almighty God. Because he fears God, he will seek refuge from the threats of God's justice in the atoning work of Jesus Christ. Simple-minded fools will laugh at any serious considerations of guilt, sin, death, and hell. It is hard to deny the pangs of guilt because they do feel guilt. They can hardly deny that they have failed to live up to the minimal standards of morality. They have ruined relationships and there are multiple instances in their own lives where they have forfeited moral integrity. They cannot deny the idea of justice, for they have been bothered by some egregious act of injustice committed by some other person. They know what it is to demand justice. But they still laugh at those who fear God and would flee the wrath to come. They laugh at those who take Jesus' warnings about hell seriously. They pass on, and they are punished.

For related commentary, reference Proverbs 22:3.

Family Discussion Questions:

1. Is it always possible to forecast an economic depression or some other catastrophe? Why would prudent men want to keep an eye on the horizon for a possible cataclysm?

2. How do we make reasonable predictions, without giving way to paranoia, false prophecies, etc.?

3. How might we prepare for an economic downturn?

4. How might we prepare for the judgment day at the end of the world?

PART 263 ~ TRUSTING STRANGERS
Proverbs 27:13

Take his garment that is surety for a stranger, and take a pledge of him for a strange woman.

Be careful when doing business with strangers. Do not lend to them and do not enter into partnerships with them. There is an innate tendency within all of us to want to trust others. We forget that man is depraved and tends towards dishonesty, envy, and covetousness.

When contracting for a product or service, we are not always careful to put it in writing. All of this contradicts what we know about the nature of man (Rom. 3:10–18) and what God says about man. If we first trust in God's truth, we will not be taken in by our reason. But we are reticent to consider man as morally unreliable. Perhaps that is because we are unreliable ourselves. Before we assess ourselves or others, we must take into account our own deceived hearts.

In the case of the present text, some acquaintance has lent money to a stranger. Because this fellow proves himself careless in his business dealings, he is not to be trusted. Even if he is a close acquaintance, a brother, or a friend, you simply cannot trust him in a close partnership. He is not reliable. If you lend him your pickup truck for the afternoon, have him sign over an automobile to you of equal value in the event that should he fail to return your truck in good condition.

If you would not trust your money to strangers, would you trust your children with them? This caution is directed towards employers, school teachers, baby sitters, neighbors, or relatives concerning whom you have little background knowledge. With strangers, you do not know their criminal history. You do not know the bounds of their sinful habits. You don't know what videos they watch or what Internet sites they frequent. The ease by which men fall into perversions is ten times what it was sixty years ago and the perversions which they are capable are unmentionable. As they disappear into the electronic world, many will become strangers to their own friends and family members. Therefore, it is wise to keep systems of accountability in place when our children are in the presence of strangers. Many families insist that multiple family members be present when in traveling or visiting the homes of strangers. How many tragic experiences might be avoided if parents would just put some basic rules in place?

The Bible does not recommend paranoia, but it does mandate a wise assessment of man's fallen condition and some careful rules governing our business and casual relations with them.

For related commentary, reference Proverbs 20:16.

Family Discussion Questions:

1. Why should we be careful about trusting others? Provide biblical backing for your answer.

2. Do we trust strangers too much? Is it possible to be too paranoid? On which side of this do we err as a family?

PART 264 ~ CURSING YOUR FRIEND AND PLAGUING YOUR FAMILY
Proverbs 27:14

He that blesses his friend with a loud voice, rising early in the morning, it shall be counted a curse to him.

What is presented here should be intuitively obvious, but there are more implications to this truth. If you call your friend at 3:00 in the morning to wish him a happy birthday and a blessed day, he will probably take it badly. What then, is the larger principle behind the application? Of course, there is nothing wrong with blessing a brother, but you are still responsible for *how* the blessing is delivered and *how* the blessing is received. When you communicate, you must do your level best to see that the message is received as it is intended to be received.

Giving somebody a big stinky, sweaty hug doesn't always send a positive message, even if that was what you intended. Wisdom calls for knowledge concerning your friend's needs and expectations, a sincere love for your friend, a constant application of Jesus' "Golden Rule," and a thorough understanding of the accepted social norms.

Sometimes we can become slothful in our interchanges and communication with family members and friends. We take our friends for granted, and grow slack in our willingness to invest in these relationships. But just like plants in the garden, friendships can wither away if they are not tended with consistent care. Cultivating friendships takes thoughtfulness, planning, and hard work—and that goes for anything that is worthwhile in life!

Proverbs 27:15–16

A continual dropping in a very rainy day and a contentious woman are alike. Whoever hides her hides the wind, and the ointment of his right hand, which betrays itself.

While the Proverbs are generally directed to young men (and the sins common to young men), occasionally a sinful characteristic of women is mentioned. That is the case with this verse. The problem with the contentious woman is that she is discontent with her situation in life. Either she is grappling for control or she wants others to think she is the trove of all knowledge. She wants her way all the time and she will get it by endless nagging and arguing. When men are controllers, they will seek to manipulate by brute force and anger. Women are more likely to use the tongue to get their way.

If the contentious woman wants something fixed in the house, she nags and whines until the job gets done. If her husband fails to provide spiritual leadership to her satisfaction, she will nag him about it and complain to others about his failures. Under the guise of submission, she refuses to wait for her husband to lead. She takes control and becomes a domineering wife and mother. Under these conditions, her husband will usually withdraw from the family into his own world of alcohol, sports, and entertainment, which only encourages the woman in her role. Families consisting of the domineering mother and disconnected father are all too common in many cultures around the world today. They often produce either more passive young sons or angry sons, which only perpetuates the breakdown of family life in subsequent generations.

It is not difficult to identify contentious women, unless a society is overrun by them. When problems metastasize, and homes everywhere are filled with angry, disconnected fathers and nagging, discontented mothers, the vision for a functional society begins to fade. But under normal conditions, you should be able to pick out a contentious woman at a church picnic. If she has habituated her contentious ways in the home, it will be obvious to everybody around her by her public interactions with family members and others. It is certainly hard to miss the nitpicked husband who is subjected to incessant brow-beating and nagging.

An important ministry of the godly woman in the home is "subjection" or "submission." It is not by the power of the word that she wins the spiritual battles she wages. It is by her silence! The faithless will not believe this is possible, but the godly will appreciate this paradoxical principle. Listen to how the Apostle Peter puts it, "Likewise, you wives, be in subjection to your own husbands; that, if any obey not the word, they also may without the word be won by the conversation of the wives; while they behold your chaste conversation coupled with fear" (1 Pet. 3:1–2). These are women who live every day in the fear of God. They cannot help but be silent, as they reverently contemplate the power and sovereignty of God. How can they complain against the providences that God has brought about in their lives? Complaining against their circumstances would be equal to complaining against God Himself! This makes for a powerful testimony to an unbelieving world, as well as to a husband who is not walking in obedience to God.

Family Discussion Questions:

1. What kind of a gardener are you with your friends? How might you best nurture your friendships?

2. What happens to families with domineering mothers and disconnected fathers?

3. What should a wife do if she wants her husband to be a better father?

PART 265 ~ THE POWER OF FRIENDLY AFFIRMATION

Proverbs 27:17

Iron sharpens iron; so a man sharpens the countenance of his friend.

The countenance is a reflection of the heart. If the heart is joyful, the countenance is joyful. If the heart is confident, the countenance takes on that hopeful and positive expectation. The countenance reflects the attitude of the heart and most people will pick up on your attitude from your countenance. Thus, a positive attitude for a Christian is a hopeful and a faith-filled attitude. This is not true for the unbeliever. If he has a positive attitude, it is only because he has faith in himself and in man's political and economic systems.

So whether or not a person is a believer in God, he still relies upon his friends to form his outlook and attitude. Everybody needs encouragement and affirmation. This is one reason why believers will seek out regular fellowship with other believers. Without daily and weekly affirmation in the faith, we will find our faith growing dull and hope in this life will become a distant, vague thing.

You cannot sharpen a blade by rubbing it over a piece of wood. The blade will wear the wood away before the wood does anything to the steel blade. It takes steel to sharpen steel. Therefore, in order to penetrate the heart and encourage a man to pursue the Christian life of faith, it will take more than taped messages, books, and preachers speaking from big video screens. It takes a friend who looks his brother in the eye and tells him what he needs to hear. This speaks strongly to the need for relational pastors and warm edification between brothers and sisters in the church. Without these healthy friendships, our churches quickly dry up in spite of attempts to encourage the crowd with wildly inspirational talks from gifted speakers on Sunday mornings.

Family Discussion Questions:

1. What is the "countenance" of a person?

2. How does a friend help his friend's attitude?

3. Can we get by on inspirational messages without encouragement from brothers and sisters in Christ?

PART 266 ～ REAPING AND SOWING
Proverbs 27:18

Whoever keeps the fig tree shall eat the fruit of it; so he that waits on his master shall be honoured.

To keep a fig tree is to protect, nurture, and water it. This verse offers the principle of reaping and sowing. God rewards the worker. God writes the paychecks. Sometimes the rewards may be delayed for a few years. We may cultivate multiple businesses and multiple sources of income and see little fruit from the endeavors for a year or two or three. Some plants bear fruit in three months and some in three years. But patient, arduous labor over the long run always yields good fruit.

Those who work for a paycheck expect immediate fruit from their labors and they believe the harvest comes from men. However, the farmer understands this principle differently. He knows that he must wait for his rewards, and every plant will not necessarily yield good fruit. The man of faith knows that God is the source of all good things—and as surely as He oversees the law of gravity, He controls the law of sowing and reaping. Men may try to cheat one another, but God will see to it that every person is rewarded according to what he sows (Gal. 6:7).

This proverb speaks powerfully to the age-old system of mentorship. Let us say that a young eighteen-year-old man sets out to apprentice with a successful Christian attorney. The older man opens up his office for the young man, teaches him the practical issues of client relations, court room etiquette, methods of argumentation, law office accounting, and how to integrate Christian principles into the practice of law. He takes note of the young man's character flaws and begins to hone him in these areas. Over two or three years, the apprentice finds ways in which he can take some of the day-to-day burdens off of his mentor. He empties the wastebaskets in the office at first. He waits on his master. As time progresses, he helps with research on case precedents and types up the affidavits, pre-trial motions, and other legal documents. In a mentorship like this, the mentor usually consumes more in time with the apprentice than the apprentice is giving in helpful assistance for the first year or two. By the second or third year, he begins to provide some benefit for the mentor. The master may hold back from remunerating his apprentice, during the early period of the apprenticeship. But the young man should find the training, the practical experience, and the networking invaluable to his future career, and he will enjoy rewards from this mentorship for many decades to come. Even as the fig tree doesn't yield fruit for three to five years, the apprentice may not enjoy much fruit right away. But if he throws himself wholeheartedly into the mentorship, he will enjoy the fruits of his labor in future years. And when a mentor's heart is committed to the success of his apprentice, he will see to it that the young man is remunerated, eventually. Yet if the master refuses to give the apprentice a dime, you can be sure that God will reward the young man for his commitment, his self-discipline, and his faithfulness.

Family Discussion Questions:

1. When it comes to rewards and paychecks, what is the difference between a job and an entrepreneurial endeavor?

2. How does a young apprentice help the mentor? How will his faithfulness result in blessing in the years to come?

PART 267 ~ THE HORROR OF THE HUMAN HEART
Proverbs 27:19

As in water face answers to face, so the heart of man to man.

We read a story about a horrible murder in the newspapers and we shudder at the evil that men do. When a twelve-year-old boy murdered his Christian parents in Colorado, the story gripped the Christian community. But why should this come as such a shock? Was this boy any more evil than anybody else? Perhaps what makes these stories so horrific is that we catch a glimpse of the same form of evil residing in our own hearts. Remnants of ungodly hatred and anger lurk within the hearts of every one of us, and what prevents us from acting upon this but the grace of God? What if God should remove His grace from the Christian church in this country? Might one of us give way to similarly wicked acts?

This truth lies somewhere in the fabric of all of the best fiction writing. When writers and producers portray human nature in its stark reality on the movie screen or in the novel, men and women understand exactly what is being said. It cuts them to the bone. Of course, all readers or viewers do not receive the story in the same light. Some delight in the wicked character of the story and others are horrified by it. Some will draw closer for an intimate fellowship with the unfruitful works of darkness while others will reprove them (Eph. 5:11). But everybody can relate to the strong inclinations towards personal revenge, fornication, power, covetousness, and other human desires found in these fictional stories. They can relate to the man who is hopelessly lost in his sin. They say "Amen" to John Bunyan's "Man in the Iron Cage."[8] They embrace the nihilist. They thrill when they read of the "edgier" sins of cannibalism or vampirism. They delight in others who appear to be joining them on the path to destruction. While the Christian understands the messages of human depravity just as well as unbelievers, his reaction is quite different. Should

8 John Bunyan, *Pilgrim's Progress*

these stories shed any light on any of his own sinful lusts and desires, he will not allow his own flesh to delight in these things for a minute. Rather, he takes the occasion to peel off that flesh and nail it to the cross of Christ. He acknowledges his own need for Christ, and relies even more upon the death and resurrection of his Savior.

Proverbs 27:20

Hell and destruction are never full; so the eyes of man are never satisfied.

This lesson comes across on a depressing note, because the proverb describes man in his fallen state. Two very negative ideas are contrasted. The potential of fire to destroy everything in its path is beyond comprehension. After a wildfire has consumed millions of acres, even whole continents, there are still other continents across the ocean untouched by the fire. But what if the sun were to explode and burn up all of the planets in this solar system? There would still be other planets and stars yet to burn. Fire is insatiable, as long as there is still something in the universe available to burn.

Jesus speaks also of a hell where the worm never dies and the fire is never quenched (Mark 9:43–48). It is hard to imagine a place of destruction that will continue to destroy and burn forever. As long as there is fuel available, the fire will continue to burn. From the evidence we can find in the Bible concerning hell, it is plain that human beings will make up that fuel that feeds an everlasting fire (Matt. 18:8, 25:41). That fire provides for everlasting punishment (Matt. 25:46) for those in everlasting chains (Jude 1:6), suffering eternal damnation (Mark 3:29). It is an unquenchable fire (Matt. 3:12; Mark 9:43–48; Luke 3:17) for those who are sentenced to the blackness of darkness forever (Jude 1:13).

What could possibly be so relentlessly and endlessly destructive as the yawning, eternal flames of hell, but the hearts of men who will burn in that fire? It is easy for us to underestimate the unrelenting commitment to rebellion found in the hearts of sinful men. The hungry, yearning lust of the eyes (1 John 2:14–16) seeks for something with an intensity that will never relent. But what is it that man wants? If his greedy eyes are looking everywhere for something, what is it that he wants? He wants to be God—this is the core problem with man. This is what lies at the root of all of his covetousness, envy, greed, and lust. This has been the all-consuming desire since the serpent promised something like that in the garden. "You shall be as gods," the serpent hissed. Since that time, man seeks his own sovereignty with all that is in him. He desires what he can never achieve, and he seeks it with a passion! As the drug addict desperately reaches for his next dose and the alcoholic downs another drink, natural man seeks autonomy apart from God. He will seek it 10,000 different ways. Every moment of his day finds him attempting to be God in his thoughts, motives, and actions. He never quite achieves it. But each failure only impels him to more desperate attempts to obtain it. Life for the rebellious sinner is nothing but unending dissatisfaction. Ironically, The Rolling Stones admitted this in the most popular Rock 'n' Roll song of the 1960s, when they screamed out repeatedly, "I can't get no satisfaction! I can't get no satisfaction!" This is the plight of natural man. Thankfully, when hearts are made submissive toward God, they really do find satisfaction in God. As Augustine wrote, "Our hearts are restless until they find their rest in God!"

Family Discussion Questions:

1. What is it that makes an evil crime so horrific for us?

2. What is the difference between the perspective of the ungodly and the godly as they read the stories about wicked deeds and evil men?

3. Why would a fire continue to burn? What has to happen for the fire to stop burning?

4. What do men seek after with unrelenting determination? Why are they never, ever satisfied?

PART 268 ~ HOW TO RECEIVE PRAISE
Proverb 27:21

As the fining pot for silver, and the furnace for gold; so is a man to his praise.

There is one thing more difficult than receiving criticism—receiving praise! Of course, it can be encouraging to receive a little praise from time to time. But most people don't handle praise very well. If you have a hard time handling criticism, you're going to have a harder time handling praise. It is your pride that has a hard time receiving criticism. Naturally, your pride is more than happy to receive praise and feed on it for all it's worth. Even the most mature men can be torn apart by praise if they do not receive it rightly. This all assumes that pride comes before a fall (Prov. 16:17–18).

So every time a man receives some praise or commendation, it will do him either good or ill. It will test his character. If taken in the right spirit, with humility and gratefulness to God, then he will profit from it. But if the kudos feed his pride, he should brace himself for a fall.

When people come to rely on men for constant affirmation and praise, they fail to act on the right motivations. It is their pride and self-confidence that drives them and they set themselves up for a spectacular fall. If they work and live their lives for the praise of men, or to prove themselves better than others, they will end their lives in utter frustration. So let us do *all* to the glory of God, and when we must receive the praise of men, we will instinctively attribute our success to God's good gifts.

Every time you receive the admiration and the commendations of others, use it as an opportunity to praise the God of all goodness who makes all things good. Always give God the glory. Johann Sebastian Bach, arguably the greatest musical master of all time, would pen the letters "SDG" on each of his compositions: *Sola Deo Gloria!* To God alone belongs the glory! If we fail to give the glory to God in our greatest moments, we are, of all men, most miserable. We prove ourselves to only be out for ourselves in everything we do.

Family Discussion Questions:

1. What is so difficult about receiving praise and commendations?

2. On the day you achieve the greatest accomplishment of your life, what will you tell others?

3. What did the musician Bach write on all his compositions?

PART 269 ~ FOOLS VS. CHILDREN
Proverbs 27:22

Though you should bray a fool in a mortar among wheat with a pestle, yet his foolishness will not depart from him.

Once a man has taken the position of the fool—who has convinced himself that there is no God—no amount of browbeating, intellectualizing, or emotional pleading can knock him off his perch.

The proper use of the rod may drive foolishness from a child but not so for the fool. Here is a fine distinction, yet an important one. We must be careful not to call our children "fools." Their hearts may be plagued with foolishness, but in the covenant home this foolishness is usually removed by the right application of the rod and the Word. In the Christian home, we see the Spirit of God opening up the doors of our children's hearts as we faithfully teach them in accordance with the Word. When godly parents teach a two-year-old child about God, it is rare to see him turn towards the skepticism of a David Hume or a Charles Darwin. The university works hard to create such skeptics and some children raised in Christian homes eventually prove themselves to be fools. But Christian parents must apply biblical teaching with the hard work of consistent discipline. We grind the wheat in the pestle through daily devotions, prayer, and training, and sure enough, God works in our children's lives over time and we see the results.

So this is normative in the home, but not so for the crowds of unbelievers who hear the Word. Those not raised in covenant homes are not so blessed. Thankfully, there are some who are changed by the power of the Holy Spirit of God. Their eyes are opened, foolishness dissipates; the leopard loses his spots and hearts are radically changed (Jer. 13:23; 1 Cor. 2:14; 2 Cor. 4:4–6).

Family Discussion Questions:

1. Is there a difference between a fool and a child? What are the similarities? Should we call our children "fools" or "foolish?"

2. What is the difference between teaching a two-year-old child about God and teaching an atheist like Richard Dawkins or Charles Darwin about God?

3. How are hearts and eyes opened to the Word of God?

PART 270 ~ STEWARDING YOUR FLOCKS AND HERDS
Proverbs 27:23–24

Be diligent to know the state of your flocks, and look well to your herds. For riches are not for ever; and does the crown endure to every generation?

God calls every young man and young woman to their tasks. Every member of the family should be responsible for some particular set of duties. Men who work for employers receive their list of responsibilities from a supervisor or manager. But some children will fail to follow through on their responsibilities. Consequently, the pet guinea pig starves to death. Somebody leaves the bicycles in the driveway and dad backs over them in the car. Somebody else forgets to show up for Mr. Jones' yard work project on a Saturday morning. These children are consummately disorganized. They must be reminded over and over again to follow through on their tasks. Very often, their lives are filled up with trivial things and they are less interested in taking care of their important responsibilities. It is possible that a child may be incapable of handling some set of duties, but more often than not, we are dealing with the problem of slothfulness again.

This proverb also calls for thoughtful assessment of the *condition* of our assets or work projects. If something is languishing, or if there is a need here or there, we should be on the lookout for it. This is what a faithful steward will do, and we are stewards of the projects that God gives to us. If the bicycle chain needs oil, let's apply the oil right away! Running an automobile at low oil levels can easily ruin the engine and waste a valuable asset. Or if we sense that our clients and customers are unhappy for some reason or other, we will take positive action to correct this. With a lawn-care business, should the lawn mower fail to cut or bag the grass cuttings properly, a diligent man will promptly address the problem.

Wealth is not easily retained. Most family dynasties created by the original patriarchs waste away quickly in successive generations, at least in the present day. It is the debauched Paris Hilton socialites of the world that drive their grandparents' fortunes and reputations into the ground. It was only seventy-five years ago that the groundwork was laid for the mighty Hilton hotel empire. If the legacy dissipates at the normal rate, the great-grandchildren will have little of the fortune left. Recent research on successful American businessmen conducted by Dr. Thomas Stanley, finds that these entrepreneurs are thrifty and hardworking. But they train their children to reject the "lifestyle of thrift and a self-imposed environment of scarcity." They want their children to have a "better life." They send them to college where they learn to live a "high level of consumption" and become "under-accumulators of wealth."[9] Sadly, these successful men

9 Thomas Stanley, *The Millionaire Next Door,* (Marietta, GA: Longstreet, 1996), pp, 23, 24

are usually failures at raising their own children. They define the "good life" badly.

Sometimes entire societies think they can skate on the capital of previous generations but they will eventually discover that slothfulness brings severe repercussions. It takes about as much energy and work to maintain your flocks as it takes to build them up and a spirit of slothfulness is always counter-productive.

Too many people today see the goal of life as retirement, capital consumption, and entertainment. Soon our people will learn that this is corrosive to the character of a nation and to its economy. Unless we come alongside our children and train them to keep the herds and wisely steward our resources, we will see our work come to naught. In the ministry of Christ, He discourages the burying of talents in the ground and unwise stewardship. Whereas it may be tempting to let things go, after we have built a bit of a legacy, whether in business or ministry, this counters the wisdom of our Lord. We must be faithful and true with what He has given us to the very end. We must not lay the hammer and the plow down until He calls us home. We must see to it that our children and grandchildren continue in the faith. We must make a good run from the beginning to the end. If God calls us to run a 100 mile race, let us run every mile of it. If it is a 500 mile race, we will run 500 miles—no more and no less.

Family Discussion Questions:

1. How are our children doing with their chores and responsibilities? Do things fall through the cracks? Are you faithful to finish every job and finish it well?

2. What are our family's assets? Are we taking good care of them? What could we do to take better care of them?

3. How do successful businessmen fail to raise their children properly? How will our family retain healthy family units, strong economics, and strong faith for multiple generations?

PART 271 ~ GOD'S BLESSING FOR
FAITHFUL SONS
Proverbs 27:25–27

The hay appears, and the tender grass shows itself, and herbs of the
*   mountains are gathered.*
The lambs are for your clothing, and the goats are the price of the field.
And you shall have goats' milk enough for your food, for the food of
*   your household, and for the maintenance for your maidens.*

If our sons are faithful to look after their herds, and they are
carefully trained in diligence, the Lord attaches a precious
little promise in these verses. There will be food and clothing
enough for their future families. There is comfort here. It is
for us to focus on preparing our sons to take responsibility
for their future households and then we enjoy the blessing of
God.

Throughout Scripture we find that the man of the household is
responsible for "the maidens" (1 Cor. 7:36). Even the Apostles
took responsibility for their sisters and wives, as Paul asks the
rhetorical question in 1 Corinthians 9:5, "Have we not power
to lead about a sister, a wife, as well as other apostles, and
as the brethren of the Lord, and Cephas?" This may seem a
little odd to the modern mind, since many families turn their
grandmothers, wives, and daughters over to corporations and
governments for their sustenance. But Paul admonishes men
to take care of the needy widows in their own families, instead
of turning them over to the church or some other institution
(1 Tim. 5:8ff). In fact, those men who refuse to take care of
their widows are considered worse than infidels. This is basic
to a Christian social order.

While a few maidens may find this text degrading, they will
always find their sustenance and security in some institutional
structure or another. With the collapse of the family in the
industrial age, the hearts of daughters have wandered far
from the home. When parents declare their intention to raise
their daughters to be "independent," they should clarify what

they mean by that word. Do they intend for their daughters to be independent of the state and the large corporation or independent of the family? In the 21ˢᵗ century in America, the largest socialist voting bloc turns out to be single women, which explains the inevitable rise of socialism and total government in once-free countries.[10] The *New York Times* reported that "In 2005, 51% of women said they were living without a spouse, up from 35% in 1950."[11] As long as fathers are raising their daughters to be dependent upon the state and independent of the institution of the family, we will see the empowerment of the socialist state.

The more fundamental problem is not so much with the maidens, but with the fathers and sons. Without manly faith in God's promises, and without solid training for our sons in looking after their flocks and herds, we will never see a biblical social order restored. Even among Christian homes and Christian homeschools, there is far more passion today to prepare daughters for the "independent" life than in the 1970s and 1980s. But the reason why these mothers are training their daughters with a vision towards an "independent" career, is because they are well aware that 70% of young men are not grown up by thirty years of age. Men are not maturing. They are not capable of caring for a household made up of a wife and daughters (the maidens). So, of course, their women must seek career jobs in the workforce. The results of such a social order is only more single mothers, more children in day care who will seldom see father or mother, more young men who fail to grow up by thirty years of age, more socialist government programs, and an increasingly dysfunctional socioeconomic order.

Thus, you can see the importance of raising a young man with the character to look after his flocks and herds. But it is more than that. Our young men must know that, if they work, God will bless. They must work without worry, believing that

10 http://www.wnd.com/?pageId=80246, Unmarried women put Obama over the top, All time high of 70% support for Democrat
11 http://www.nytimes.com/2007/01/16/us/16census.html

somehow their work will not be in vain. They must plant their crops and establish their herds, believing that God will provide an increase for them. Faith is essential in all of life but especially in the area of work. When we go off to work on Monday morning we must believe that God will reward the works of our hands. This gives the man great confidence and joy in his work.

Family Discussion Questions:

1. Who is responsible for taking care of the household and the "maidens?" Provide biblical backing.

2. Why is faith important for those who work?

3. How might we train our young men that they will be responsible for the material well-being of the home?

PART 272 ~ TWO FORMS OF FEAR
Proverbs 28:1

The wicked flee when no man pursues; but the righteous are bold as a lion.

Those who work in corporations know the autocratic middle-manager who throws around threats and loud curses in order to intimidate his employees and his coworkers. Obviously, this fellow is afraid of something. More often than not, he is afraid of losing his position in the company. He motivates others by fear because he is himself a fearful man. But the Christian has no business fearing this manager or any other human being. When tyrants get a little power in a corporation, with a police force, or at the head of some huge empire, they can do some damage. There is no doubt about that. But the righteous cannot fear these men. To fear a man instead of God is blasphemous.

There are two kinds of fear, which explains why the wicked are so fearful and the righteous are bold. It is impossible for a man to completely avoid the reality of God. He may pretend that God doesn't exist by "suppressing the truth in unrighteousness," but he cannot escape some faint notion of His Creator. The worst thing a man can do is pick a fight with the Creator of the Universe, and this is what the wicked man has done. He is at odds with his Creator and Judge. In spite of all his arrogant rhetoric and loud bravado, there is a horrible fear and a silent dread that ever enfolds him. This is more than fearing the loss of a job, of a position, or a relationship. This is the ultimate fear—the fear of falling into the hands of the living God who is a consuming fire (Heb. 10:31). This fear puts him on the run, constantly. He has a consummate fear of death and anything that might threaten his life. Preeminent among the proud wicked men who scorned God was the great Roman Emperor, Caligula. Yet he was also known to be more paranoid of every storm or political stirring than any other emperor.[12]

The righteous man fears God too. Unlike the wicked man, however, this fellow would gladly admit that he fears God. This fear is fundamentally different in nature and form. He fears God as a sovereign, as all-powerful, as all-wise, as all-just, and as a Father. So his fear is based on the relationship. Because the ungodly man lives in proud rebellion against the God he knows exists, he fears impending judgment from divine retribution. Conversely, the godly man lives in peace with God, having been reconciled to Him by the blood of Christ. He lives the life of repentance and humble service to God. He fears God with a reverent awe as he sees judgment fall upon the wicked. But he doesn't fear that impending judgment upon himself! Hence, this fear is liberating, invigorating, and empowering. In whatever ferocious battle he engages, he knows that the worst thing that can happen to him is his death, and then he goes to heaven! As with those Christians facing the full opposition of the beastly powers in John's Revelation, they overcome by the word of their testimony, by the blood of the Lamb, and they do not love their lives even unto death! (Rev. 12:11) For the Christian, then, the fear of God renders

12 John Calvin, *Institutes of the Christian Religion,* Chapter 1, Paragraph 6

courage. He couldn't possibly fear men who can kill the body because he fears Him which is able to destroy both soul and body in hell (Matt. 10:28). But for the unbeliever, fear brings about uncertainty, horror, paralysis, and constant efforts to escape. He will attempt to escape reality through addictive drugs, stories, entertainment, sports, and games. He carefully avoids any contact with the preaching of the Word of God, preferring to listen to 1,000 heretics than to countenance one honest man who testifies to God's truth. One thing you can be sure of: wicked men are very afraid. If you are held hostage by wicked men during a bank robbery, you can be sure that these men are extremely fearful individuals.

To make matters worse, the wicked man has not dealt with his own guilt and this makes it difficult for him to face his accusers. He knows that God and everyone else have a case against him. He must therefore be on the defense all the time. The righteous, on the other hand, has addressed his fundamental ethical problem. He can face others because he has already dealt with his sin by humbly confessing before God and others whom he has offended. This gives him standing to interact with those who take issue against him. He can fearlessly speak with the enemies in the gates (Ps. 127:5).

Family Discussion Questions:

1. How is the fear of God invigorating to us? How does the fear of God turn wicked men into wimps?

2. Put yourself in the position of John the Baptist, who confronted the wicked King Herod with his sin. Would you fear Herod or would you fear God?

PART 273 ~ BUREAUCRACIES AND PETTY TYRANTS
Proverbs 28:2

For the transgression of a land many are the princes thereof; but by a man of understanding and knowledge the state thereof shall be prolonged.

This is Political Theory 101. Since the founders of this nation inherited a strong Christian heritage from earlier generations, the Proverbs 28:2 principle was well ingrained in their thinking and in their political systems. Patrick Henry, one of the founders of this country, would say that, "It is when men forget God that tyrants forge their chains." William Penn added, "Men must be governed by God, or they will be ruled by tyrants." Then Benjamin Franklin put it in the form of a quip: "Either you'll be governed by God, or by God you'll be governed." This means that you must govern yourself according to the laws of God, or by God's sovereign order, you will be tyrannized by the strong hand of government. That is the message of this proverbial truism.

No maxim better explains the last 150 years of this nation's existence than this one. As the integrity of the family collapses, the government increases its purview into every area of life. While legislatures mandate homosexual indoctrination in public school classes, fund abortion, and facilitate easy divorce, they are also busy increasing the size of the budgets. The people are happy to elect these tyrants who promise them security by offering more government programs and nanny-state regulations. As the illegitimacy rate rose from 3% to 42% between 1910 and 2010, government spending—on local, state, and federal levels—grew from 10% of the GNI to 64% of the GNI. "For the transgression of a land, many are the princes thereof!"

There are three times as many bureaucrats (per 100 citizens) in this country today, as there were fifty years ago.[13] By

13 http://mwhodges.home.att.net/state_local.htm#Person

the year 2011, there were twice as many people working for the government (22.5 million) than those working in manufacturing jobs (11.5 million).[14] That is a lot of princes, and they produce an incredible amount of paperwork, regulations, and costs for the taxpayers! One indication of the size of the federal tyranny that regulates every area of our lives is the length of the Federal Register that has expanded from a paltry 9,910 pages in 1954 to a whopping 82,580 pages in 2010.[15] The princes have been busy.

The second half of the verse, however, is instructive. Undermining the character of the nation and obliterating strong families will send the nation into a spiral of destruction. Anarchy plays off of tyranny, and tyranny grows out of anarchy until the fabric of the nation unravels. The modern socialist systems are bound to fail, eventually. By the end of the 20th century, Sweden considered itself to be the greatest exemplar of socialism in the West but its illegitimacy rate was also the highest in the west, exceeding 50%! A nation simply cannot violate the laws of God indefinitely and hope to receive the blessing of God upon its economic and political systems. This is a lesson to be learned in the 21st century! The ungodly may laugh at those humble folk who take this book of God's wisdom seriously, but their day of reckoning will come. God vindicates His truth again and again throughout history.

If you want a nation that will survive and thrive, you must have a self-governing, moral people. Pastors must preach righteousness. Fathers must lead their households well and ingrain biblical character into their children. And political leaders must be careful not to undermine the morality of the people by their policies. This lesson applies to some obscure African nation as much as it does to a Western nation with a Christian heritage.

---

14 http://online.wsj.com/article/SB1000142405274870405020457621907386718 2108.html?mod=googlenews_wsj
15 http://www.llsdc.org/attachments/wysiwyg/544/fed-reg-pages.pdf

Proverbs 28:3

A poor man that oppresses the poor is like a sweeping rain which leaves no food.

It is one thing for a rich, highly developed nation to oppress its people. Even when subjected to the highest tax rates, the middle class and the upper classes live a prosperous life. The poor enjoy their welfare handouts, though they usually corrupt their families and destroy the integrity of their men. But nobody starves to death in these modern countries. Nobody is truly poor in the real sense of the word. People in the poorest welfare class use their food stamps to purchase name brand foods, cigarettes, and expensive steaks. These are examples of rich men oppressing other rich men. Tyranny in the modern socialist states like Sweden and America is hardly the picture of big brutes beating on the citizenry and starving them to death. Tyrannical governments can get far worse and far more devastating in communist countries and third-world nations. Consider, for example, Joseph Stalin, Mao Tse Tung, and Fidel Castro, all of whom created frightening tyrannies in already impoverished nations, bringing terrible suffering to their people. Sadly, many petty dictators from African nations will oppress their people badly, producing an economic debacle and mass starvation. These unwise and wicked tyrants produce mass social upheavals, civil wars, economic depressions, and forced labor. Since the 1990s the tyrants in North Korean have starved three to four million people to death.[16] Between 2000 and 2010, Robert Mugabe took Zimbabwe from holding one of Africa's best economies to the worst. News reports indicate that 12,000 Zimbabweans were dying of starvation every month in 2009.[17] When we witness men of low character violating property rights by confiscating private property, by suffocating the free market, living lavish lifestyles at the peoples' expense, and driving their nations into bankruptcy, we get a picture of what is conveyed in this proverb. These monsters promise the world and when

16 http://en.wikipedia.org/wiki/North_Korean_famine
17 http://www.zimbabwemetro.com/news/12-000-killed-by-starvation-in-zimbabwe-every-month/

the people elect them to office, they only deliver sweeping rain that leaves no food.

Family Discussion Questions:

1. How do you get a free country?

2. How does a fool ruin a prosperous country?

3. Describe tyranny. Are we seeing tyranny in this country?

PART 274 ~ LOSING THE ANTITHESIS
Proverbs 28:4

They that forsake the law praise the wicked; but such as keep the law contend with them.

On March 31, 2011, the judiciary committee of the Colorado House of Representatives considered a bill approving of civil unions between homosexuals as a first step towards legitimizing "homosexual marriage" in the state. Methodist and Lutheran clergymen testified before the committee, proceeding to endorse homosexual behavior and encouraging passage of the bill. These men purportedly represented Jesus Christ as leaders in the church! Future generations who read these words will scarcely believe that anything like this could have ever happened! How in the world did "Christianity" ever devolve to such a low level? Well, this is the answer. "They that forsake the law praise the wicked; but such as keep the law will contend with them."

Large segments of the Protestant faith have gradually abandoned God's law over a period of several hundred years. Evangelicals began to see the law as antithetical to the Gospel. Later in the 19th century, the social gospel encouraged Christian involvement in society without a serious consideration and application of God's law. Over the centuries, Christians rejected extensive portions of God's ethical requirements in Exodus, Leviticus, Numbers, Deuteronomy, Matthew 15, 1 Timothy 2, and 1 Corinthians 14. Anyone who advocated

God's ethical directives was castigated as a "legalist." This attitude towards God's law flies in the face of what Jesus taught in Matthew 5:17–19. And it certainly doesn't resonate with the spirit of the psalmist who cried out, "Oh, how love I Thy law!"

The law of God draws the line of demarcation between the wicked and the righteous. If you tell a group of unbelievers that God loves them and has a wonderful plan for their life, chances are they won't take serious issue with that. But you would catch some flak if you stood up in the middle of a college classroom and announced that homosexuality and fornication are sins against God and sufficient to condemn a man to hell fire. It is the testimony of the law of God that enrages the wicked. The very nature of unbelieving rebellion spurs men to cast off the ethical demands of a sovereign authority; the wicked will abhor even faint reminders of God's righteous laws. Therefore, those who have respect for the laws of God will never seek a détente with wicked men. The righteous serve as a constant source of aggravation to the wicked. When men boast of their drunken parties in the workplace, true believers will make their disapprobation obvious. When a relative advertises their fornicating and homosexual relationships, the godly will clearly register opposition to such behavior. If a neighbor invites a Christian man to a "homosexual wedding," the Christian will register his disagreement with it either by not attending or speaking publicly against the abomination at the event. Uncomfortable though it may be, godly men will find themselves at odds with wicked men. This does not mean that they have to be ugly, vindictive, or take personal offense against them, but they do need to take an uncompromising stand on the law of God.

The law of God is the discerning standard. If the righteous fail to lift up this standard, and if they fail to maintain a constant opposing force against the wicked, they will synthesize into the surrounding degrading, ungodly systems. This is why professing Christians have softened their perspectives of divorce, fornication, homosexuality, feminism, and egalitarianism over the years.

Family Discussion Questions:

1. How do "Christian" pastors come to the point where they endorse wickedness?

2. How does one contend with wicked people? What is a proper heart attitude? Does this mean that we must be ugly, hateful, and obnoxious toward others? How do we address sin in ourselves and others?

PART 275 ∽ RULES AND RELATIONSHIPS
Proverbs 28:5

Evil men understand not judgment; but they that seek the LORD understand all things.

Judges in today's family courts award child custody to people who demonstrate gross moral infidelity. The adulterous father and homosexual mother are prime candidates preferred by the more "liberal" judges in these cases. According to the standards of biblical law, such moral lapses are defined as crimes worthy of the death penalty. At the very least, righteous judges should take this wisdom into account in divorce and adoption cases. But even many professing Christians would find such laws reprehensible.

The Bible does not speak to every single issue with equal clarity, but there is sufficient truth in it to convey the will of God for every possible situation in life. Take, for example, the child born as a hermaphrodite, with both XX and XY chromosomes. Jesus addresses this unusual condition in Matthew 19:12. But what does God think about artificial insemination, where children are formed in test tubes or even nurtured in artificial wombs? How does God view women placed in military combat? These are real questions facing believers in the 21st century and those who seek the Lord will understand these things too. One must understand the heart of God to draw out the principles found in His Word. Why does God repudiate the boiling of a baby goat in its mother's milk (Deut. 4:21)? Does this inform the believer at all in regards to God's perspective of women in combat? To know God's heart is to understand His will as communicated to us in Scripture. It is not enough to keep His commandments. Repeatedly through Scripture, in both the Old and New Testament, He tells us to "love Me and keep My commandments." So our relationship with God is essential for the proper application of God's principles, both to know His will and to do it.

When a mother instructs her son to refrain from wearing his best suit of clothes out to play in the front yard, she is telling him something more than that. For example, if she were to observe him later in the afternoon swimming in the neighbor's pool in his Sunday best, she would most certainly correct him. But suppose the lad should argue that his mother had not specifically forbidden swimming in the pool in his good clothes. This kind of response would prove that this boy's heart is far from his mother's. He doesn't want to see things her way, and his poor relationship with his mother is manifest in how he interprets her words. The problem with the Pharisees in Matthew 15 was that their hearts were far from God. They did not seek after God and their practices displaced the intent of God's laws. If their hearts were right with God, they would have known that their system of Corban fostered the dishonor of parents!

Family Discussion Questions:

1. Does the Bible help us to understand God's will for every single situation in life? Give several examples where God's Word speaks with authority and relevance to everyday situations.

2. How does our relationship with God play into our understanding of His Word and a right application of it?

PART 276 ~ WHAT'S MOST IMPORTANT
Proverbs 28:6

Better is the poor that walks in his uprightness, than he that is perverse
in his ways, though he be rich.

Life is, in a way, a walk, and this proverb introduces two
different walks. There is the upright walk and the perverse
walk. Think of a fishing line that is in a jumbled mess. After
a little examination, you find that there are six ends sticking
out of the tangled knots, which means that this is not one
complete piece of line. Compare this to another piece of
fishing line that is one full piece. There may be a few bends
in the line, but it is straight and true. This is how the proverb
contrasts the walk of the wicked with the walk of the righteous.
The godly man may wander off the path occasionally, but he
humbles himself, confesses his sins, and returns to the straight
path. The walk of the wicked is a jumbled mess.

One way you can tell that you have an ungodly person on
your hands is to try to counsel him. The ungodly are seldom
honest about their sins, and if they confess a sin, it will not be
the sin they should be confessing. They have many excuses for
their moral failures. They blame others for their own sins and
hide their true colors under layers of hypocrisy. To unravel
this man's problems would take years, and even then you still
would not make much progress. This man is perverse in his
ways.

Sometimes perverse men are very rich. This is often the case
because these men come to trust in their riches and they see
no need for trusting in God. Their confidence turns to their
own achievements and they fail to seek God's guidance and
deliverance each day. On average, there is more spiritual
risk for those who gain wealth (1 Cor. 1:26). In the New
Testament, the Apostle Paul warns of this problem when he
says, "Charge them that are rich in this world, that they be
not high minded, nor trust in uncertain riches, but in the
living God, who gives us richly all things to enjoy: that they

do good, that they be rich in good works, ready to distribute, willing to communicate." It is no sin to be rich, but it comes with more temptations. So the proverb tells us that it is better to be a poor man who walks in the upright path, than the rich man who walks the crooked path to hell.

For related commentary, reference Proverbs 19:1.

Family Discussion Questions:

1. Describe the person who is perverse in his ways. What does the upright look like walking the straight and narrow path?

2. Why are some rich men less likely to be interested in wisdom? Does this mean that we should avoid material prosperity?

Proverbs 28:7

Whoever keeps the law is a wise son; but he that is a companion of riotous men shames his father.

Wisdom is found in keeping the law of God ever before you. This is what we earnestly desire for our sons. Before a man will keep the law of God ever before him, he needs to reverence it and value its worth more highly than gold (Ps. 19:10). Herein is wisdom.

But then there is the son who casts off the law of God, and he does this when he becomes the companion of riotous men. The great writer Robert Louis Stevenson grew up in a godly home trained in the Bible, the Shorter Catechism, and the excellent writings of Robert Murray McCheyne. But in 1867, the man entered Edinburgh University. It was there that he fell in with "easy-going companions." He began to visit public houses frequented by "the lowest orders of prostitutes." He and his friends formed a club on campus which maintained the rule "Ignore everything that our parents have taught us." By 1873, his father was horrified to discover that "his son no longer believed in the Christian religion."[18] Stevenson

18 Iain H. Murray, *The Undercover Revolution*, (Carlisle, PA: The Banner of Truth Trust, 2009), P. 11, 12.

wrote about his father, "It was really pathetic to hear my father praying pointedly for me today in family worship, and to think that the poor man's supplications were addressed to nothing better able to hear and answer than the chandelier."[19] It was men like this that led national apostasies in Europe and America away from the Christian faith during the 1800s and 1900s. Almost without exception, their rebellion began by associating with evil companions in college or in high school. They did not keep the law of God they had learned as children. Instead, they cast it away and took up with riotous men. What a shame and a disappointment to their fathers. Thomas Stevenson, father of Robert, encapsulated his terrible sorrow in these heart-wrenching words for his son, "You have rendered my whole life a failure!"[20] In this case, the companion of riotous men really did shame his own father!

PART 277 ～ SEEKING WEALTH OR HELPING THE POOR?
Proverbs 28:8

He that by usury and unjust gain increases his substance, he shall gather it for him that will pity the poor.

The Word of God does not permit a man to charge interest when he lends money to a brother (Exod. 22:22–27; Lev. 25:35–37; Deut. 23:19–20; Ps. 15:5) and Deuteronomy 23 distinguishes clearly between a brother and the stranger. Hence, we distinguish between the brother loan and the stranger loan. From Deuteronomy 15 we understand that debt is only for the poor (Deut. 15:4, 7). The flagrant use of bank loans by those who live in 10,000 square foot homes in the present day counters the teaching of the Word of God concerning debt.

According to Deuteronomy 15, true believers will provide special interest-free loans to poor brothers on request. If the

19 Ibid., p. 13
20 Ibid, p. 13

brother cannot repay the loan, the creditor will cancel the debt on or before the seventh year. This is a brother loan. Biblically speaking, debt is intended for the poor man, but why would a man make an interest-free loan to a poor brother who may never pay it back? There are people who really do pity the poor. To these generous men, God promises material blessing. For a limited period of time, the unprincipled bankers who issue payday loans to the poor at exorbitant rates may profit from the business. But in the macro-economic scheme of things, they will see their money disappear, and their own lack of character will curse them in a severe economic downturn. Then, God in heaven will see to it that their substance rolls over to the man who was less interested in increasing his own wealth and more interested in caring for the poor.

Some men are primarily interested in furthering their own wealth, and they do little or nothing to relieve the suffering of others. By the end of their lives, they have contributed to more slavery, more government, and more of a slave-orientation within the populace. Thankfully, there are others who will use their wealth to build others up in faith and character. They devote much of their time and resources to mentor, disciple, and empower others with opportunities. They do not want to enslave the poor to banks through loans or to governments by welfare programs, or to big business by enslavement. They would rather make men free and the primary means by which this happens is through the preaching of the Gospel of Christ. "If the Son therefore shall make you free, you shall be free indeed" (John 8:36).

Ironically, it will be those who pity the poor that will end up with the most wealth. This does not mean that anyone will completely solve the problem of the poor. Nor does it mean that governments must enforce the "charitable" redistribution of the wealth. But when men focus on helping the poor instead of enriching themselves at the expense of the poor God will, as a general principle, make sure that these men are rewarded with the most wealth.

Family Discussion Questions:

1. What are biblical restrictions relating to debt?

2. Which is a higher priority—seeking wealth or empowering the poor? What happens to men who sincerely pity the poor? Do people who try to redistribute other people's money into the coffers of the poor really pity them?

PART 278 ～ RESPECTING GOD'S LAW
Proverbs 28:9

He that turns away his ear from hearing the law, even his prayer shall be abomination.

Turning the ear from hearing the law is the very opposite of keeping the law of God. When a young man raised in a Christian home joins the Army and wanders away from the assembly of believers, he has adopted a wicked lifestyle. If someone who knew him as a child should approach him and ask why he is out committing fornication and consuming copious amounts of alcohol, he would have to admit that he has changed his outlook. He is hardly convicted by the law of God. If he had compromised in these ways earlier in his life, he might have felt pangs of guilt but that is not the case anymore. He hasn't read the law of God or heard the preaching of God's Word in six years! In fact, when he speaks to other believers, he can't understand how these people can be so sensitive to the sins of fornication and drunkenness. "Why do they make such a big deal about this?" he thinks to himself. This man has turned his ear away from hearing the law, and God considers his prayers abominable. When he is crawling around in the foxholes with hand grenades falling everywhere, then he may wish to pray to God for help, but God will not listen to this detestable man and his odious cries, because he has turned his ear away from hearing the law. First, he needs to return to the Word of God and listen to the words of the law. Only then can he pray and expect the mercy of heaven.

Even some professing Christians are bothered when they hear the law of God in the present day. They repudiate the words of our Lord in Matthew 15:4, where He recommends the death penalty for the rebellious son. They mock the restrictions God placed on slavery or divorce, as if these are not realities in our sinful world. They can't imagine why God should allow polygamy over homosexuality and adultery in the Old Testament. Instead of delighting in the perfect wisdom of God's Word, they impose their own cultural norms—as perverted and dysfunctional as they may be—over the laws of God. A society that has destroyed its families and enslaved its people under big socialist government is hardly in a position to judge the laws of God. Yet, instead of carefully studying God's laws and identifying the relevant applications for us today, some Christian churches will turn their ears away from hearing the law. They look upon anyone who dares to love God enough to keep His commandments as a "legalist" in the most deprecating sense of the word. From the present text, it is clear that God takes their prayers and worship services as an abominable thing.

Family Discussion Questions:

1. Do you respect the law of God? What is your attitude towards God's Word when it points out your sins? Does God receive our prayers and worship?

PART 279 ~ DESTROYING CHRISTIAN FAMILIES
Proverbs 28:10

Whoever causes the righteous to go astray in an evil way, he shall fall himself into his own pit; but the upright shall have good things in possession.

The 2010s and 2020s will be known for the aggressive promotion of homosexuality among the K–12 schools for children as young as six or seven years old. Throughout the history of the world, one would have a hard time finding such a wicked era where both public school attendance and indoctrination in homosexual behavior were mandated. This decadence is mainly to be found—not in Muslim or African countries—in "Christian" countries such as the Netherlands, Sweden, Germany, and the United States. It was Christian families who were led astray by humanist heresies, many of which were taught in "Christian" churches by ordained men and women who professed Christ! As Christian families sent their children into the public schools, and as they imbibed the popular music and stories produced by apostate Christians, their children quickly accepted the doctrines of evolution, homosexuality, and revolution. Pseudo-intelligent university professors delighted in drawing these poor lambs away from the paths of truth.

It will not be long before this foolishness is over. The humanists that reject God's eternal moral law code will fall into their own traps. They will destroy the character of the next generation and there will be nothing left. But the righteous men who love God and keep His commandments will enjoy God's good blessings. While the nations around them watch their own birth rates implode, their families disintegrate, and their gods of materialism collapse, these true believers enjoy the true blessings of godly children, selfless charity, close-knit and peaceful church communities, contentment, and joy in the Holy Spirit. Eventually, the powerful state that holds the confidence of so many will always fail. But not so with the kingdom of God!

Family Discussion Questions:

1. How are Christian families attacked by powerful ungodly forces in our day?

2. What will happen to those who are working hard to corrupt Christian families all over the world?

3. How do we protect the families of the upright from the corruption of the wicked?

Part 280 ~ Wisdom Better than Riches
Proverbs 28:11

The rich man is wise in his own conceit; but the poor that has understanding searches him out.

Rich men are usually confident in their own achievements and abilities. Because they have acquired a little wealth, they begin to imagine themselves to be impregnable, or at least self-sufficient with their riches. It is hard to tell them anything. Very often, those who take the Gospel into neighborhoods will avoid the rich homes because the rejection rate in these communities is extraordinarily high.

You will find an occasional poor pastor who has little wealth but great wisdom. He finds himself sitting next to some rich businessman on an airline flight and he asks penetrating questions. He is not pushy and he doesn't need to use some pre-packaged set of questions or statements to open the conversation. He just knows how to search people out by his discerning spirit and Word-based wisdom. He gets to the ultimate issues, even in conversation on the mundane. He knows that riches can never satisfy and no material prosperity can ever fulfill the longings of the human heart. Self-interested philanthropy and self-atoning charitable endeavors usually worsen the conditions of the poor and provide little respite from the constant nagging of the conscience. With all of his riches, the wealthy man can do little to solve the problems of this world. The suffering, the inequities, and the corporate and personal sins abound everywhere. So this poor wise man slowly delves to the very heart of the problem and the need for redemption that far exceeds anything money could ever buy.

Some men have the wisdom and understanding to speak to the heart issues of just about any person. Wealth and power do not intimidate them. By the time the conversation is over, the greatest men are shaken by words they will not soon forget.

Family Discussion Questions:

1. Are you intimidated by wealth and power? What are the issues that are of far more importance than politics, wealth, and education?

PART 281 ~ RIGHTEOUS MEN PRODUCE GOOD COUNTRIES
Proverbs 28:12

When righteous men do rejoice, there is great glory; but when the wicked rise, a man is hidden.

The word translated "rejoice" is better rendered "triumph." It is the rousing sense of rejoicing that a people feel when they have just won a terrifying conflict with a formidable enemy. It may be a political or military battle. But should an honest and truly God-fearing people ever again win a position in the civil order in this world, there will be great blessing and benefit for future generations. It is a remarkable thing that many of the founders of our nation acknowledged the sovereign reign of almighty God and the redemption of His Christ. John Adams remarked to Benjamin Rush at the first Continental Congress that the American republic might survive if "we fear God and repent of our sins."[21] Patrick Henry, arguably the most influential leader of the country during its formative years, reminded his constituents that "Bad men cannot make good citizens. It is when a people forget God that tyrants forge their chains." He referred to the Bible as "a book worth more than all the other books that were ever printed."[22] So concerned was he that others not view him as a deist, he wrote to his daughter Betsy, shortly before he died, "I hear it said by the deists that I am one of the number; and indeed that some good people think I am no Christian. . . I think religion of infinitely higher importance than politics, and I find much cause to reproach myself that I have lived so long and given

21 David McCullough, *John Adams*, (New York: Simon and Schuster, 2001), p. 160
22 William Wirt, *Sketches of the Life and Character of Patrick Henry*, (New York: Derby and Jackson, 1857), p. 418.

no decided and public proofs of my being a Christian. But indeed, my dear child, this is a character which I prize far above all this world has or can boast. . ."[23]

These are the roots of a nation that truly received the blessing of God through several centuries. Millions came to this land seeking freedom from oppression. As late as the 1990s, hundreds of thousands of persecuted Christians from Slavic nations rushed into America, although some were disappointed to find less freedom than expected. Freedom brings prosperity, and prosperity brings great glory and even happiness. Eventually, however, prosperity can lead to self-reliance and pride. That is how America forgot God. At the turn of the 20th century, this country did everything possible to erase its Christian heritage from the school textbooks. The wicked rose quickly to gain the reins of power. The outspoken atheist, John Dewey, spearheaded a new secular education and endorsed the *Humanist Manifesto* that set a new direction for all of America's educational, political, and scientific institutions. They proudly declared the universe "self-existing" and "not created." There was no fear of God before their eyes.

Since that time, millions of Americans have been subjected to tyranny. They are subject to "compulsory school attendance laws." Prior to 1913, there was no income tax, no inheritance tax, no inventory tax, no Social Security tax, no Medicare tax, no sales tax, no state income tax, or a hundred other taxes. Today businesses and individuals are subject to far more tyranny than they were a hundred years ago. They have very little privacy in their personal records and effects. Hardly an American alive doesn't fear an audit from the Internal Revenue Service as they might have forgotten to include some income on their tax forms or some private sales record on a sales tax form submission.

Other godless, totalitarian nations like Sweden and Germany have fined Christians or jailed them for a mild use of the rod or absenting their children from the sexual training classes

23 Ibid, p. 402, 403

in the public schools. Of course, it gets worse when officially atheistic nations like China or the Soviet Union persecute Christians assembling for worship. When the wicked rise, men must resort to hiding. Some families in America, and now China, protect their families from social service investigations or one-child-policies by birthing their children at home. They refuse to register their children with a Social Security number, so as to be untracked by the authorities. Some churches are forced to meet secretly in basements or in forests. This is what happens when the wicked gain power.

Family Discussion Questions:

1. How did the *Humanist Manifesto* differ from the teachings of the founders of America?

2. How do you know when the wicked are ruling?

PART 282 ~ THE CHRISTIAN LIFE
Proverbs 28:13

He that covers his sins shall not prosper; but whoever confesses and forsakes them shall have mercy.

There are only two ways to deal with your sins. You can try to cover them by self-justification, blaming others, distractions, loud denials, or desperate attempts at self-atonement. Or you can confess your sins to God and others, and repent of them.

This is the warp and the woof of the Christian life: confession and repentance. We are all sinners. All of us fall short of the glory of God. Perhaps we have done things in the past of which we are ashamed. The best thing we can do is bring this out into the open, admitting it first to those to whom you are accountable—whether parent, pastor, or teacher.

Suppose a young boy does something terribly wicked at ten years of age. He steals $100 from his father. Now, if he refuses to admit the sin to his father, he will not prosper. He will not find mercy, and God will not forgive the sin and cleanse him from all unrighteousness (1 John 1:9). Refusing to confess known sin is rebellion against God. And that sin will dominate his life. The young man may very well turn into a bank robber and rot away in a maximum security prison in later years. But if the young man does humble himself, confessing his sin to his father, that boy will find mercy. The course of his life is set by hiding his sin or his confession. What a difference that simple little confession makes in this life and in eternity.

For a confession to be valid, it must be specific, truthful, and repentant. The confessor must see the dastardly nature of his sin, and truly desire a change in himself. He should not beat around the bush or confess some lesser sin. He should not compare himself to others nor shift part of the blame to somebody else. He should take full responsibility for his own sin and ask forgiveness of those affected. But this is only the first step towards healing, restoration, a change of life, and restitution. If a man sins against his wife and children, he must not only ask forgiveness, but take active steps towards rebuilding those relationships. Confession alone clears the air to allow this to happen.

Proverbs 28:14

Happy is the man that fears always; but he that hardens his heart shall fall into mischief.

How can anybody possibly be happy if they are living in fear all the time? What is assumed here is everything that has been taught thus far in the book—the beginning of wisdom is the fear of Yahweh. Fearing the wrong thing is a fatal mistake that brings about all sorts of misery. But living in the proper fear of God is a source of great comfort, stability, and blessedness. We hardly have to worry very much if we are sure that God has the whole world in His hands. We need fear no tyrant if God is who He reveals Himself to be. If we are running from God, avoiding Him at all costs, and failing to open our hearts to Him in honest confession, then we have real cause to be anxious. It is a dreadful thing to be in a wrong relationship with the Judge of the earth (Heb. 10:31).

The fellow who hardens his heart against God will inevitably face heartbreaking distress and despair. Of course, ultimate distress and despair will descend at the moment of his death. A person will either soften his heart, admit God's authority, and plead for mercy, or he will progressively harden his heart against God. According to Paul, the hard-hearted unbeliever knows God's power and Godhead, but he "suppresses the truth in unrighteousness" (Rom. 1:19–21). That means he hardens his heart against the knowledge of God. He comes up with cheap excuses for not believing in God. He constructs incoherent worldviews. The existentialist philosopher of the 20th century, Jean-Paul Sartre, was raised as a Catholic with some knowledge about God. But he said that he grew very tired of God watching him all the time, so he threw God out of his house. "He that hardens his heart shall fall into mischief."

How is it with us then? Do we live in the fear of God every day, all day long? Or do we take short breaks here and there, all the while assuming that God is not present and disinterested in what we are doing? This is what produces instability in life. So many professing believers are unstable and fearful in their circumstances because they do not fear God all the day long.

Family Discussion Questions:

1. Are we careful at keeping short accounts with our sin? How do we handle our sin? Is there a true humility and honesty about our sin in our home?

2. How often do we take short breaks from the fear of God, and assume that God is disinterested and distant from us? How might we learn to live in the fear of God?

PART 283 ~ FRIGHTFUL TYRANTS AND FOOLISH TYRANTS
Proverbs 28:15

As a roaring lion, and a ranging bear; so is a wicked ruler over the poor people.

From biblical records, we have clear pictures of wicked rulers. They exercise eminent domain and confiscate the property of poor men (1 Kings 21:1–13). They kill babies and enforce birth control on poor people; this was the case with the Pharaoh at the birth of Moses and King Herod at the birth of Christ (Exod. 1:15–22; Matt. 2:11–18). These tyrants reappeared in the 20th century in full force, but it began with the eugenic doctrines of Charles Darwin's cousin, Francis Galton. Piggybacking on Darwin's survival of the fittest, Galton took this doctrine to its logical conclusion–the survival of the fittest race. In his book *Human Faculty*, this wicked man introduced the fateful concept of eugenics in which, "The final object would be to devise means for favouring individuals who bore the signs of membership of a superior race."

This new "scientific elite" played right into the hands of the social planners—those who would use government to engineer that "superior race." The first targets in this country were those whom the government deemed mentally unfit. In all, the government subjected at least 65,000 people in thirty-three states to compulsory sterilization. In the famous Buck v. Bell case—adjudicated by the U.S. Supreme Court in 1927 and decided by a vote of 8–1—a poor woman was sterilized against her will. Commenting on the case in the ruling, Justice Oliver Wendell Holmes wrote, "Three generations of imbeciles is enough." The victim, Carrie Bell, had one daughter who was listed on her school's honor roll in April, 1931.

Tyrants in the present day operate under a thin guise of moral rectitude and scientific pseudo-wisdom. But if you strip back the masks, you find the same type of wicked tyrants who ruled in the time of Moses and Christ.

The social planners now spend more of their resources on indoctrinating the masses using media, schools, and universities. Also, since the 1970s, the federal government has poured billions of dollars into Planned Parenthood, an organizations dedicated to reducing the birth rate among poor minorities, especially the African-American population. Since 1973, there have been over thirteen million black children eliminated in the womb. Three out of five pregnant African-American women will abort their children, and fully one third of abortions are committed on black women (who only make up 12% of the population). By their expenditures of billions of dollars, social planners really can bring devastation to communities of poor people. They encourage them to murder. They fund fornication and have helped to increase the percentage of inner city children born without fathers from 30% in the 1960s to 70% at the present time.

In some nations, evil tyrants are extremely blatant in their wickedness. A missionary in China recently told of a family who dared to have a second child. Because of the one-child-per-family policy, the local tyrants imposed a fine on the family which they could not pay. The bureaucrats proceeded to kill the child on the spot.

Proverbs 28:16

The prince that wants [lacks] understanding is also a great oppressor; but he that hates covetousness shall prolong his days.

Sometimes stupid men will subject the people to unreasonable and oppressive conditions. What caused the Ukrainian famine of 1932 was a combination of stealing and stupidity. First, the Premier of the Soviet Union, Joseph Stalin, confiscated property from the Kulak farmers who had tilled the soil for generations. Turning the farms over to bureaucrats who were supposed to run the collective farms was stupid enough. But then, the tyrant demanded unreasonable exports of all foodstuffs out of the Ukraine into Russia, leaving the country with nothing to feed its own people. This famine killed an unprecedented 7,000,000 people. To that point in history, most famines came as a result of natural causes, such as droughts and plague. With the advent of modern social planning and centralized communist governments we find multiple instances of famine by stupidity.

Was it wickedness or stupidity that resulted in the dissolution of Israel in the reign of Rehoboam? He listened to the wrong advisors, and chose to tyrannize his people (1 Kng. 12:14). His actions brought about the secession of the northern tribes under King Jeroboam. Ruling by intimidation may yield a little progress, but in the long run the tyrant will not achieve good productivity by beating or starving his people to death. It takes more finesse and more wisdom than that to lead a business or a country.

If you are looking for the best long-term strategy that yields the most longevity for a business or a political order, the second half of the verse fits the bill. Hate covetousness. Greedy men will always make a bad judgment call at some critical point in their career. They will drive their businesses into the ground. Power-driven politicians will fail to make the prudent decision because it would cause short term pain and diminish their chances of re-election. Because their highest value is their own popularity and power, they will back away from the hard calls. They will buckle under pressure. During the first decades of the 21st century, the American government tried to spend its way out of economic ruin. This was the popular option and many politicians from both political parties added trillions of dollars in deficit spending to the national debt in the process. It was the worst thing they could do, although it might have extended their political careers for a few years. The constant impulse to personal affluence is dangerous and destructive. Wise men will refuse to make their decisions based on the metric of personal affluence and power they receive. Wherever greed is the motivator, these men will shy away from the investments, the projects, and the political endeavors involved.

One of the four most important biblical prerequisites for political office is that the man must "hate covetousness" (Ex. 18:21). This man must, at all costs, avoid the coveting of other people's money for the purposes of controlling that money and channeling it into the pockets of his favorite causes. But he must also hate the political maneuvering, the fame game, and the power mongering. Sad to say, these characteristics very much describe many of our leaders in public office today.

Family Discussion Questions:

1. How did tyrants take advantage of Carrie Bell in the 1920s in America? What has happened to the children of immigrants from Africa here in America between 1960 and 2010?

2. How did the Ukrainian famine of 1932 come about?

3. What kind of leaders should we look for, if we are endorsing candidates for the civil magistrate (reference Ex. 18:21 and 2 Sam. 23:2)?

Part 284 ~ The End of the Violent and Perverse Man

Proverbs 28:17

A man that does violence to the blood of any person shall flee to the pit; let no man stay him.

Violent men usually die violent deaths. It is a vicious cycle from which it is almost impossible to escape. Perhaps the most famous outlaw in America's history emerged from the darker elements of the civil war of the 1860s. According to certain reliable reports, Jesse James and his brother Frank participated in a massacre and scalping of twenty-one unarmed troops from the Northern armies in 1864. After the war, these lawless men quickly lost the fine distinction between righteous warfare and unrestrained, unlawful violence. They robbed banks, shot up innocent citizens, and waylaid trains from Virginia to Minnesota. After twenty years of revolutionary activity,

Jesse James was murdered by his friend and co-conspirator, Robert Ford, in 1884. Eight years later, a man named Edward O'Kelley shot Jesse James' assassin in Ford's saloon in Creede, Colorado. Only twelve years later, the same O'Kelley attacked a police officer in Oklahoma City, nearly killing him. As God would have it, a railroad baggage man came to the policeman's aid, enabling the lawman to get the upper hand in the conflict. He got off two gunshots at O'Kelley, killing the man who killed the man who killed Jesse James.

The best biblical example of this lesson is demonstrated in the life of Judas Iscariot. After betraying our Lord, his guilt pressed him almost immediately to suicide. He could not live with his deeds and so he quickly entered everlasting torment and nobody acted to prevent his demise. The torturous mental agony suffered by those who commit murder or sell themselves to the devil's service is beyond comprehension. Many spiral into addictions, self-mutilation, and suicide. If the civil magistrate is acting properly, the murderer should be put to death. This is the most basic, in fact, the very first civil law, ever revealed to man (Gen. 9:6; Ex. 21:12–14; Lev. 24:17, 21). If the magistrate doesn't act properly and you have a murderer in your presence who refuses to repent of his sin, it would be best to have nothing to do with him whatsoever. He is still a dangerous man to himself and to others.

Proverbs 28:18

Whoso walks uprightly shall be saved; but he that is perverse in his ways shall fall at once.

The term "walking uprightly" might be better rendered "walking with integrity." A man's walk is either characterized by increasing honesty, transparency, and uprightness or it will manifest itself to be hypocritical and hopelessly rebellious. Eventually, every man, woman, and child will show their true colors. Jesus said, "For from within, out of the heart of men, proceed evil thoughts, adulteries, fornications, murders, thefts, covetousness, wickedness, deceit, lasciviousness, an evil

eye, blasphemy, pride, foolishness; all these evil things come
from within, and defile the man" (Mark 7:21–23). One may
appear to be good on the outside, but full of dead men's bones
on the inside (Matt. 23:27). False religions are good at this
sort of thing. They train their children to act a certain way in
outward manners and religious practices. But when a crack
develops in the façade, a horrible green slime oozes out of the
heart of the person in sins of drunkenness, incest, and other
filthy behavior. Those standing around wonder at the stinking
green slime and seek out its source.

Despite all the attempts to polish the outside by cheap
religious rites, the hearts of men will remain corrupt. This
applies to the moralistic religions of Islam, Mormonism, and
Buddhism, along with some sects of Roman Catholicism and
Protestantism. Wherever men refuse to rely upon the working
of the sovereign grace of God, and wherever men take pride
and confidence in their own religious status, there you will
find corrupt hearts and perverse ways. The Mafia henchmen
may attend a Mass from time to time, but the rottenness of
their hearts is manifest in their murderous ways.

Often the slide into these terrible, destructive sins is rapid.
Once the crack in the heart develops, it metastasizes quickly
and the green slime flows everywhere. The man's reputation is
ruined, and the civil magistrate usually gets involved. But it is
worse than that. The fall of that man descends as far as the pit
of hell (Ezek. 31:16; Matt. 7:27: Rev. 21:8).

Now, the good news is that the fellow who walks uprightly
will be saved from this nightmare. From both Old and
New Testaments we learn that the upright walks in a spirit
of humility, honesty, and utter dependence on the grace of
God to save him. It is the walk of faith and repentance (Prov.
3:5–6, 11:2, 16:18; Ezek. 18:21–22, 32; Rom. 12:1–2; Eph.
2:8–9; 1 Pet. 5:5). Some have seen faith and repentance as
a single moment's experience. Sadly, theologies have drifted
from biblical language over time in this area. Yet Scripture
configures this as a "way" or a "walk" (Acts 16:17, 18:25–26,

19:9, 23, 20:21, 26:20; Rom. 1:17, 4:12; 2 Cor. 5:7; Gal. 3:11; Heb. 6:1, 6, etc.) Those who are saved walk in the way of humility, faith, and repentance before God.

Family Discussion Questions:

1. What happens to men who habitually fix problems by violence?
2. What is it to walk uprightly? Is it the same thing as being completely sinless?

PART 285 ~ A FAITHFUL WORKING MAN
Proverbs 28:19

He that tills his land shall have plenty of bread; but he that follows after vain persons shall have poverty enough.

The safest thing to do with your children is to get them working as soon as possible. The sooner they understand the principle of sowing and reaping the better. When they discover that hard work always pays off, they are more likely to live a productive, happy life. The Bible commands us to work for six days and rest a seventh (Ex. 20:9). How much of our time is spent in productive labor, planting seeds that will likely produce fruit?

Following after the vain person means to associate with flaky, unproductive people. They fritter away their time playing games, watching movies, and making trite, meaningless entries on their Facebook accounts. Sometimes they attend college for years and years without doing any meaningful work in the marketplace. Perhaps the greatest risk assumed by those attending college is in their associations. For the less academic minded student, the social environment can be more toxic than the worldview taught in the secular classrooms. Many families discover this too late, seeing it clearly *after* their children have followed vain persons who have never grown up and who are living in spiritual and moral decay.

Young men who have never learned to provide for their own families will live the life of the infidel (1 Tim. 5:8). Failing to provide for their own wives and children, they create many fatherless homes and bring a tremendous curse upon multiple generations. May God save our children and grandchildren from such a horrible predicament!

Over the last century it was the teen culture that discipled the young adolescents. The pop music stars and the teen peer group served as the mentors that captured the hearts of the youth. Sadly, the pastors and parents had little influence over the teen-aged children. Untold millions of people follow after vain persons in popular music, movies, and other media. Many are absorbed by their Twitter accounts and constantly revisit their dysfunctional lives by reading the gossip magazines and on-line news stories. These pop idols are, by definition, vain, hollow personalities that lead a society towards broken relationships, fornication, divorce, and moral bankruptcy. But what does moral bankruptcy have to do with economic bankruptcy? It turns out that divorced families and single, mother-led households suffer far more economic distress than the average healthy, nuclear family, according to many socioeconomic studies that follow these families.[24] Following after the vain licentiousness and irresponsibility of movie stars and the parts they play in their motion pictures is a recipe for disaster. While these big stars tout immoral lifestyles and dysfunctional families, they seem to retain a facade of material success and wealth. But the millions of people who are influenced by their lifestyles and morals suffer a great deal of socioeconomic disintegration.

This is a modern phenomenon. It was certainly not normative for the humble plowboy raised on his family's farm in the 1850s. These boys plowed the fields for thousands of year by their fathers' side, and sat around the candle light for hours each evening with the rest of the family. It is only in the modern age that a culture of vanity dominated in the discipleship of the youth.

24 http://www.heritage.org/research/reports/2000/06/the-effects-of-divorce-on-america

Proverbs 28:20

A faithful man shall abound with blessings; but he that makes haste to be rich shall not be innocent.

Here is a qualifying word for the previous passage. While it is true that sowing seed has a great deal to do with reaping, this lesson is hardly intended for those who want to get rich quick. The faithful man is the plugger-and-chugger. He is the tortoise in the famous tale of the tortoise and the hare. He puts his hand to the plow, his nose to the grindstone, and works hard for twenty years.

Every now and then, you run into a young man who does hit the "jackpot" in his business. But if he lacks the character to take on the responsibilities associated with increased riches, he will quickly meet his "Waterloo." At some point, he makes an unwise decision which results in huge losses. In one sense, he gets what he deserves in life. In another sense, people do not get what they deserve because it could always be far worse for them. According to the standards of divine justice, rebellious sinners deserve death forever (Rom. 6:23). For God to reward the slothful cheater in business would be contrary to His nature. He may allow the wicked businessman a little rope for a time, but as the old saying goes, the fellow will use it "to hang himself."

For related commentary, reference Proverbs 20:21.

Family Discussion Questions:

1. What is the best way for young men (and young women) to avoid being disciple in vanity?

2. Describe a "faithful man." Are we raising humble, faithful men and women?

PART 286 ~ BRIBES AND GREED
Proverbs 28:21

To have respect of persons is not good; for a piece of bread that man will transgress.

This principle is particularly focused upon the civil government, but it could apply to any situation. A gift here or there can bias a person's judgment concerning someone else. The man could have been a serial killer, but if he handed your child some candy, you might describe him as "such a nice man!" We are easily biased by paltry little gifts here and there. The true character of the man is only judged by careful consideration of his reputation, his history, his treatment of all people (including widows and orphans), and the nature of the crimes or sins he has committed. In the Old Testament, when cases were judged by judges over ten or one hundred families, chances are the judges knew the people involved in the civil and criminal charges. Today, a judge will usually recuse himself if he knows the people involved. But there was a benefit to knowing the people involved in the court trials. Knowing the people can help you get to the truth of the matter. You can see, therefore, why it was so important that these judges not be influenced by the fact that the family facing charges had him over for dinner two weeks earlier.

For related commentary, reference Proverbs 18:5 and Proverbs 24:23.

Proverbs 28:22

He that hastens to be rich has an evil eye, and considers not that poverty shall come upon him.

Making wise judgments concerning those with whom you do business is important. It can protect you from harmful situations. But what is a decent criterion for making this judgment? Here is one simple rule: you really don't want to do business with people who have the "get rich quick" mentality. If it appears that some salesman wants to get rich quick, and he is trying to bring you in on a "get rich quick" scheme, you need to put some distance between you and that fellow. He has what this proverb calls "an evil eye." That means his motivations are tainted and he is up to no good. He doesn't put his neighbor's interests above his own and he will be glad to impoverish others in order to enrich himself. Regrettably, there are a fair number of network marketing businesses and pyramid schemes that promote this "get rich quick" mentality in our day. If the business presents a good product or service for a fair price, helpful mentoring, and reasonable rewards for a good day's work, then it may be worth pursuing. Inevitably, those that seek to get rich quick by cutting corners here and there will find themselves awash in poverty, unemployment, and even bankruptcy.

For related commentary, reference Proverbs 20:21 and 28:20.

Family Discussion Questions:

1. Is it a good thing or a bad thing for a judge to know the people he adjudicates? Explain.

2. What is the difference between a bribe and a campaign donation?

3. How would you know a reputable businessman or marketing organization?

PART 287 ~ FLATTERY AND ROBBING PARENTS
Proverbs 28:23

He that rebukes a man afterwards shall find more favor than he that flatters with the tongue.

Which is easier to do and what might win you more friends— rebuke or flattery? It is possible that flattery might make you more popular for a little while. But flattery only wins the hearts of superficial people who will leave you in the lurch at the drop of a hat. Rebuke is not pleasant at the time it is offered, either for the one offering it or for the one receiving it. But if hearts are humble and receptive, and the rebuke is given in love and concern, in the end this will further solidify the friendship.

Where does affirmation fit into the picture? Affirmation lies somewhere between flattery and rebuke. Flattery is man-centered and fails to maintain truthfulness in relationships. But if our friendships were based entirely on rebuke, we would be a discouraged, harried lot! Sometimes our friends need an encouraging word to keep going (Prov. 12:25). It is faith that tunes the eye to identify the grace of God at work in the lives of our brothers and sisters. Faith also follows up with gratefulness and warm affirmations. Yet even in our affirmations, we must remember that grace enables all that is good and God's glory is pre-eminent.

Proverbs 28:24

Whoever robs his father or his mother, and says, It is no transgression;
the same is the companion of a destroyer.

Stealing is an interesting thing. Sometimes children think that their parents owe them everything and they take the things of the household for granted. They may have asked permission before taking some of the family resources in the past, but as time progresses, they take advantage of their parents' good graces and they develop a pattern of stealing. They justify their behavior because they are a son or daughter and they expect the inheritance in the end anyway. Because they do not love nor honor their parents, they use their parents' love for them as justification for their delinquent behavior. This only heightens the egregious nature of the sin.

Respect your father's and mother's right to oversee the entire family economy. If you are given purview over some piece of it, or if you have some money that you can spend at will, be sure that all parties are clear on the particulars. Some children have access to their parents' credit cards or bank debit cards. This right can be abused where there is no clear communication between parents and children in the use of these financial tools.

Typically, children who do not respect their parents' property will not respect the property of others. Often, young men who violate their parent's properties won't think twice about striking their mothers or cursing their fathers. Before long they have reduced themselves to what the Bible calls "capital punishment" crimes (Matt. 15:4). This behavior is terribly destructive to a social system.

Family Discussion Questions:

1. What is the difference between flattery and godly affirmation? Are we excessively critical as a family? Do we flatter one another? Are we affirming toward each other enough?

2. As children, are you thankful for the good things that your parents give you? Do we make it clear enough what your rights and responsibilities are with the family economy? How might we improve this?

PART 288 ~ TRUST IN GOD AND HUMILITY
Proverbs 28:25

He that is of a proud heart stirs up strife: but he that puts his trust in the LORD shall be made fat.

The contrasts here are important. Pride is contrasted with trust in God and strife is contrasted with productivity and blessing. Are these things opposites? Wherever you see strife, you have to count on the fact that there is a problem with pride there. This goes as much for sibling rivalry as it does for arguments between elders in a church or a denominational meeting. Humility is required to make it through disagreements and misunderstandings. But it also takes faith, because without faith in God we could not proceed to work out our disagreements or clarify our misunderstandings.

We need great faith to meet a brother who disagrees with us in some doctrinal area (relating to baptism or God's sovereignty), and work through it towards a blessed unity. These issues have divided the church for thousands of years. How might a couple of humble souls in some small town in Kansas work out these differences? This will happen only by exercising great faith and humility. By faith, our relationships in our families and churches will develop into a fruitful garden.

When we speak of faith, we mean something more than a half-hearted assent to some historical fact from the Gospels. We need a faith to live by, a faith to bear children, a faith to disciple children each day without getting discouraged, a faith to talk to the grocery clerk about our faith, a faith to work in the marketplace, a faith to mortify our sinful flesh. True believers cannot live without faith. Faith is *how* they live. The life of faith is always fruitful. When we believe in the resurrection of Jesus Christ and when we live by this faith, we are blessed—extraordinarily blessed—throughout our whole lives and on into eternity.

For related commentary, reference Proverbs 13:10.

Proverbs 28:26

He that trusts in his own heart is a fool: but whoever walks wisely, he shall be delivered.

Perhaps the most common piece of advice given today is "follow your heart." Movies, books, and television programs offer this nifty-sounding aphorism again and again as some sort of sage advice. It is the teaching of Arthur Schopenhauer, another 19th century humanist philosopher. Because people do not want to follow the laws of God, they will usually end up doing what *they* want to do. Sometimes they follow their own emotions and desires and they do what seems right to them after a brief contemplation or after a good long "think about it." Of course, the problem with following your heart is that "the heart is deceitful above all things and desperately wicked"

(Jer. 17:9). As far as the heart is sanctified and cleansed by the washing of regeneration and the Word, then it can be trusted. But it cannot be trusted in the ultimate sense. We must continually return to the authoritative Word of God, and hem ourselves in by that standard. For those who are true believers, this should be a daily exercise. The Christian always cries out with Paul, "Let God be true, and every man a liar!" (Rom. 3:4).

Thousands of different denominations are claiming that all of God's revealed truth cannot be right. There are new cults and new sects developing practically every day because men are captivated by the innovations of their own hearts. It is of utmost importance, therefore, that we "walk circumspectly, not as fools but as wise" (Eph. 5:15). The books you read, the movies you watch, and the friendships you cultivate will either guide you in the walk of wisdom or they will take you out of the narrow way. Choose wisely. Redeem the time. Many from the next generation will wander out of the way as they absorb the ideas and lifestyles of heterodoxies of every description. One young woman raised in a Christian evangelical home in the 1990s wandered into fornication, body mutilation, and nihilism before she was "rescued" by a Muslim from Saudi Arabia. Now she finds solace in the structure and moralisms of this new religion. Is she in a better state today than she was ten years ago in her mother's home? With each newfound "faith," she trusts her heart to decide if she has found the right one. But alas, her heart is not to be trusted!

At the end of the day we must trust in God to enable us, to give us the faith and the wisdom to stay in the way. Without faith a man cannot be saved. "Therefore we are always confident, knowing that, whilst we are at home in the body, we are absent from the Lord; for we walk by faith, not by sight" (2 Cor. 5:7).

Family Discussion Questions:

1. What does it mean that the true believers in God are "made fat?" What does the life of faith look like?

2. What is wrong with the phrase "follow your heart?"

3. If your own heart is deceitful, who can you trust when it comes to finding the truth in a world of a million errors?

PART 289 ~ HAPPINESS AND CHARITY
Proverbs 28:27

He that gives unto the poor shall not lack; but he that hides his eyes shall have many a curse.

The Bible has much to say about giving to the poor. After all, this is pure religion in God's eyes (Jam. 1:27). In the Old Testament, the Lord gives guidelines to provide for the poor in the form of the once-every-three-years' poor tithe and the gleaning principle (Deut. 14:28–29; Lev. 23:22). From these texts and our Lord's parable of the Good Samaritan, we conclude that charity is direct, local, relational, and voluntary. The socialist coercive forms are humanist fabrications that kill the spirit of true charity. Until the poor reject the socialist handouts and others provide directly for the needs of the poor in their families and communities, our entire society will face the curse of God. Those who hide behind the socialist systems and refuse to deal directly with the poor are hypocrites and subject to the curse promised here in this passage.

For those who are generous towards the poor with their own money (not with other peoples' money), God promises manifold blessings. He does not promise material wealth specifically, but there is far more to life than stacks of gold lying around in one's basement.

According to a recent Gallup survey done in 153 countries around the world, the most generous nations of all are Australia, New Zealand, and the United States. Among

European nations, Switzerland, the Netherlands, and the UK were the most generous contributors to charity (all Protestant Christian nations). An interesting correlation developed in the study, when researchers found that these were also the happiest nations in the world. The nations rated highest for happiness were the Netherlands at 7.6, followed by Canada at 7.5, New Zealand at 7.4, Australia at 7.3, and the United States at 7.2.[25]

In order to properly provide for the poor in our midst, we must always keep our eyes peeled for needs. When you hear that a brother has lost work, or that a sister has lost her husband, you are now apprised as to those needs. Now you are responsible to act on what you know. It is easy to forget about these needs and to hide our eyes from them.

For related commentary, reference Proverbs 11:24.

Family Discussion Questions:

1. What are the Old Testament requirements for helping the poor?

2. Are we sensitive to the needs of the poor? Are we generous as a family? Should we increase our giving to the poor in our midst?

PART 290 ~ WHEN THE RIGHTEOUS DECREASE
Proverbs 28:28

When the wicked rise, men hide themselves; but when they perish, the righteous increase.

Repeating the principle laid out in Proverbs 28:12 (and to be revisited in Prov. 29:2), the wise father impresses upon his son the horrific state of affairs when wicked men gain power. Of course, we must define wicked policies by the clear laws of God. Those who support homosexuality, the killing of innocent children, thievery, unjust war, and tyrannical power grabs (such as those described in 1 Sam. 8:11–18) are wicked

25 http://www.christiantoday.com/article/happy.people.more.likely.to.give.survey.finds/26660.htm

rulers. Should they forcibly enslave children in their schools and work places, this might also be considered tyrannical. When this happens, men hide themselves and the numbers of the righteous decrease.

Truly, when wicked men control the media, the schools, and the universities, children from Christian families will be absorbed into their systems over time. Churches do their best to remain "relevant" to the popular culture and inevitably compromise with scientism, higher criticism, evolution, and post-modernism (rampant in the 21st century). Whereas 70% of Americans considered themselves Christians in 1970, only 50% did so by 2010. The problem is twice as bad in England. The reason the faith has died in these countries is because wicked men gained tremendous power and controlled most of the institutions. A Christian church in Sacramento organized a charter school on its grounds several years ago. There was no mention of God in the textbooks and no part of God's Law-word on the walls. When the principal was asked why they would neglect such an important part of a child's education (Deut. 6:7–9), she replied softly, "Oh, that would be against the law!" Of course, this was not a reference to God's law. They are concerned about man's laws, and they fear a lawsuit from the ACLU and other organizations that enforce a godless education system. The wicked are in power now, and the poor righteous are systematically eliminated from the systems. But one day they will perish, just as they always do, and the righteous will increase once more (Ps. 37).

For related commentary, reference Proverbs 28:12.

Family Discussion Questions:

1. Why has the Christian faith died out in Europe, Canada, and (to some extent) America?

2. Will the wicked always dominate everything in this world's institutions?

PART 291 ~ THE CHRONIC REBEL
Proverbs 29:1

He, that being often reproved hardens his neck, shall suddenly be destroyed and that without remedy.

Here is the story of the rebellious child, and it is repeated a million times in every generation. From the time this boy was a toddler, he resisted his mother's admonitions. He threw a tantrum every time his father used the rod. He screamed, spit at, and hit his father. As time went on, his parents resorted to psychotropic drugs to quell his violence, and they felt compelled to give in to his constant demands. Through his teen years, they hesitated to correct him or require anything of him for fear of his dishonoring, sullen, or angry response. In total, he may have been corrected 50,000 times over a period of ten to fifteen years. But with each correction, he took the opportunity to harden his neck a little bit more. According to this verse, the demise of this young man will be quick and there will be no room for repentance at that time. The same scenario is revisited in Hebrews 6:4–6 for the man who has "tasted of the spiritual gift," and rejected it. There is something known as the "point of no return" in the path of rebellion.

It would be well, then, for our children to take fair warning from this passage. Our children must not tempt God by constant and perpetual rebellion to the teaching, the correction, and the warnings He has given to them. God is patient and merciful, but a rebellious child can push Him too far, even in covenant homes where believing parents continually teach God's Word to their children.

But now, what does this say to parents or teachers who must work with those who are full of this hard-hearted rebellion? At what point do they give up all hope for repentance? Certainly, parents must try to contain the rebellion, and do what they can to prevent a cancerous spread of the rebellion into others around them. If they countenance rebellion in any way, it almost certainly will play into the lives of the other children in the home—even into the more mild mannered of them. If it becomes impossible to contain the rebellion, then of course, the young rebel simply cannot remain in the home, and his father and mother may continue to pray that God would sovereignly work a heart-change in the rebel. But this is in His hands. To ignore a child's rebellion while counting on God's gracious work in the life of the child is presumption, and detracts from the glory of God. This was Eli's mistake, and God cursed his family for it, for multiple generations (1 Sam. 3:11–14). God is not obligated to save every one of our children. He chose not to save Esau, a circumcised son of the covenant (Rom. 9:13). Yet, we are still hopeful and believing, eagerly expectant of His mercies and grateful for every act of heart-softening we see in our families.

There is a fine line between faithlessness and presumption in child raising. We ought not to turn our children into idols, but we should take advantage of the gracious means God has given us to raise our children in the covenant. As a farmer plants the seeds and diligently waters his crops, he is hopeful of God's good blessings in the harvest. Parents ought therefore to be good farmers. We plant the seeds, teach the Word, and water the plants. We baptize and then we teach them some more. After eighteen years, we look up and see what God has done for us! To disciple the nations we baptize and teach them to observe whatsoever Jesus has commanded in His Word. This is the great commission, and we start by discipling a very small nation called a "family" (Matt. 28:18–20).

Family Discussion Questions:

1. What will happen to a chronic teenage rebel, according to this text? Are there any exceptions to this?

2. How should parents handle rebellion in a child?

3. As parents, do you err on the side of presumption or faithlessness?

PART 292 ~ GOOD LEADERS AND BAD LEADERS
Proverbs 29:2

When the righteous are in authority, the people rejoice; but when the wicked bear rule, the people mourn.

This is a black and white statement. Some would see history in terms of pure ethical relativism, where there are no really bad guys, and no good guys. But this is not the way the Bible looks at it. Throughout the Old Testament, there were good kings and bad kings, and then there were some very bad kings. God takes sides in history, and so should we. For example, a cursory reading of the writings and actions of two historical leaders, John Winthrop and Nero, would reveal that Winthrop was a good ruler and Nero was not. The difference between good rulers and bad ones is delineated by the righteous standards of God's law. A righteous man fears God and lives in accord with the laws of God (Rom. 7:12; Gal. 5:21–24), and says with the Psalmist, "Oh how I love your law!" Wicked leaders steal and kill, usually under the guise of seeking a "higher good." But the righteous oppose these machinations.

According to this verse, wicked rulers will make life unpleasant for their people. Of course, these rulers will make grand promises and always present themselves in the best light when they run for office in a "democratic society." But they will make the people mourn. Granted, even this is under the sovereign dictate of God. If a nation is due for God's judgment, He will raise up rulers who hate His laws in order that they may tyrannize the people.

It is God's blessing on a nation when men of outstanding character rise to the top of the political machines. This may not happen very often in this sin-drenched world where immoral people love to elect tyrants. But there are a few places and times in history where righteous men have prevailed—and they usually bring unprecedented freedoms with them. This is the legacy of Oliver Cromwell in England, who fought hard for religious freedom at a time when the state controlled the church.

For many years, America has retained a position among the most free and prosperous nations in the world.[26] This is because America's foundations were strong at the beginning. Many of the early leaders were committed Christians of the Protestant faith, descendants of the Pilgrims and Puritans who settled the land in the 17th century. The above-mentioned, John Winthrop was the first of their leaders in the colonies. Writing in his own diary, he testified to his faith in God: "I will always walk humbly before my God, and meekly, mildly, and gently towards all men… to give myself, my life, my wits, my health, my wealth to the service of my God and Saviour." For the first five years of the Massachusetts colony, he dipped into his own pockets to fund the government. He paid for shipments of food from England with his own money, saving many from starvation during the first terrible winter in New England. Then, he voluntarily gave up his political rights to the governorship, allowing for America's first free elections to take place. What a stark contrast with the Soviet Union's Joseph Stalin who said, "You know, they are fooling us, there is no God… all this talk about God is sheer nonsense."[27] This man was responsible for killing at least thirty million of his own citizens (estimates run from eight million to sixty million dead). "When the wicked bear rule, the people mourn."

For related commentary, reference Proverbs 28:12, 28.

Family Discussion Questions:

1. How does the Bible describe good leaders and bad leaders? How can we describe any leader as righteous, when men still sin as King David did?

2. Based on the criteria of righteous leaders, name some good and bad leaders in history.

26 Heritage Foundation, Index for Economic Freedom, http://www.heritage.org/index/.
27 E. Yaroslavsky, *Landmarks in the Life of Stalin*, (Moscos: Foreign Languages Publishing House, 1940)

PART 293 ~ UNCOMMITTED, LOOSE LIFESTYLES
Proverbs 29:3

Whoever loves wisdom rejoices his father; but he that keeps company with harlots spends his substance.

Some boys are attracted to harlots and some to wisdom. The two are incompatible. The biblical term for harlot is used for a woman who does not see a need for a husband, but takes up with different men who may or may not support her financially. The woman could be in "dating relationships" or temporary "hook ups" that last for a week or two, or "shack-ups" that may last a year or two. While 95% of Americans confess to having committed fornication prior to their wedding day, only 7% of unmarried women still claim to be virgins by twenty-nine years of age.

To keep company with harlots, then, is to fraternize with promiscuous women who have little interest in marriage. When a woman crosses the line and is willing to trade her body for something less than the marriage commitment, she is giving way to the lifestyle of the harlot. The men who seduce these women (or are seduced by them), have little interest in marital commitment themselves. This lack of marital commitment also involves a lack of commitment to family, material provision for a family, child-bearing, and inheritance. That is one reason why the birth control technologies of the last century enabled massive fornication and harlotry rates in America, Africa, South America, Asia, and Europe. For the first time, women believed they were "free" to prostitute themselves without worrying about pregnancy, as long as governments and businesses could provide them with material security.

But what does this do to society? The uncommitted playboy lifestyle is self-centered and destructive to a family heritage. It is destructive to economies and to the character of an entire nation. When men live for themselves, they create a society of children born without fathers and raised without fathers. This perpetuates the increase in criminal activity among young men, and a breakdown of the economic well-being of the country.

A fair number of young men today meet these harlots on the internet. As they are tangled into the web of sexual and emotional manipulation, they quickly lose a vision for life and a vision for building a family economy. They discover that they do not need a wife to get what they want, as they find ways in which they can serve themselves. This self-centered lifestyle then fuels more irresponsibility, sinful addictions, and ends in a wasted life.

Our children carry on our legacy. When a son fails to pursue worthy endeavors for God's kingdom and instead seeks his own pleasures, he turns into a tremendous disappointment to his father.

Family Discussion Questions:

1. What does it mean to "keep company with harlots?" What is a harlot?

2. How did birth control technologies contribute to the breakdown of family life and encourage immoral living?

3. How is it that the playboy who refuses to settle down, get married, and further his family's economy becomes such a disappointment to his father?

PART 294 ~ SOCIAL STABILITY
Proverbs 29:4

The king by judgment establishes the land; but he that receives gifts overthrows it.

In the human social arrangement, there is constant tension between the tyranny of the one and the anarchy of the many. Some want big government socialism, and others want libertarian individualism where every man does that which is right in his own eyes. How then do we strike a balance between the individual liberties of each person and the necessities of the social order? Should the government allow divorce in any and all circumstances, and permit the ruin of families by the millions? Shall governments educate all our children with the same curriculum and goals in order that they might maintain a united order? Should parents have the right to spank their children? What if they spank hard and leave a bruise? What if every parent educated their children according to their own agenda? Would chaos ensue? Should the government regulate concrete foundations for buildings so as to ensure safety during earthquakes? Should a man have the right to commit adultery with impunity? Where do individual liberties violate the liberties of others? And where do governments violate the liberties of the individual by tyrannical regulations and controls?

There is tension between the tyranny of the one social unit and the anarchy of the many individuals. It is only resolved by good leaders who make wise judgements. Maximum stability in a country and maximum liberty for the people can only be achieved in the implementation of God's law. If you believe in the Trinitarian God, you know that He is One and He is Three. Therefore, His law strikes the perfect balance between social unity and individual liberties. As God's law is wisely and carefully applied to a unique situation in time and place (whether it be Zimbabwe in 2025 or America in 1634), it will achieve the best balance that can be achieved. Of course, this is a sinful world, so there will be no Utopia. Living in this world is a matter of making the best out of a bad situation, and there is no better law to apply to any bad situation than the righteous principles of God's law.

It still requires great wisdom to make these applications, however. For example, the sin of the people may require more government involvement at some points. Anarchical societies may require an expensive and intrusive police force to keep relative stability in the land. Until men can govern themselves and their families by God's righteous laws, they will need the strong hand of civil government to keep the civil order in place. But the righteous leader will look to God's laws to prioritize his agenda, to balance justice and mercy, and to provide a righteous standard for the state he governs.

The second half of the verse speaks to the dissolution of governments and the breakdown of nations. If leaders are more controlled by a thirst for power, media attention, or popular opinion, they abandon God's principles and sound judgement. When campaign donations become the deciding factor in elections, you can be sure that justice will be perverted and the government will turn into a den of thieves.

For related commentary, reference Proverbs 17:8, 23, and 21:14.

Family Discussion Questions:

1. What makes for a wise and righteous leader in the civil magistrate?

2. Is a police force always necessary in every community? Should governments prosecute drunkenness and drug use? Where is the correct balance between government regulation or enforcement and individual liberties?

3. Are campaign donations a deciding factor in our elections?

PART 295 ~ THE SNARES OF FLATTERY AND SIN
Proverbs 29:5

A man that flatters his neighbor spreads a net for his feet.

Having a right estimation of oneself is critical for success in relationships, in business, and life. It is flattery that encourages a man to think of himself more highly than he ought to think. Thus, encouraging a man to miscalculate his own skills and abilities will tend to decrease his motivation for improvement. This doesn't happen in every case, however. A humble man may have learned to ignore flattery, refusing to take it into account in his own self-assessment. But many will listen to flattery and stumble.

Flattery comes in various forms. It may be the Christian conference speaker who softens the message a bit for popular acceptance. He backs away from a message about sin or repentance. When he speaks of faith, he directs men to self-confidence instead of God-confidence as if self is worthy to be trusted! Or he speaks of social sins without prodding the consciences of those who are sitting before him. Some employees will lavish their managers with obsequious and unnecessary honorifics, in hope that they might secure a raise or a promotion. In the world of the internet, millions of people will register their support for things they don't really care much about, by toggling the "like" button on their "friends" web pages.

Flattery does not win you friends. It may return a little weak affirmation for the moment. It may even gain a politician the popular vote. But it will not get you true friendship. When your acquaintances discover the falsity of your glad-handing and pseudo-positive hype, they will usually treat you with similar superficiality.

Proverbs 29:6

In the transgression of an evil man there is a snare; but the righteous do sing and rejoice.

Sin curtails freedom. It burdens the conscience, and one sin usually leads to other sins. When a man gives way to the sin of drunkenness, he opens himself up to other sins like anger, lust, and lying. With each new sin introduced into his life, he builds another wall to keep himself in the way of sin and destruction.

Sin is also addictive. Some studies have indicated that pornography is more addictive than cocaine, and its ruinous effects on marriage and the family are legendary. The burden of all the social sins, destructive habits, and ruined relationships is evident in the psychological pathologies of the modern day. Between 1996 and 2006, the use of psychotropic drugs and anti-depressants increased by 200% among adults sixty-five and older.[28]

Meanwhile, the righteous man sings and rejoices. It is not that he doesn't face his own trials, discouragements, and temptations. But his heart is still free to rejoice in faith that his sins are forgiven and he is accepted with God. He enjoys the freedom that comes with honest confession of his sin and sincere repentance.

It is interesting that most false religions do not emphasize singing. The Muslims generally forbid the use of music altogether. While the ungodly do sing occasionally, their repertoire is severely limited to chronicling the sad, hopeless conditions of their lives (whether it be unfaithful lovers, drunken parties, and other unfulfilled expectations). Almost without exception, the happiest families in the world are Christian families who sing the psalms and hymns in the home, in the car, and at church. They don't need to sing the blues! They can eat their bread with rejoicing because they know that God has accepted their work (Eccl. 9:7). With full understanding that they are justified before God, received into His family, and invited to His table in communion, they can rejoice even when going through the fire of a serious trial (1 Pet. 1:6).

Family Discussion Questions:

1. What is so dangerous about flattery? What happens to people who are led to believe they are better than they really are?

2. Why are evil men so easily ensnared in drunkenness and addictions? Why do the righteous experience the freedom to sing and rejoice?

3. Are you a happy family? Do you sing and rejoice on a fairly regular basis?

28 Julie Steenhuysen, "More Americans Taking Drugs for Mental Illness," on Reuters http://www.reuters.com/article/2009/05/05/us-mental-drugs-idustre5440v120090505

PART 296 ~ CARING FOR THE POOR
Proverbs 29:7

The righteous considers the cause of the poor; but the wicked cares not to know it.

Too many people do not prefer to know the cause of the poor. While living in their own gated communities, they assume that the government is taking care of the poor. Their churches have very little contact with the inner city, and if a poor single mother happens to attend one of their churches she is referred to the welfare agencies. But do the government bureaucrats working on the fourteenth floor of some public building in New York City truly know the state of the poor? Do they really know their spiritual needs? Are they familiar with the needs of the fatherless? Is there a public employee who can provide spiritual leadership for the young men who have no father? Will he take them fishing or hunting a couple of times a year? The wicked doesn't want to know what is happening to the poor in his community. It's too complicated. It might require time and resources out of his reservoir. It might require true compassion and selfless love. These are burdens to bear which he would rather not bother with.

The righteous knows that he will never entirely solve the problems of the poor, even as he cannot solve the problems of disease, death, spiritual sickness, sin, and conflicts in this world. But the righteous doesn't mind rolling up his sleeves and getting involved. He will understand that there are no simple solutions, and that he cannot solve these problems by money and by sheer governmental power. But he *can* get involved. The righteous man can assess the problems from both a material and spiritual perspective and provide time and resources to alleviate some of the issues. Of course, as he provides some material help and bring spiritual teaching to address the spiritual needs, the righteous man will trust that God will work the major work of grace that is needed in the life of every person, whether rich or poor (Jam. 2:5).

Family Discussion Questions:

1. Why do the wicked shy away from getting involved in the needs of the poor?

2. How do you solve the problem of the poor? What is your responsibility in regards to the poor?

<h1 style="text-align:center">PART 297 ~ SCORN AND MOCKERY</h1>
Proverbs 29:8

Scornful men bring a city into a snare; but wise men turn away wrath.

Scornful people refuse to learn anything from those who disagree with them. Their language is always laced with disdain, mockery, and sarcasm towards their opponents. Respect all but disappears. These scorners will communicate spite for the president or governor of the state. They speak evil of dignitaries (2 Pet. 2:10). They cannot think of anything good to say at all. When in truth there is little difference between political parties, scorners speak as if one is far better than the other. They consider themselves the absolute standard of what is right and true. Instead of doubting themselves, and referring others to the standard of truth revealed in Scripture, they accuse others of gross ignorance for not aligning with their own perspective. They cannot see the inherent weaknesses and inconsistencies in their own economic and political solutions.

When all parties of a nation resort to hateful spite for each other, through constant streams of scorn and mockery, this will undermine the unity of the civil body. This in turn introduces anarchy, which inevitably leads to a breakdown of freedom and economic prosperity in the nation. That is how scornful men bring a city into a snare.

Nevertheless, this does not preclude all uses of sarcasm on the part of God's people. Elijah and Isaiah mocked the idolatry of Israel and the prophets of Baal. Jesus attacked Pharisaism with a measure of scorn (Matt. 23). However, it is far better to mock ideas and idols than individuals or political leaders.

It is exceedingly dangerous when a ministry or a person's work is characterized entirely by a constant stream of scorn and sarcasm. Talk radio in the present day often turns into a scorn fest, with one party spewing a torrent of scorn against the other. Scorn like this is merely therapeutic for those who have learned to hate the opposite party. It does not do much to persuade people of the truth. On occasion, we might employ a little scorn to wake somebody up, as we might splash a little water in somebody's face to wake him out of sleep. But it would be wrong to drown him in buckets of water!

Excessive scorn betrays insincerity on the part of the scorner. He may successfully elicit scornful laughter and hatred from some other person, but he certainly does not convey a spirit of humility and the fear of God. He hates some idea or institution, but he doesn't really love God and others. As with the church in Ephesus, they were good at hating the deeds of the Nicolaitans (which Jesus also hated), but they were terrible at loving (Rev. 2:1–8). As God-fearers, we are called to hate, and to love. Some professing believers would have one without the other, but both are important if we are to love God sincerely and hate the world of pride and lust.

Stirring up wrath among our opponents is usually unprofitable, and that is what happens when we resort to sarcasm and satire. In the case of Elijah, Jesus, and Isaiah, they were more interested in winning the ears of the common people rather than the support of the prophets of Baal and the Pharisees. So, we must know our audience before engaging in this kind of rhetorical device.

For men who lead in the church or the civil state, it is important that they work hard to keep the peace. God calls us to live at peace with all men, as much as possible (Matt. 5:9; Rom. 14:19; 1 Cor. 7:15). And it takes a wise man to know how to quell wrath among opposing parties. This is essential for good leadership. Every good leader is a peacemaker.

Family Discussion Questions:

1. How is scorn used in a proper way? How is it used in a sinful way?

2. What does scorn, satire, and sarcasm accomplish?

3. Does our family engage too much in sarcasm? Are we too negative? Are we better haters than lovers of good things?

PART 298 ~ CONTENDING WITH THE FOOLISH
Proverbs 29:9

If a wise man contend with a foolish man, whether he rage or laugh, there is no rest.

Various rhetorical and emotional methods are often used to try to convince an audience of a point. A good preacher might apply strong language, condemning words, or even a little satirical remark to his message. He may employ every ounce of his strength, every brain cell in his head, and every argument he can muster. But none of this will convince the fool sitting in the audience. Such an endeavor is an exercise in futility.

This passage speaks of two approaches often taken when dealing with fools. Some call it the "good cop, bad cop" treatment. You try to convince by being the "nice guy," and then you try to convince by warnings and threats. The fool doesn't respond to sound reason, affectionate words, or threatening jeremiads. At the root of it, this man doesn't fear God. At the most fundamental level, the man is not teachable. He will not learn the fear of God.

Thankfully, not everybody you run into is so characterized by foolishness. But should you ever find yourself in a conversation with a foolish man, the wisest thing to do may be to dust off your feet and move on to more profitable endeavors. This was Christ's recommendation to his disciples when they confronted stubborn resistance in their teaching (Matt. 10:14).

God does not hold us responsible for cleansing the world of all foolishness. Generally, Christian parents will have more success rooting foolishness out of their own children. But, whenever that foolishness embeds itself deeply in the hearts of men, you will not be able to remove it with your rhetorical jackhammers and backhoes. The foolishness is there to stay, unless God the Holy Spirit supernaturally works in the hearts of these men (1 Cor. 2:14; 2 Cor. 4:4–6).

Family Discussion Questions:

1. How do you know that you are dealing with a fool?

2. What should you do if you realize you are contending with a foolish man?

PART 299 ~ WHEN THE WICKED TURN VIOLENT
Proverbs 29:10
The bloodthirsty hate the upright: but the just seek his soul.

Throughout the history of the world, righteous men have always struggled to remain free from the hateful, murderous intent of the wicked. When God received Abel's sacrifice, it was obvious to Cain that Abel was in a right relationship with God and Cain was not. A dark cloud settled over Cain. A frightful, uncontrollable rage dominated his heart, pressing him to commit the murderous act.

For a while, wicked men are restrained by social customs, political constitutions and systems, or even by their own consciences. But given enough power and time, they will come after the righteous. Why should the raging mobs of Gaul torment the innocent Blandina whose only crime was to repeat the phrase, "I am a Christian," over and over again?[29] Why did they delight in ripping her flesh apart, until her body was just one continuous wound? These early persecutors

29 John Foxe, *Foxe's Book of Martyrs*

of Christians were unspeakably vicious. But then again, for what crime did the Romans and Jews come after Jesus Christ of Nazareth? For raising the dead, healing the lame, and restoring sight to the blind?

Later again in church history, when the powers of centralized, modern nation states enabled persecution against men and women of deepest piety, these trials came like a flood. It was the year 1685 when the two Margarets were bound to stakes on the banks of the Blednoch Burn, to await a slow and torturous death by the ocean tides. Margaret MacLachlan was a widow of seventy years old, and Margaret Wilson, a farmer's daughter of only eighteen. Their crime was worshiping God in the field, and they were arrested and dragged into court. Their prosecutor was Grierson of Lagg, known to be most savage in his persecution of the Covenanters. At the trial, he cursed at the two Christian ladies, referring to them several times as female dogs. Then he sentenced them to death by drowning. The elder Margaret died singing the words of Psalm 25, and the younger died while she prayed for repentance, forgiveness, and salvation for her enemies. Whether initiated by pagans or apostates, the capacity for cruelty in the human heart is almost impossible to comprehend. This blind, irrational rage that mounts in the hearts of wicked men against the righteous, even against innocent women and children, can only be explained by a devilish hatred against a righteous and holy God. It is the beastly, demonic rage referred to in the book of Revelation (Rev. 13:7).

Occasionally, there will be those with a sense of justice who will intervene and employ their influence, even risking their lives to save the people of God. This was true in the case of leaders like Nicodemus (John 7:45ff), Esther (Est. 7:1–6), and Gamaliel (Acts 5:35ff). The Good Samaritan intervened for the life of the poor man left for dead by bandits on the road (Luke 10:25–37). As other men run to shed blood, there are still some who retain a sense of justice, an appreciation for the value of human life, and a willingness to give their lives for others, if necessary. When the masses rush to support illegitimate wars, torture, and tyranny, may God's people retain this sense of justice as defined by God's Word.

Family Discussion Questions:

1. Name several situations in history where wicked men turned against the righteous.

2. Why do these men go after the righteous with such violent hatred?

3. Is there still hope for justice in these situations? Give examples of some who intervened to save the innocent in such horrible times.

PART 300 ~ WISE AND TRUTHFUL SPEECH
Proverbs 29:11

A fool utters all his mind; but a wise man keeps it in till afterwards.

The temptation to speak out of turn, to attempt to dominate the conversation, to vent an emotional response, or to issue an opinion on an issue can be very strong. Some men feel that the sooner they turn the conversation in their own direction, the sooner the truth will be vindicated. What they forget is that they are not the paradigm of all truth. They also forget that public opinion is unreliable and vacillating. People can be persuaded of your position at one moment, and then they are persuaded against you the next. What you say and how you say it are both important, if you want to bring about significant and lasting effects by your words. So much of what is said is of little lasting import! It may serve some therapeutic purpose for the fellow flapping his jaws. But it betrays his insecurity, his foolishness, and his emotional instability to those around him.

If you are not sure that what you are about to say is accurate, or that it will contribute in any way to the edification of the listeners, it would be better not to open your mouth. Allow for a little down time in conversations. As the old saying goes,

"Silence is golden." There is no need to fill every moment with words. Oftentimes, the longer you wait to speak, the more impact it will have. Let the fools rush into the conversation first and bandy about their foolishness. If your contribution is more significant than all of that, then it will be obvious when you finally bring it out.

Proverbs 29:12

If a ruler hearkens to lies, all his servants are wicked.

A business owner who does not want to hear bad news is bound to fail in the free market, at least wherever there is a free market operating. As one wise business guru puts it, "What matters most is how quickly you hear the bad news. Receiving good news is not quite as important as getting the bad news. The sooner you get the bad news, the more time you will have to react to it." As it turns out, everybody gets bad news. Every family and every business has to deal with failure and weakness, because of the underlying problem with human frailty. People make mistakes. They make bad calls, and that can negatively impact the bottom line in a business. Therefore, it is essential that business leaders prepare themselves to receive bad news so they can wisely and promptly act upon it.

But some men do not have the character to receive the truth. Sadly, this is even true for leaders of large business organizations and governments. They respond to the truth with proud anger, loud denials, or indiscreet actions. They often resort to what is commonly termed as "shooting the messenger," or they may focus their energies on assigning blame instead of identifying permanent solutions to the root problem.

Now, if everybody in the operation knows that this business leader doesn't want to hear the truth and that he reacts badly when confronted with problems, it won't be long before they are all lying to him. As the months go by, the lies build up and the financial reports present a far brighter picture than what is really happening in the organization. This creates a recipe for one spectacular disaster, especially if this is a national government, a military complex, or some large corporation. But even more tragic is what happens to the character of the organization. The leader creates an environment for dishonesty. He trains all his servants to behave wickedly.

Family Discussion Questions:

1. Do you talk too much? Do you jump into a debate too quickly? What can you do to be a more thoughtful speaker?

2. What is your response to bad news? Is there quite a bit of blame tossed around, or do you proceed with faith in God and wisdom to address the problems?

3. Why do people respond to bad news badly? Do they hate to hear the truth about themselves and their own organizations?

PART 301 ~ THE PROBLEM OF THE POOR
Proverbs 29:13

The poor and the deceitful man meet together; the LORD lightens both their eyes.

The poor and the deceitful man have something in common. They both suffer from the effects of the fall. While the poor man feels the physical effects of Adam's sin in the garden, the deceitful man experiences the spiritual effects of it.

The deceitful man becomes deceitful by believing the lie of the deceiving serpent. This is the university professor who rejects God's truth by turning to himself as the source of truth, determining good and evil for himself (Gen. 3:5). Whether he deceives himself or others around him, he is lost in a sea of lies. He is characterized by his lying. He suppresses the knowledge of God in unrighteousness, but he would never admit that he does this. Is there anything more pitiable than a man who is blind, but who refuses to acknowledge his blindness? It is an utterly hopeless condition. Thankfully, God in His sovereignty intervenes in some of these cases, and enables a man to see his own condition. As a man's eyes are enlightened, he begins to understand the value and the meaning of God's revealed Word. As the layers of cataracts fall from his eyes, he sees his own blindness and deception. He appropriates the truth of God's atoning work for his sin, the power of the resurrection of Christ, and the covenant promises in the Word to himself. Then, he begins walking in the light.

But what can we say for the poor and destitute man, living in a cardboard shack in some third world country? How might the wise testimonies from God enlighten his eyes (Ps. 19:8)? It is God's Word that gives a man hope in something better beyond this sad world that suffers the dreadful consequences of sin. But many of these nations sunk in gross poverty are cursed with sins like drunkenness, fraud, slothfulness, fornication, and a failure to nurture children in the fear of God. These sins destroy the nations' economies, and deprive the people of a decent living. When the Gospel of Jesus Christ (which includes the book of Proverbs) comes to a nation by way of faithful missionaries, these nations are transformed in their social and economic systems. When men begin to learn the godly habits of self-discipline, faith, honesty, and diligence, generally they find an improvement in their economic conditions.

Proverbs 29:14

The king that faithfully judges the poor, his throne shall be established forever.

Most people are motivated by money and power, so it is rare to find somebody who wants to take time and energy to vindicate the cause of the poor. They would rather not put the work into investigating the injustices. In one instance, a poor widow's family was falsely accused of committing a felony by a disreputable thug, and the public defender (provided by the court) told her to submit to a plea bargain and accept a lesser charge. Instead, the church of which she was a member intervened and hired an attorney at a substantial cost to defend her case. After the attorney made proper investigations into the background of the accusers, the prosecutors dismissed the charges and the case never made it to trial.

Sadly, the ill treatment of the poor is not unusual in the present day. Law is big business today. To get decent representation for their own side in court, some poor families have had to sell their homes and most of their belongings. Can anyone get adequate justice in our legal system without paying a fair amount of money in legal fees and representation costs? Nobody gets rich defending the poor.

But what may be said of the socialists who have shown themselves very generous with other people's money? They found a way to provide preferential treatment for the poor, while enslaving them to the state and turning more of the nation's wealth over to the government's power brokers. This socialism turns out to be just one more way to consolidate power in the political institutions.

The problem, of course, is that every king falls short of this at some point. Nobody is absolutely faithful in the adjudication of each poor person. Many poor widows are victimized by shysters. The social service agents confiscate their children without so much as a court trial. Hundreds of millions of babies lose their lives to the knife of the abortionist. Poor men and women everywhere lose their homes and businesses due to excessive taxation and regulation. Hundreds of thousands of poor girls are railroaded into prostitution by con-men and rogues every year. There aren't enough righteous judges in the world to take care of all the injustices everywhere. But there is One.

Speaking prophetically of Jesus in Psalm 72, David describes this eternal king who will reign forever, "For he shall deliver the needy when he cries; the poor also, and him that has no helper. He shall spare the poor and needy, and shall save the souls of the needy. He shall redeem their soul from deceit and violence; and precious shall their blood be in his sight" (Ps. 72:12–14, also reference Is. 11:4). This is the true fulfillment of this verse (Ps, 89:4, 29, 36; Is. 9:7; Lam. 5:19; Heb. 1:8).

We can rest assured that every abridgment of justice will be righted by this King who sits now at the right hand of the Father. Jesus rules over all of history, and He will make all things right.

Family Discussion Questions:

1. What problem do the poor and the deceitful man share?

2. Can we solve the world's problems? How can we be sure that justice will be done everywhere in the world?

PART 302 ~ THE ROD AND REPROOF
Proverbs 29:15

The rod and reproof give wisdom; but a child left to himself brings his mother to shame.

God gives parents two major tools whereby they may train a child in wisdom—the rod and reproof. If you want a child to be wise, these are the ways to achieve it: you must teach them by reproofs and by the rod.

This assumes first, however, that children are fallen creatures and tend to sin (Ps. 51:5). Every time a child asserts himself in clear disobedience to his parents, he proves again this basic truth. Thus, a parent reminds his child every day of the laws of God that he fails to observe (Deut. 6:7), and encourages him to trust in God as the true and only Savior from the slavery of his sins (Ex. 20:1; Deut. 32:4, 15). Children must learn to honor their parents, but babies and toddlers do not find this command convenient to their desires and nature. It is up to parents to teach this important commandment by constant, patient, insistent reminder and reproof. Lives fall apart, cultures break down, and families disintegrate when children do not honor their parents. After all, this is the "first commandment with promise" (Eph. 6:1–2).

The Bible does not provide a long list of specifications governing the use of these two implements, the rod and reproof, but it does say that they are both indispensable for the training of a child. Some will discourage a parent from using the rod before the child is two years of age. Others will discourage the use of it after twelve or fourteen years of age. The Bible doesn't specify. Ultimately, it must be both love and wisdom that determines when a child is corrected, how often he is spanked, and the intensity of the correction.

The modern world tells us that they have a better plan for raising children than these archaic rules from the Old Testament! Recently, a family from Sweden was fined $50,000 after the Christian school in the area turned them in for spanking their child. The enlightened humanists of the present age have replaced the rod with what is known as "Time Out!" It is a time when a child can reflect on his behavior and access his rational self in order that he might make wiser decisions in the future. Search as you may, you will not find this method among the biblically-prescribed forms of discipline. Actually, a child left to himself will bring his mother to shame.

Parents may find it supremely inconvenient to correct a child. There may be far more interesting and enjoyable things to do in life. Naturally, it would be easier to let the child have what he wants, and leave him to electronic media all day long. But this is a recipe for disaster! The parent must instruct the child in wisdom by way of the rod and reproof. Long years of neglect in this area will yield a child that brings his mother to shame!

For related commentary, reference Proverbs 13:24, 22:15, and 23:13–14.

Family Discussion Questions:

1. Do parents enjoy correcting their children, or is it easier to give them what they want, and let them entertain themselves all day long?

2. Are there other forms of discipline that we should use besides the rod and reproof? Would it be wrong to withhold privileges or require extra arduous tasks as a means of correction, for example? At what point do we replace God's methods with our own?

PART 303 ~ TRANSGRESSION METASTASIS
Proverbs 29:16

When the wicked are multiplied, transgression increases; but the righteous shall see their fall.

Taking into account the corpus of data on the wicked found in the book of Proverbs, we discover that the wicked walk in the way of darkness (Prov. 4:19). John clarifies this further as the man who hates his brother (1 John 2:9–11). Also, the wicked is held down by the cords of his sin (Prov. 5:22). He cannot NOT sin. Bound hand and foot by sin, he refuses to repent of it. Violence also covers his mouth (Prov. 10:11, 12:6), he refuses to fear God (Prov. 10:24), he works deceitfully (Prov. 11:18), and he sins constantly with his tongue (Prov. 15:28). Perhaps most telling, this man is out of covenant relationship with God (Prov. 15:29).

With the rapid increase of wicked men and covenant breakers in the present day, our churches fill up with women (and sometimes men) abandoned by their spouses. The illegitimacy rate in America climbed from 6% in the 1960s to 42% by the 2010s. Divorce is a bloody, treacherous affair. When a man chooses to commit adultery and initiates a divorce, he figuratively puts a gun to the head of his family and pulls the trigger. God calls this an act of wicked violence (Mal. 2:16), and this treachery is on the increase in the present day. As far back as 1890, the divorce rate (per 1,000 marriages) in this country stood at three. Nearly 120 years later, that rate has increased to seventeen.[30] Adultery becomes commonplace as well in these wicked countries. When a website announced opportunities to arrange adulterous affairs and offered free services on Mother's Day in 2011, nearly 60,000 women rushed in to avail themselves.[31] The news story was quick to remind readers that adultery is now irrelevant in divorce court proceedings and alimony settlements.

30 "Marriage and Divorce: Changes and their Driving Forces," by Betsey Stevenson and Justin Wolfers, *The Journal of Economic Perspectives,* Winter 2007.
31 http://www.foxbusiness.com/personal-finance/2011/05/11/cheating-moms-mothers-day/#ixzz1M9iC9ebT

In 1893, a Christian author chronicled the conditions of the western world at another time in history, when humanist man achieved his highest marks. Writing on the decline of the Roman Empire, David Breed reports that "Marriage had fallen into deeper and deeper contempt. The freedom of single life was preferred by both sexes. Seneca went so far as to affirm that marriage was only contracted in order that adultery might afford additional charm, and declared that whoever had no love affairs was to be despised. Unnatural vices prevailed... In such a state of society, even if marriages were celebrated, the children were few in number... Infanticide was commonly practiced. The destruction of unborn children was even more practiced than infanticide, and not only did moral disintegration ensue in the destruction of family life, but the very foundations of the state were undermined in the decrease of the native population."[32] This account seems eerily similar to the present age. As the entire world faces huge increases in adultery, abortion, and divorce, as eighty nations around the world today face birth implosions, the next collapse will be spectacular, no doubt eclipsing anything seen in the ancient world! The righteous shall see their fall. Thankfully, the righteous are not killing their children. Instead of aborting, they are adopting. Instead of euthanizing their elderly, they honor their fathers and mothers. Rather than spending their grandchildren into debt, they eschew the materialist lifestyle and save an inheritance for their children's children! Instead of abandoning their children in mass-production centers and state-run orphanages and day care centers, they invest time and energy discipling the next generation in faith and robust character.

Family Discussion Questions:

1. What are the indications that wickedness and transgression are on the increase in a nation?

32 David R. Breed, *A History of the Preparation of the World for Christ,* (New York: Flemming Revel, 1893), pp. 426-427

2. What are the similarities between what has happened in the modern world and what happened in the rise and fall of the Roman empire?

3. Should Christians be concerned when wickedness becomes so prevalent in society? How should we perceive these things?

PART 304 ~ FAITHFUL PARENTING
Proverbs 29:17

Correct your son, and he shall give you rest; yea, he shall give delight unto your soul.

A child left to himself will bring his mother to shame. But one who is corrected for his slothfulness, his dishonor to mother, or his grumbling will be a great delight to his parents. Sadly, many families neglect this correction in the early years and they live to regret it. With seven times the percentage of children born without fathers today (compared to 1960), more grandparents are pressed into providing assistance for these fatherless children. There are almost five million children living in their grandparents' homes today (up from 2 million in 1970).[33] With 64% of children under the age of six no longer being raised by loving parents in the home because both parents work outside of the home, we must expect a failure in child-raising in most cases. The problem was bad enough when fathers disengaged from the home. Fathers took little interest in their children, or they only paid attention to their children for their own selfish interests, and the social consequences were tragic. It does take spiritual and emotional energy to correct a child. But if a father returns home from work each evening to watch television for four hours while sipping through a six pack of beer, his children will sense his disinterest in them over the years. When a father fails to marry his child's mother, that child gets the message loud and clear. His father is a self-centered, loveless lout and cares little for

33 http://www.aarp.org/relationships/grandparenting/info-12-2010/more_grandparents_raising_grandchildren.html

his child. Generally speaking, these men will never enjoy the delight of godly children and fruitful generations following.

When parents take the time to patiently correct their children, teach them the wisdom of God's Word , and lovingly apply the rod, they find great blessing. Of course, all of this comes by God's gracious work in and through the parents and children. But every parent must bear a strong sense of responsibility in this area. If a race car driver wants to win the Indy 500, he cannot just sit back and "leave it all in God's hands." Yes, God is sovereign over the outcome of the race. But the driver must engage everything within his control and abilities to win the race. He does his practice runs. He checks the pressure in each of the cylinders. He checks the tires. He reviews procedures with his pit crew. He summons all of his abilities to obtain his objective of winning the race. We must believe that God is sovereign, but man is still responsible for his actions. Correct your son, and he will give you rest!

Family Discussion Questions:

1. How do God's sovereignty and human responsibility work in the raising of children? Are both important? Which is more important?

2. As parents, what are the blessings that we long for more than anything else? Money? Successful ministries? Faithful children?

PART 305 ~ GOD'S LAW IS VISION
Proverbs 29:18

Where there is no vision, the people perish; but he that keeps the law,
happy is he.

The first part of this proverb is one of the most oft-repeated phrases in the Bible. Usually, the second half of the verse is left out, but this is the clue to understanding the first part.

Vision provides direction. It is the light over yonder hill. It signals to a man the way he should walk. Once he sees the light in the distance, he knows where to go. But where a father, an elder, or a leader has no vision and no light, he will most certainly take others over the cliff with him. The most popular song of the 1970s endorsed fornication with the phrase, "How could it be wrong, when it feels so right?" The song was written by a man whose life was characterized by this hedonistic philosophy. When he ended his life by suicide in 2011, the songwriter was facing multiple criminal charges of rape. This self-centered, autonomous, hedonistic approach to ethics exactly contradicts a God-centered view of ethics. What devastation follows a popular culture that wholeheartedly embraces this philosophy! The millions of people who blindly followed this great cultural leader would go on to construct a society based on sexual license and self-centered hedonism. Where there is no true light to define what is true and what is right, the people will perish.

But when a man hears the law of God preached against the antithesis of the day (wherever God's law is broken), and accepts it, he will know what to do. If he understands the thrust of God's law against murder, and sees the blood of thousands of innocent babies shed in the clinics, he will know what to do. When a man of true faith is faced with God's laws concerning selfishness, materialist greed, birth implosions, and the blessing of children, he will know what to do with birth control. Immediately, he will begin to see relevant applications appear for him in his own marriage, in how he educates his children, in his economics, and in his work life. As he sees the principle of God's law taking shape—that light over yonder hill, he knows exactly where to place his first step. Of course, he does not achieve some sort of sinless perfection, but he begins moving in the right direction. He begins to keep the laws of God by making application of it here and there in his life. This man is blessed.

Family Discussion Questions:

1. What is vision? What is the source of vision according to the second half of the verse?

2. What does God's Word teach us about having children? Do some people who use birth control and refuse to have more than two children have a proper vision? Why or why not?

3. Have you received vision from God's Word yourselves? Give several examples.

PART 306 ~ SULLEN SILENCE AND GARRULOUS GABBERS
Proverbs 29:19

A servant will not be corrected by words; for though he understand he will not answer.

The proverb speaks here of a man who never learned to receive correction as a child. By the time he is a grown man, rebellion is ingrained, and words are insufficient to guide, restrain, or correct him. Typically, such a man is reduced to slavery. Without some measure of character, a man cannot be free: no man will ever develop character unless he has the wisdom to receive correction. So the grown man who has never learned to receive correction is in trouble. A business manager can hardly work with a man who stubbornly refuses to obey orders or receive correction. If the employee short-changes the customers on a regular basis, or provides slovenly service, the business will do poorly. When he is corrected, this man stubbornly refuses to acknowledge his failures and correct them. He may blame others for his faults, or just ignore the advice and continue with the same bad service. Now what will be done with such a fellow? Generally, these men will lose their jobs and either rely on the state for welfare or send their wives to work. Occasionally, they resort to begging on the streets. At one time, employers would apply the rod in order to get some work out of these men, but it is rare to see that sort of correction anymore. Nowadays, it is easier to let them die of starvation, or live off the state in welfare colonies or in prisons where they receive room and board at taxpayer expense—to the tune of $40,000 a year.

Do you see the benefit of receiving correction? It does take humility to acknowledge your weaknesses and shortcomings. But this is the only way to improvement! "God resists the proud, but gives grace unto the humble" (Jam. 4:6).

Proverbs 29:20

See a man that is hasty in his words? There is more hope of a fool than of him.

The prior verse deals with the man who maintains a "sullen silence." Now here we find the opposite sin—the fellow who is too quick to speak. "Let your words be few" is wise advice (Eccl. 5:2). James repeats the same lesson in the New Testament: "Wherefore, my beloved brethren, let every man be swift to hear, slow to speak, slow to wrath" (Jam. 1:19). Why should a man be eager to speak his mind? He may wish that others hear what he has to say, because he can't think that anybody else has anything to contribute to the issue at hand. After all, he is the paradigm of wisdom. Why should people want to listen to anybody else? The last person to speak is often the wisest. This is because he has the benefit of the wisdom of others, and he has time to consider his words. Every conversation and every situation is unique, and requires careful reflection before airing your opinions.

Moreover, your speech can get you into trouble! Should you speak out of turn or say the wrong thing in haste, you could mislead somebody or permanently damage a relationship. Thus, you can see how important it is to check your spirit before speaking. If you are aggravated about something, if you lack faith, or if you are impatient with others, it would probably be unwise to say anything at all. Pray first, repent, and then enter the conversation.

Proverbs 26:12 brings out a parallel idea, stating that there is more hope for a fool than a man who is wise in his own eyes. This man cannot be told anything, because he already knows it all. Often, the poor listener is the big talker. If you have a problem with talking too much, it might be good to check your pride. Could it be that you have an over-inflated view of your own wisdom?

Family Discussion Questions:

1. What happens to a man who refuses to obey orders or make necessary corrections to slovenly work habits?

2. What does a sullen silence say about a person's ability to receive correction?

3. Have you ever hurt anyone by your speech? How did you do that?

4. How might we all become better listeners?

PART 307 ~ ADOPTING A SON
Proverbs 29:21

He that delicately brings up his servant from a child shall have him become his son at the length.

This verse further describes a biblical social theory. The family is basic to God's order of life. Although this notion has been viciously attacked in the modern age, the truth of God remains unchanged. Today, the individual feels as if he belongs to the state. He is raised in public day care. He attends public schools. He receives social security at the end of his life, until the state runs out of money, at which point he is euthanized (in some nations). But this is far from a biblical way of life. In the end, the dissolution of the family will mean the dissolution of society because the family is the basic social unit.

The principle stated here is simple. Whoever raises a child has himself an heir or a legacy in that child. Many parents in the present day serve as part-time guardians for children who are, for the most part, raised by institutions. The goal set for the child is emancipation from his home. When the child turns eighteen years old, he or she is emancipated— especially if the family is fortunate enough to receive grants and loans for the college education of their child. Then, the parents purchase a motor home with the appropriate bumper sticker that reads, "I'm spending my children's inheritance!" Thus, in the modern socialist state, children increasingly become the property and legacy of the state. Of course, this is not always the case. Wherever the hearts of the fathers are turned to the sons and the sons to the fathers, you will find the restoration of inheritance, honor of parents, and parental love for children. But in a society that has killed 80 million children in the womb over fifty years, and remanded 64% of children under six into day care systems, we must conclude that the love of many has grown cold.

This verse may also be the closest lesson from the book of Proverbs that addresses the subject of adoption. The orphanages of the 19th century fit into the institutional model of the humanist state, where sons were not raised as heirs within the context of family units. Thankfully, this trend changed in the latter part of the century. First came the orphan trains that carried children from the streets of New York into the farmlands, placing 200,000 children into loving homes over a period of about fifty years. President Theodore Roosevelt insisted that the family represented "the highest and finest product of civilization, and was best able to serve as primary caretaker of the abandoned and orphaned." This was a positive move. To this day, America remains the nation with the highest number of adoptions per year (over 100,000). In fact, Americans adopt three times the number of children (per live births) than any European nations where adoptions are legal. But the legal adoption of the child is not enough. In order for that child to be a son, the adopted parents must treat him as a son and an heir. Part and parcel with sonship is the encouragement, the affection, the training and the chastisement that comes with raising a son. The son is a "son at length," when he has been received and treated as a son by his parents. This is how God brings us into His family as well.

"For whom the Lord loves he chastens, and scourges every son whom he receives. If you endure chastening, God deals with you as with sons; for what son is he whom the father chastens not? But if you be without chastisement, whereof all are partakers, then are you bastards, and not sons" (Heb. 12:6–8).

Family Discussion Questions:

1. How important is inheritance to sonship?

2. Have family bonds loosened through the generations in our family, or are they getting stronger?

3. How is a son treated as a real son, and not as an illegitimate son?

PART 308 ~ ANGER AND PRIDE
Proverbs 29:22

An angry man stirs up strife, and a furious man abounds in transgression.

Anger is the great sin-and-strife multiplier. An angry man places his home in a constant state of tension. Nobody can relax. This environment becomes a perfect nurturing ground for blow-ups, arguments, and bitter feelings. This man watches the commentators on television news and he gets angry. Whenever somebody airs an opinion that counters his own, or when somebody gets elected who doesn't meet his standards, he blows his top. The problem is that he has turned himself into the sovereign, but he doesn't make a very good sovereign. Almost everything that happens in the world is beyond his control, because he is not God. He is frustrated because he cannot control the outcome of a nation's elections, or because others do not perfectly align with his perspective of what is true and right. So he might take out his frustrations by kicking the cat or yelling at his children, both of which would be violations of God's law of love (Prov. 12:10; Eph. 4:32, 6:4). You can see that this man will not do anything constructive to solve the political problems in the world.

Rather, he exasperates them by adding more transgressions and strife to his own family!

This verse also coordinates with Proverbs 13:10, which speaks of pride as the source of contention. There is a connection between pride and anger; a humble man will not give way to sinful anger, because anger is rooted in a desire for control. When a man desires something and cannot have it, he will give in to the impulse to acquire that thing by brute force. He becomes the "control freak."

Proverbs 29:23

A man's pride shall bring him low; but honor shall uphold the humble in spirit.

There are three ways to live life. You can live life with self confidence, with no confidence, or with God confidence. Earlier in the book we were warned against trusting in ourselves (Prov. 28:26).

The world sees nothing wrong with pride. A local high school in Colorado recently presented the vision of the school as preparing "proud" men and women to take on the challenges of life. The dictionary definition of pride is "a feeling of pleasure concerning one's own achievements." This is the doctrine of humanism in its rawest sense. During the graduation ceremony, the commencement speaker cried out, "You will define the future! You are the future!" He is glorifying man, especially if he avoids mentioning God as the final determinant of reality. All of this is humanistic pride.

Man considers himself to be the chief cause of his own destiny, so when he accomplishes something, he feels that he deserves the praise and the glory for what he has done. Therefore, the more that a humanistic man accomplishes in life, the better he feels about himself. With each accomplishment, with each political office he takes, and with each successful business he launches, he becomes increasingly proud. But as sure as there is a God in the heavens who is sovereign over all, that man will be humbled.

If we accomplish anything in life, we must give God the glory for it (Rom. 11:36). We may work out our own salvation, but it is God who works in us both to will and to do of His good pleasure (Phil. 2:12–13). Even that great leader of Israel, Moses, acknowledged that all of his accomplishments in life were worthless unless God would establish the work of his hands (Ps. 90). Every day of the year, we must trust in God that He will bless the work of our hands. Every time we look at our lives and sense a blessing or an accomplishment, we must look to God as the source of all blessings. Our hearts should not swell up with pride, but with warm gratitude for what God has done in us and with us!

Our lives consist of a lifetime of successes and failures, both spiritual and physical. Nobody lives a problem-free life. If we need a good humbling at any point along the way, we can be sure that God will humble us. While the proud achiever will fall miserably at some point in his life, God will raise up the humble in some spectacular way (either in this life or the life that is to come). It is for us to remain humble.

For related commentary, reference Proverbs 11:2 and 16:18.

Family Discussion Questions:

1. Why does a man get angry? Does he really want to fix the problems in the world? Will anger fix any of these problems?

2. What is pride?

3. What is an accomplishment? How do we look at our accomplishments in life? How do we know our accomplishments will last?

PART 309 ~ THE DOMINO EFFECT OF SIN
Proverbs 29:24

Whoever is partner with a thief hates his own soul; he hears cursing,
and betrays it not.

The book of Proverbs assumes the ethical requirements of God's law as the standard for what is right and wrong. If you don't read the Proverbs with an understanding of the laws of God, you will miss the thrust of what is said here, because this verse ties in directly with the portion of the law given in Leviticus 5:1: "And if a soul sin, and hear the voice of swearing, and [is] a witness, whether he hath seen or known [of it]; if he do not utter [it], then he shall bear his iniquity."

This is precisely what the partner in crime refuses to do. He is bound to witness in a court of law against the man who stole the goods. But he fails at this, because he is bound in trust with the thief. To knowingly support criminal activity would prevent this fellow from testifying in the trial. Either he will be true to his commitment to the criminals or he will be true to his commitment to a higher law. But because he has already abandoned his commitment to God's law by supporting the thievery, he will no doubt stay consistent to that way of life by opposing the truth at the trial.

The initial choices a man makes in life have a domino effect upon other subsequent ethical choices. In this way a man is hardened in the path of sin. It is the path of destruction; these initial choices "seal the man's fate." Unless God intervenes by a powerful heart-changing work in his life, this man will continue down the road to hell. In a real sense, this man hates his own soul.

This proverb also calls into question the use of plea-bargains for criminals testifying against criminals. How can a thief testify against a thief? Or how can an adulterer testify against an adulterer? This is the principle that our Lord raises in His condemnation of the men who were accusing the woman caught in adultery (John 8:1–11, also reference Matt. 7:1–3).

Family Discussion Questions:

1. If you witness a criminal act, what does God's law required you to do?

2. Why are your "initial choices" important, when it comes to setting the course of your life?

PART 310 ~ FEARING MAN AND FEARING THE STATE
Proverbs 29:25

The fear of man brings a snare; but whoever puts his trust in the LORD shall be safe.

We do not see fear in the Apostles when they boldly proclaimed the Gospel of the resurrection of Christ in the Roman world. The threats of rejection and persecution meant nothing to them, as they faithfully advanced the Gospel and "turned the world upside down" with that Gospel. Overcoming the world begins with overcoming the fear of worldly powers, and this happens by faith (1 John 5:4). In relation to the fear of man, Jesus said, "Fear not them which kill the body, but are not able to kill the soul: but rather fear him which is able to destroy both soul and body in hell" (Matt. 10:28). If we fear men, we are treating men as a more threatening, more powerful, and a more important reality than God Himself. This is blasphemy. The fear of God must involve trust in God's salvation.

This relationship of fear and trust is best understood in the context of Noah. Certainly, Noah and his family felt safe in the warm ark of protection during the worldwide cataclysm. But as they contemplated the hundreds of thousands of dead bodies that thumped against the bow of the ark, they would have shuddered a bit. God's violent rage that burned against sinful man would have commanded some measure of reverence on the part of those few who were saved! This is our sentiment as well. It is faith and a sense of security mixed with fear and reverence for a holy God.

Our liberties are curtailed when we fear men over God, because fear of man entails an undue reverence and worship. When men place too much credence in a power-hungry state, they submit themselves to tyranny and bondage. Either we fear God and enjoy the liberty that flows from that, or we will fall into the snare of tyranny.

Proverbs 29:26

Many seek the ruler's favor; but every man's judgment comes from the LORD.

This lesson ties in to the previous verse. There are thousands of ways in which you might offend the bureaucracies, the taxing agencies, or the police in the present day. With the governments controlling 60–70% of the Gross National Income in modern nation states, it is no wonder we are in constant risk of violating some regulation. So the average citizen worries about this tax form and that. He worries about being sued in a court of law. He worries about regulatory laws. Indeed, some righteous men are serving decades of time in American prisons for committing minor tax infractions. Evidently, these men fall out of favor with the bureaucracies and they pay for it. But how serious are these crimes in God's eyes? That's the important question, but hardly the question people will ask when they are subject to these incredibly powerful, god-like, civil governments.

At the end of the day, we are all weighed in the balances of God's system of judgments. There is no man alive today who lives his life in sinless perfection. Some fellow who divorced his wife may be ten times more wicked in the sight of God than a fellow who neglected to issue a W2 tax form to an employee. God knows. The man counted among the righteous is the one who fears God and throws himself on the mercy of Christ, trusting only to His provision to save him from his sin.

Family Discussion Questions:

1. What does the fear of man do to you? Do we fear man?

2. Do we owe any fear or reverence to the civil government? How would the fear of God moderate the fear of the state?

3. Are we more concerned about how God views us, or how the Internal Revenue Service (or some other government regulatory agency) views us?

PART 311 ~ WHO'S ABOMINABLE TO WHOM?
Proverbs 29:27

An unjust man is an abomination to the just; and he that is upright in the way is abomination to the wicked.

In the year 2011, two more mainline "Christian" denominations endorsed the ordination of homosexual clergy—the Presbyterian Church USA and the Scottish Presbyterian Church.[34] It would be hard to find such a strong synthesis with an ungodly system as this one since the horrific blend of Judaism and Baal worship (with child sacrifice) that developed during the era of the Old Testament kings and prophets. Official endorsement of capital crimes and the incorporation of these things into the church is shocking to anyone schooled in biblical ethics and historic Christian doctrine and life.

Yet, this is not the way that the PCUSA denomination looks at the issue. Actually, the pro-homosexual churches find those intolerant preachers who keep referring to Leviticus 20, as abominable, unloving wretches. They look at them as judgmental, to say the least. As one mainline evangelical pastor put it, we are all sinners! Some people get divorced. Some lie. Some people speak irritably to their children. And some commit homosexual acts. What right does one sinner

34 http://www.guardian.co.uk/world/2011/may/23/church-of-scotland-gay-lesbian-ministers,

http://www.christianpost.com/news/pcusa-votes-to-allow-openly-gay-clergy-50176/

have to condemn another? We are all in need of a Savior. But according to these people, the worse sinner is that judgmental, intolerant prophet, who doesn't seem to want to be gracious to homosexuals and divorcees.

Now you see how both groups consider the other to be abominable. So who is right? Of course, in the ultimate sense, God will sort it out at the Day of Judgment. But the Word of God is informative here, and we are called to judge righteous judgements ourselves. There does appear to be a marked difference between the two groups. One group seems to be willing to admit their sin and confess it openly. The other group is busy justifying their behavior and minimizing the sinful nature of it. One group is ashamed of their sins of anger, lying, and divorce. Meanwhile, the other group is building monuments to their sin of homosexuality, seeking approval of all those around them. Now it is possible that there are those who would minimize their sins of anger, lying, divorce, or even a proud judgmental spirit. But labeling every attempt to judge and every call for repentance as hypocritical and judgmental is disingenuous and arbitrary. To label somebody as judgmental is also an act of judging that could be subjected to the same accusation!

Suffice it to say, there are two types of persons in this world. There are those who are humble and repentant before God. They are honest and upright in the way, willing to be corrected by the preaching of the Word of God. Then, there are those who will not face their sins with honesty, humility, and repentance. These are the wicked. Each of these two groups will find the other's viewpoint abominable and detestable.

Family Discussion Questions:

1. Why do the pro-homosexual churches view the anti-homosexual Christian crowd as abominable? Why do the anti-homosexual Christians view the ordination of homosexual clergy as abominable?

2. How do you condemn some sin without being judgmental and violating Matthew 7:1ff?

PART 312 ~ THE CHARACTER OF A WISE MAN
Proverbs 30:1–4

*The words of Agur the son of Jakeh, even the prophecy: the man spoke
    unto Ithiel, even unto Ithiel and Ucal,*
*Surely I am more brutish than any man, and have not the
    understanding of a man.*
*I neither learned wisdom, nor have the knowledge of the holy. Who has
    ascended up into heaven, or descended?*
*Who has gathered the wind in his fists? Who has bound the waters in a
    garment? Who has established all the ends of the earth? What is his
    name, and what is his son's name, if you can tell?*

Proverbs is Solomon's book. His name appears in Proverbs
1:1, 10:1, and 25:1. When Yahweh asked him what he would
most desire, Solomon requested wisdom, and the Lord gave
it to him (1 Kgs. 3:1–10). We can be sure that the book of
Proverbs is a compilation of that wisdom provided from on
high. But now, we have this rather unusual chapter included
in the book of Proverbs, a lone chapter authored by a man
named Agur. His name means "collector," which may point
to the fact that he collected certain wise sayings and included
them in this short synopsis. This in itself is remarkable. Most
writers have published more than one solitary page of wisdom
during their entire career, but this man boiled down all that
he ever learned in a lifetime to one page. It is worth a careful
read.

By God's providence this man's writings are included in the
Book of Wisdom. But why would He want the thoughts of a
man who claims to have no understanding or wisdom in this
book? Isn't this a strange irony? However, what Agur is saying
is that he has barely scratched the surface of wisdom himself,
and whatever he records here is the best he has obtained in
a lifetime of enquiry. His position is one of humility. Before
God will use anyone as a recipient and conveyor of His truth,
he must really and truly live out this heart attitude. Academic
pride may work for the temples of humanism, but it is entirely
unacceptable in the city of God! After studying this Book of

Wisdom for two or three years at a time, we should concede the same things as well! Surely we have barely scratched the surface of wisdom.

"Who has bound the waters in a garment?" After all of his scientific investigations into the basic building blocks of the molecule and the atom, man still has yet to understand the basic building blocks of matter. We have yet to understand what holds an atom together. There is the mystery of the tetraneutrons, that are bound together in a manner that defies the laws of physics.[35] Moreover, nobody really knows why the "strong nuclear force" in an atom increases in strength with distance between its quarks (the building blocks of the proton and neutron). While the quarks are close together, there is a smaller force working, but as the quarks pull away, the force between them grows rapidly, pulling the quarks back together. What is this mystery force? Even after all the modern investigations into the field of chemistry, we do not yet comprehend the most basic constituents of matter! Even the most brilliant atomic physicist is stumped when it comes to the work of the Master Creator. It is too complicated for the most "knowledgeable" men who have ever lived. Also, how do all the hydrogen and oxygen molecules hold together in a lake of water? This is one of the questions Agur is asking, and still today, nobody has answered his question! It is true that a few men have ascended as high as the moon. But when Agur speaks of the "heavens," he would still like to hear from somebody who has made it beyond the solar system or even beyond the Milky Way Galaxy! Man fully expects to make it into outer space, and take command of new frontiers. To contemplate these capabilities for many today, is another futile attempt to gain ultimate control over the universe. Modern man really hopes that he can someday displace God the Creator, but this is something that Agur utterly rejects from the outset.

Moreover, Agur admits to knowing very little about the "holy" One, God Himself. In some sense God is knowable, but in another sense He is incomprehensible. You're not going

35 Amin Elsersawi, *The Atom and the Universe,* (Xlibris Corp, 2009), p. 87

to figure out God. For example, how does God sovereignly ordain the free actions of men? He holds men morally accountable for their crucifying an innocent man at Calvary, while still foreordaining the action (Acts 2:23). Neither do we understand how this God creates a universe, or even one solitary piece of sand, out of nothing! We do not understand how God can be One, and yet the power and the glory belonging to God alone belongs equally to all three persons—Father, Son, and Holy Spirit. Sadly, it is at this point that cults and false religions begin. They fail to comprehend the Incomprehensible; so they turn the Incomprehensible into something comprehensible by their cheap theologies. Then, they proceed to lead billions of people astray with their false concept of God. But it all starts here. They fail to say with ignorant old Agur, "I have not the understanding of a man... nor the knowledge of the Holy."

Could the last reference to "his son," be a shadowy allusion to the Son of God, the second person in the Trinity? Assuming that these writings are inspired by God Himself, *it is a distinct possibility.* Indeed, according to further revelation obtained in the New Testament, "All things were made by Him (the Son), and without Him was not anything made that was made" (John 1:3).

Family Discussion Questions:

1. Who is the author of this chapter? What does his name mean? What is the character trait that best describes him?

2. Do you know what holds the atom together?

3. At what point of error do many cults get their start?

4. How does humanism attempt to compete with God in the area of science and space exploration?

PART 313 ~ THE RIGHT SOURCE OF ALL TRUTH
Proverbs 30:5–6

Every word of God is pure; he is a shield unto them that put their trust
*   in him.*
Add not unto his words, lest he reprove you, and you be found a liar.

Agur's one-page collection of wisdom begins with God the
Creator, and then moves on to the source of truth. This
amounts to an epistemological authority. Everyone trusts in
some source of authority. For Agur, that source of truth is the
revealed Word of God. Men today look to science and the
conclusions drawn from science as the pure, unadulterated
truth. When scientists take a measurement of the radioactive
decay rate in a piece of rock at the present time, assuming
constant decay rates over billions of years, and assuming
certain starting conditions, they conclude the rock to be X
number of billions of years old. They insist the fossil captured
in the rock layer is the same age, and nobody must ever
question these conclusions. According to them, the truth that
comes by observation and interpretation of the data is truth
in its purest form. This, however, is not Agur's ultimate truth
authority. When consulting with the wizards in the white coats
that peep and mutter, Agur would say, "To the law and to the
testimony! If it is not according to these words, it is because
there is no light in them" (Is. 8:19–20). If God's words tell us
that God made heaven and earth, the sea, and all that is in
them in six days, then we must reject the wizards in the white
coats. Might we have reasons to question the orthodoxy of
science? Yes, but we never have a reason to doubt the words
of God. Without God's revelation, you must know everything
about everything in the universe, before you can be sure that
you know anything about anything. Although scientists may
feign a little certainty, they cannot be certain about anything
without having an absolute standard as a starting point. We
are wandering in a snowstorm in Antarctica without a tether
if we have no sure starting point for truth. Thankfully, we can
trust in the Word of God.

Every worldview also presents a way of salvation, as Agur does in this verse. Many turn to man for salvation. They look to large, centralized states to provide salvation from poverty, sickness, and even death. Most humanist religions depend on their own works to save them, always relying on themselves to save themselves. But it is not so with Agur. Only God can protect us from our greatest enemies, and we must trust in Him for that salvation. This is a simple, rustic Gospel for the humble saints of the Old Testament. In the New Testament, the message is essentially the same. It is only by faith in the Son of God that we are saved (Acts 16:31).

Now, in verse six, we are warned not to add anything to what God has given us, as false prophets do when they offer information that does not comport with previous revelation. They cram widely differing doctrines into the corpus of divine revelation, and the final product presents a completely different worldview, theology, and soteriology. This is what has happened in the religions of Mormonism and Islam.

Men will also add to the Word of God when their traditions make the laws of God of no effect, a practice that Jesus condemns in Matthew 15. Could the traditions of youth ministries, children's church, and Sunday Schools displace God's intent that parents teach their children God's Word as they sit in their own homes, as they walk by the way, and as they lie down (Deut. 6:7; Eph. 6:4)? When celibacy becomes normative instead of an exception for pastors and elders, are we really retaining the biblical principles laid down in 1 Timothy 3 and I Corinthians 7?

Some have attempted to practice a principle of God's Word by emphasizing one particular application not specified in God's Word. For example, some families will insist on "timed feeding" for a nursing baby so that the child may learn to honor his parents, and that if any parents feed their children "on demand," then these parents fail to teach the fifth commandment. But we must be careful here. The Word of God has nothing to say about "timed feeding." It is possible that for some families "timed feeding" may be a good way to teach the fifth commandment, but it is not the *only* way. There are thousands of ways in which parents might teach the commandment. To narrow the application in this way will often place our own applications on par with the principles laid out in the Word of God. Even when we don't intend to do so, it may happen subconsciously with ourselves and others. Over time, these pet applications displace the authority of the Word of God in our minds and lives.

Family Discussion Questions:

1. What is the source of all truth, according to Agur?

2. How are we saved, according to Agur?

3. How does an Islamic view of God and salvation differ significantly from that presented in the Old and New Testaments?

4. In what areas might we be tempted to add something to God's Word, or displace God's Word with our own traditions?

PART 314 ∼ GODLINESS WITH CONTENTMENT
Proverbs 30:7–9

Two things have I required of You; deny me them not before I die:
Remove far from me vanity and lies: give me neither poverty nor riches:
*   feed me with food convenient for me:*
lest I be full, and deny You, and say, Who is the LORD? or lest I be
*   poor, and steal, and take the name of my God in vain.*

After confessing God as Creator and as the Source of his truth and salvation, Agur proceeds to a brief prayer. He asks for two things. But importantly, he asks for the provision of his two requests "before he dies." Will God give him everything he asks for right away? Maybe not. But we do know that God always gives what is needful for us in His own timing. Sinless perfection is not achievable in this life, and spiritual maturity usually comes over a long process. But the righteous man prays that God would save him from vanity and lies. For a while men will lust after vain things that never satisfy. They will believe in lies until they come to the knowledge of the truth. This is the predicament in which all of us find ourselves, and we must cry out to God to save us from these lies.

Today people hope that a constant string of fun and diversions will save them from the hard, cold realities of life and death. They look forward to plugging themselves into four hours of television each evening. They call Wednesday "Humpday," because they are that much closer to the weekend, when they can entertain themselves with more sports, entertainment, and pastimes. Blaise Pascal described this modern phenomenon in language that is as apropos today as it was then, "They are overwhelmed with business... if they have some time for relaxation, we advise them to employ it in amusement, in play, and to be always fully occupied. How hollow and full of ribaldry is the heart of man! They have a secret instinct which impels them to seek amusement and occupation abroad, and which arises from a sense of constant unhappiness."[36]

But all of this sets them up for cruel disappointments. With each passing decade, the materialists become glummer than ever. It might have been a little exciting when they bought their first record player so they could listen to the big pop singers of the 1960s. Then they bought a convertible automobile, then a color television set, then a computer, then an iPod, then a home movie system, then an iPhone, and then an iPad. But the i-Equipment was all about me, myself, and I. They were lonely, but they weren't lonely for the company of others. They were lonely for more of themselves. With each new technological development, relationships weakened, reality faded, and God became increasingly distant. Each new purchase gained them less happiness, and the best they could ever hope for was to live disconnected from reality in a partial stupor. This is not happiness. This is vanity. Electronic equipment and material things may improve our relationships with God and with others, or further disintegrate these relationships. If it is not

36 "Historical Perspectives of Popular Culture," eds. Bernard Rosenberg and David Manning White (Glencoe, IL: The Free Press, 1957), p. 48.

for our edification, we would be delivered from these things! Therefore, no less than in the days of old Agur, we cry out again to God that He would deliver us from the vanities of each new human invention!

Related to his first petition is his next request, that God would provide sufficient food for Agur's needs. What he is presenting here is the very essence of a godly Christian life. Paul puts it this way: "Godliness with contentment is great gain" (1 Tim. 6:6). The wicked are like the troubled sea without rest (Is. 57:20). They are constantly driven by an endless lust after that which can never fulfill them. Therefore, we confess with Augustine, "My heart is restless until it finds its rest in thee!"[37] But does this imply that we reject all material necessities and pleasures? There is no denying that food and wine are pleasurable things. Yet, what a powerful temptation these things present to us in that we seek more out of them than we should! As we try to find more pleasure, delight, and fulfillment in food and entertainment, we find less pleasure in God. Instead, we ought to find delight in God as we enjoy His good gifts. At the very moment that we take a bite out of a juicy strawberry, we can literally "taste and see that the Lord is good!" (Ps. 34:8). But the man who consumes 30,000 strawberries at one time, will usually forget the God who gave him these good things. He no longer enjoys them *coram Deo,* in the face of God. He comes to believe two things: first, that the source of good gifts is confined to man and nature; second, he is led to believe that man's true joy and fulfillment somehow will come from consuming the 30,000 strawberries or the 300 gallons of wine.

Sometimes a lack of God's good gifts can encourage faithlessness too. When a man loses his job, he is more given to anxiety. Consider the salesman who hasn't made a sale in four weeks. He is two months behind on his rent payment, and his wife is terribly upset with him and makes known her concerns on a daily basis. Would this fellow be more likely to use deception

---

37 St. Augustine, *Confessions*

in his sales pitch? Might he push a little too hard, and take undue advantage of an impressionable widow?

When a father gives his child too much, he runs the risk of spoiling the child and turning him into an ungrateful wretch. On the other hand, if he were to hold back a meal here and there, and seldom bless him with food and clothing, the child might wander away and seek these necessities by illegitimate means. Our relationship with our own heavenly Father is not much different from this, and this is the point old Agur makes here.

Family Discussion Questions:

1. What are the two things Agur asks of God?
2. What sorts of lies or vanity are predominant in the culture where you live?
3. What happens if you eat too many strawberries?
4. How does poverty affect faith, whether negatively or positively?

PART 315 ~ HANDLING BUSINESS AND FAMILIAL RELATIONSHIPS
Proverbs 30:10

Accuse not a servant unto his master, lest he curse you, and you be found guilty.

Now, Agur moves to relationships within the economic sphere. About 30% of our time is spent in some form of work in the free market economy, so it makes sense to deal with economic relationships. The economic relationship is different from church and family relationships. Within a healthy home, good relationships enable us to maintain honest and open moral accountability. But this is not equally the case in our economic relationships.

Should a fellow employee produce shoddy work and fail to deliver on his responsibilities, it is hardly ever helpful to report this to management. If he gets the impression that you are out to sabotage his career, he will not take kindly to this. Don't be surprised if he retaliates with a hundred ploys intended to undermine your own reputation and work. You may find yourself out of a job within a month or two. Politically-charged corporate environments call for wise discretion from those who must operate in such places. The best advice for the average employee is to keep your head down, your hand to the plow, and do the best job possible with a strong positive attitude. Good management will recognize your work and reward you properly. Organizations that are badly managed will eventually fail in a free market. You may report on your own work, but be very careful when reporting on others.

Proverbs 30:11–14

There is a generation that curses their father, and does not bless their mother.

There is a generation that are pure in their own eyes, and yet is not washed from their filthiness.

There is a generation, O how lofty are their eyes! and their eyelids are lifted up.

There is a generation, whose teeth are as swords, and their jaw teeth as knives, to devour the poor from off the earth, and the needy from among men.

After dealing with the nature of reality, the nature of truth, salvation, the good life, and economic relationships, Agur turns to the matters of familial relationships and culture. You must remember that this is Agur's summary review of just about everything in thirty-three short verses.

The fifth commandment presents a biblical view of culture and society. From God's perspective, the family is the indispensable, fundamental building block of human society. Without strong families to sustain the social systems, the most powerful empires will crumble. Ironically, humanists have opposed the family from the beginning, and they do their best to defend adultery, homosexuality, fornication, divorce, dishonor of parents, and socialist surrogate programs.

What we read in these verses perfectly describe what happened in recent generations—most clearly seen in the 1960s. Led primarily by youth bands like the Beatles and the Rolling Stones, wholesale rebellion broke out among the young people. The younger generation opposed the previous generations on almost every issue, including parental authority, war, sexual mores, women's liberation, psychoactive drugs, and the Christian faith itself. It was a generation of youth that cursed their fathers and did not bless their mothers. In 1968, the Beatles described their vision in the hugely popular song, "Revolution."

The rebellious youth of the 60s generation were pure in their own eyes, believing that their parents were the very essence of hypocrisy, war-mongering, greed, and materialism. But these rebels were not washed from their own filthiness. Rejecting their parents' materialism, they ran headlong into sexual license, psychedelic drug use, and bloody revolutions. How were these bloody revolutions any different from the "illegitimate" wars their parents were fighting on foreign soil? Many of these radicals supported the revolutions of Mao Tse Tung, Fidel Castro, Che Guevara, the Vietnamese communists, and the Bolshevics.

At the heart of the humanist revolutions of the last several centuries was a massive severing of the hearts of children from their parents. These men and women learned rebellion as children in their schools and universities. Generational rebellion was institutionalized, and evil powers used it to bring about unimaginable bloodshed and turmoil in modern nations. No doubt this will continue for at least another century, should Christ tarry.

Generational revolution is dangerous and always produces more destruction to cultures and social systems. Forty years after the Beatles, the most popular singers refer to their own mothers as "female dogs," and they revel in describing violent actions employed against their own parents. Where the bonds of familial affection are broken and gross dishonor of parents prevails, society degrades into anarchy and dangerous, bloody revolutions. According to Agur's revelation, the victims of these rebels are usually the poor and the needy among men. It is because the poor are the ones who are unable to escape the cultural malaise, the deadly political revolutions, and the social upheavals. The wealthier folks might be able to move to a different location. Some may avail themselves of exclusive private schools and others may choose to homeschool their children to avoid the unsavory social situations in the public schools. But millions of poor people will suffer the most from the social consequences of these revolutions. In this country, 70% of children born in the inner cities are fatherless, and 12% of their young men end up in the prison system. These are the consequences of the social and cultural revolution of the 1960s!

Some of the blame rightly belongs on the cultural leaders who bring us revolutionary forms of music and art. It was mass media that pushed the sullen rebellion of Elvis Presley and James Dean. Some of the blame also rests with fathers who turned their hearts away from their children and toward a materialist mindset. But the schools also led the revolution with their humanist agendas. By excluding parents from the classroom, the biblical social order was undermined, or at least, ignored. Where the fifth commandment is not carefully affirmed, social unrest and revolution will prevail. Of the 98,817 public schools in this country (as of 2009), it would be hard to find a single school that teaches the book of Proverbs as God's basic curriculum for young people today.

In many ways, the revolution still continues to this day. From the Silent Generation (born 1920s–1930s), to the Baby Boom Generation (born 1940s–1950s), to Generation X (born 1960s–1970s), to the Millennials (born 1980s–2000s), each successive generation is more likely to endorse homosexuality, materialistic evolution, and big government socialism.[38] But it all begins with a dishonor for parents. Without honor for parents, we will see a successive breaking down of the best things, the best morality, the best character that the previous generation could have given us. This is why Jesus Himself recommends the death penalty for the young man who curses his father and mother (Matt. 15:4). If civil governments acted on this, they might actually salvage the social order.

Underlying this dishonor of parents is the sin of pride. Youthful pride is especially virile in the late teen years and early twenties. As Mark Twain once remarked, "When I was a boy of 14, my father was so ignorant I could hardly stand to have the old man around. But when I got to be 21, I was astonished at how much the old man had learned in seven years." Here is pictured the pride of youth, and given full rein it can bring about much harm. May God deliver our young people from this deadly sin!

Family Discussion Questions:

1. What should you do when a fellow employee is not working properly?

2. How should you behave, yourself, when you work for an employer?

3. How did the youth generation of the 1960s illustrate the generation described in verses 12–14?

4. Why are the poor the primary victims of these revolutions?

---

38 http://pewforum.org/Age/Religion-Among-the-Millennials.aspx

PART 316 ~ THE CURSE OF A FALLEN WORLD
Proverbs 30:15–16

The horseleach has two daughters, crying, Give, give. There are three
things that are never satisfied, yes, four things say not, It is enough;
the grave; and the barren womb; the earth that is not filled with water;
and the fire that says not, It is enough.

Now Agur produces an honest assessment of life on planet
earth. It is an unhappy affair. We live in a fallen world, and
all of us suffer the cursed consequences of sin at one level or
another. We suffer with innumerable irritations, difficulties,
and maladies throughout the years of our lives. Yet there are
some curses that are unrelenting and chronic. The wounds are
deep and they do not heal quickly. They beat on us without
mercy. When a loved one dies, for example, the emptiness in
the hearts of those who are left in the home is irresolvable.
Day after day, the weight of the loss remains like a heavy
pall over the family. Barrenness produces a similar effect for
the poor women afflicted by it. Hardwired into the heart of
most women is a desire to have children and to nurture those
children in families. Whether the barrenness is genetic, or
unexplainable, or self-inflicted by birth control use, there is
no denying the gnawing emptiness dominating that woman's
life. What more significant contribution can a woman make
in her lifetime than bringing a child into the world? Finally,
Agur includes both droughts and wildfires that burn out of
control in this list of chronic, destructive forces. How many
firefighters witness the all-consuming forest fire and wonder
if the fire will ever stop? How many farmers wonder if the
drought will ever cease, after sixty long days of dry weather?

How many deaths, barren wombs, droughts, and natural
disasters must we suffer through in any given lifetime? Where
is the joy in the midst of this life of chronic pain, agony, and
loss? If life consisted merely of this suffering and a generous
dose of the opiates to dull the pain, would it be worth living?
The materialist worldview insists that we are nothing but
cosmic dust in a universe of chance. We live a life of suffering

and then we die. In another billion years or so, life will be eliminated from the earth by a passing comet or the implosion of the sun. The eastern religions try to solve the problem by the doctrine of reincarnation. After one life of suffering and death, you may be reincarnated as somebody's cow, only to suffer and die again and again. What can possibly resolve the problem of death and the grave? Must we forever and ever experience the gnawing pain of death and loss? Obviously, there is only one solution to the problem, and that is the resurrection of Jesus Christ, the first fruits of those who rise from the dead. We must believe that the last enemy to be destroyed is death (1 Cor. 15:26), and the cry of the horseleach's daughters will end forever.

Family Discussion Questions:

1. What are the four curses that seem insatiable in their destructive and miserable effects?

2. Where is our hope, in the midst of this sin-cursed world?

PART 317 ~ HOW GOD VIEWS DISHONORING TEENS
Proverbs 30:17

The eye that mocks at his father, and despises to obey his mother, the ravens of the valley shall pick it out, and the young eagles shall eat it.

The picture of a hollowed out eye cavity with blood dripping out of it is not a pleasant one. But it is the image that God uses to depict the haughty teenager who dishonors his father and mother. Perhaps we have grown cold to the dishonor of parents in a society where it is normative, especially among the teens. The teenage girl rolls her eyes, and tells her mother, "Oh Mom, you are like... so... embarrassing me!" It is at that moment that the raven swoops down to pluck that arrogant eye right out of her face. But why should God wish to send a bird to do such bloody work? We are given, here, an insight into God's perspective of this dishonor. He utterly abhors the arrogant teen's attitude towards his or her parents.

Many men and women will feel the brunt of this curse in their later years. Because of their refusal to honor their parents when they were younger, they are now dishonored by their own children. We see the unraveling of their marriages and family life, and more isolation, bitterness, and depression. Counseling offices fill up with people who never learned to honor their parents. Yet the counselors can do little for them but prescribe drugs that will disconnect them from the reality of their miserable lives. God's sanctions are real upon those who ignore His law.

May God bring repentance to the hearts of young and old alike! Where the seeds of this rebellion start to sprout, let us humbly acknowledge it and respond in confession and true repentance. Should a man be tempted to despise his father with his words, or share his father's sins with others, he should look around for the ravens and the young eagles circling above. When a young seventeen-year-old boy arrogantly chides his mother or speaks condescendingly to his father, he should be wearing swimming goggles. As sure as there is a God in the heavens, he will suffer for this dishonor. Nevertheless, there is still mercy for those who see their sins and cry out to God for His salvation.

Dishonor of parents is one of the pre-eminent sins of the day. If we are not repenting in this area, then we have yet to experience the power of the Gospel. In the midst of our social chaos and moral collapse, there is always hope for those who seek deliverance from these wretched sins at the cross of Christ!

Family Discussion Questions:

1. What happens to those who dishonor their parents?

2. Are there any areas of dishonor creeping into our home that ought to be nipped in the bud?

PART 318 ~ FOUR WONDERS
Proverbs 30:18–20

There be three things which are too wonderful for me, yea, four which I
*   know not;*
the way of an eagle in the air; the way of a serpent upon a rock; the
*   way of a ship in the midst of the sea; and the way of a man with a*
*   maid.*
Such is the way of an adulterous woman; she eats, and wipes her
*   mouth, and says, I have done no wickedness.*

Thus far, old Agur has given us a good metaphysic, an ethic, a redemption scheme, a social theory, and a review of the curse of the fall. Now he deals with the incomprehensible elements of the natural world. Interestingly, he does not bring up the deeper-rooted incomprehensible doctrines, such as the unity and diversity of God, or the sovereignty of God and the responsibility of man. Instead, he chooses what we may see as the more mundane, everyday examples of the incomprehensible. Agur's remarkable humility and intensive powers of observation are both seen here. There is a lesson to be learned from this. In our insatiable interest in the "big things" in life, we often miss the many interesting little details that make up God's creation. This brings to mind the excellent little story that George Washington Carver relates concerning the nature of his scientific enquiries.

> I asked God, "Why did you make the universe, Lord?"
>
> "Ask for something more in proportion to that little mind of yours," replied God.
>
> "Why did you make the earth, Lord?" I asked.
>
> "Your little mind still wants to know far too much. Ask for something more in proportion to that little mind of yours," replied God.
>
> "Why did you make man, Lord?" I asked.
>
> "Far too much. Far too much. Ask again," replied God.
>
> "Explain to me why you made plants, Lord," I asked.

"Your little mind still wants to know far too much."

"The peanut?" I asked meekly.

"Yes! For your modest proportions I will grant you the mystery of the peanut. Take it inside your laboratory and separate it into water, fats, oils, gums, resins, sugars, starches and amino acids. Then recombine these under my three laws of compatibility, temperature and pressure. Then you will know why I made the peanut."[39]

Scientific enquiry as well as theological enquiry must begin with a review of the incomprehensible elements in the enquiry. Herein lies the great mistake made by many theologians and scientists in our day. Rarely do you hear anyone speak of the incomprehensible first. In their fervor to inform the world of their great storehouses of knowledge, they forget to curb their dogmatism with humility by admissions of those things of which they know little or nothing. This is what makes for rabbit trails in scientific and theological systems that lead to epistemological and practical cul-de-sacs. Over-eager theologians have said too much about the sacraments, the nature of regeneration, and the mystery of God's sovereignty, and this has led millions astray over the centuries. The same thing is happening in the areas of astronomy, genetic engineering, chemistry, and natural sciences today.

The four things that are impossible to comprehend for Agur are the eagle in the air, the ship on the sea, the snake on the rock, and the man and the maid. The first two might be considered under the heading of physics and biology, and the second two are matters of psychology or sociology. What scientists struggle to explain in the laboratory, and great writers attempt to uncover in their stories as they grapple with the nature of man and creation, are at some point incomprehensible to the human mind.

If we were to study the ship on the sea, for example, the field of fluid mechanics relies heavily on an unproved hypothesis called

39 Rackham Holt, *George Washington Carver, An American Biography*, (Doubleday, 1963)

the "continuum hypothesis." This assumes that "properties such as density, pressure, temperature, and velocity are taken to be well-defined at 'infinitely' small points, defining a REV (Reference Element of Volume), at the geometric order of the distance between two adjacent molecules of fluid."[40] You may not understand that description of the hypothesis, but the important thing to remember is that it is just a hypothesis. Some scientific work is based on unproven hypotheses, and it is important to remain humble enough to acknowledge this. One day, men may conduct studies that disprove the hypothesis, and then they must operate on a different scientific hypothesis or theory. Early ship builders did not understand the basic elements of fluid mechanics, but they were still able to build ships capable of floating on the water. It is well known that less dense objects can float on water, but *how* do the water molecules hold together to enable a ship to glide smoothly over the surface of the water? After thousands of years of study, we have yet to answer the ultimate scientific questions!

Snakes generally move by a process of lateral undulation. Using what scientists call "rostral" or "caudal" wave patterns, the neuro-muscular systems coordinate the snake's body movement, activating complex, coupled segmental oscillators. By His wisdom, God created these systems in order that the snake might effectively martial its scales to push against uneven surfaces and thereby move in serpentine or side-winding patterns. We still have yet to explain how these bio-mechanical systems work on a cellular and atomic level. What's more, the snake also finds its own food, develops its own energy source, replaces its scales from time to time on its own, and maintains its own immune systems. It is a self-maintaining machine! To design a robotic snake with nerve systems controlled by a brain that could move with the smooth motion of a snake would be a mechanical feat well beyond the capabilities of modern man.

40 fttp://en.wikipedia.org/wiki/Fluid_mechanics

The fourth mystery is found in human relationships, and the most complex relationship of all is that of a man with a maid. One of the reasons why the Bible does not present one hundred rules for the courtship and marriage of young men and women is that it is far too complicated for that. How can one explain attraction, love, relationship-building, and the sustaining of those relationships? A million books would be insufficient for these things. Nevertheless, we can still talk about human relationships, and the Word of God does give us basic ethical constraints. For example, we are not to defraud, engage in sexual activity outside of the bounds of marriage, or dishonor parents in the process. But how does one orchestrate love and marriage? There is no simple answer to this question. Somehow, an emotional attachment grows into place, and the physical intimacy will naturally follow. Therefore, in order to avoid unwise and immoral choices, the Song of Songs reminds us not to awaken love before its time (Songs 2:7, 8:4). But once love is awake and the two people have entered the raging river of love, there is almost nothing that can separate them. At this point, wisdom dictates a short engagement and an expedited wedding day.

Finally, Agur throws in another psychological wonder for good measure, as he brings up the shameless adulteress. Faithful men look upon adultery as a fatal sin, from which it is almost impossible to recover. This sort of sin brings about unimaginable devastation to families and entire social systems. It undermines a fundamental human relationship. Yet, there are people who see no problem with this sin at all! Those who have thrown themselves over the cliff, (and have yet to hit the ground), wonder why others are so concerned about what they are doing. Meanwhile, those standing at the top of the cliff peer in awe-struck wonder at the extreme foolishness and blindness of the poor souls falling through the air. The almost complete absence of the fear of God in a professed atheist, an adulterer, or a homosexual is itself fearful and shocking. It is a demonstration of the blindness and incipient inability of natural man to seek after God (Rom. 3:11ff).

Family Discussion Questions:

1. What sort of heart attitude should we have, as we set out to study God's creation? Do we find science boring? Do we ourselves take the right attitude in the science class?

2. What do scientists know about the movement of the snake?

3. Based on his observations of human behavior, what two psychological wonders does Agur mention?

4. How might we be careful not to awaken love before its time? Why is this important?

PART 319 ~ FOUR DISRUPTIONS TO THE SOCIAL ORDER
Proverbs 30:21–23

For three things the earth is disquieted, and for four which it cannot bear;
for a servant when he reigns; and a fool when he is filled with meat;
for an odious woman when she is married; and an handmaid that is heir to her mistress.

Now Agur produces four things which disrupt good order in the world. God is a God of order (1 Cor. 14:34), and to willfully create disorder is to sin. While nobody can produce perfect peace besides God, we are still called to minimize disorder by taking wise actions and making wise decisions. Some homes are more stable and more peaceful than others. Some churches and communities are more stable than others. This is the consequence of wise decisions on the part of those who rule.

However, a servant who is put in a position of authority will create disorder. This is because not every person is equipped and called to leadership. The premature ordination of an elder into a church can be disastrous. Indeed, any organization can be ruined by a man who lacks good character. Given enough time, a fickle-minded and capricious leader will systematically dismantle an organization and leave it in ruins. When a man is easily swayed from one direction to another by opinion polls and widely varying perspectives, he is unfit for leadership. Moreover, leadership requires the ability to motivate and encourage. Of course, the leader must be self-motivated, hard-working, visionary, and mentally equipped for the job. Generally speaking, a man with a slave mentality does not bear these characteristics.

How does this comport with Jesus' requirement that servant-minded men be appointed to do the work in the church of Christ? Is it possible to be servant-minded in some sense, while serving as a visionary leader in another sense? Certainly, we can see all of these characteristics in our Lord Jesus Christ. He warned His disciples against "lording it over the flock," and encouraged a willingness to serve by performing the most menial tasks. All of this is appropriate for a godly manager, president, elder, or father. One may be humble, serving, self-motivated, and visionary at the same time!

The second and fourth disruptions to the good order of things are related to the first. The rich fool (filled with food), is a man who is incapable of wisely managing his wealth. He will waste his resources. Like the man who inherited $50,000 in tools from his father's automotive repair business and buried them in the back yard, these men waste an inheritance that took a great deal of work to accumulate. There is also this handmaid who receives an inheritance from her mistress. The same problem exists here, for this woman does not have the character to wisely manage the inheritance she receives.

Finally, Agur makes mention of the "odious woman when she is married." The word "odious" might be better translated "loathsome." There are some qualities in this woman that are unattractive, to say the least. She repels others because she is malicious, spiteful, bitter, and overbearing. She is persistently irritable and cranky; a spirit of discontentment governs her soul. In an honest moment, even her husband might admit to a counselor that she is a constant burden to him. He may tolerate the woman and provide for her needs, but he finds nothing attractive about her on the inside or on the outside.

All of these four scenarios create social instability. Unqualified leaders in government, business, and family economies will bring their organizations down. Because a wife and a mother are key to family relationships, there is something to be said for the aphorism, "When mamma ain't happy, there ain't nobody happy!" Thus, family relationships suffer tremendous strain and disorder when a wife is discontent, overbearing, or embittered against her husband. But as a wife lovingly and humbly submits to her husband, order and peace return to social systems at all levels of society.

Family Discussion Questions:

1. What are the four disruptions to the social order?

2. Why might a servant have a hard time taking on a position of leadership? How do we balance the idea of competence and wisdom with humility and servanthood for a leader in the church and family?

3. Describe the odious woman. How might a young lady fall into the sins of an "odious woman?"

PART 320 ~ FOUR UNASSUMING WISE THINGS
Proverbs 30:24–28

There be four things which are little upon the earth, but they are exceeding wise;

the ants are a people not strong, yet they prepare their meat in the summer;

the conies [rock badgers] are but a feeble folk, yet they make their houses in the rocks;

the locusts have no king, yet they go forth all of them by bands; the spider takes hold with her hands, and is in kings' palaces.

Creation has something to teach us about the ways of God. If you were to come upon a room decorated in a certain way, you would learn something about the decorator, her likes and dislikes. You would get a glimpse into the personality of the person who keeps the room. In a similar sense, you can pick up some things about the ultimate Designer by the design He has hardwired into His creation.

So what can we learn from the ants, the rock badgers, the locusts, and the spiders? They are all amazing creatures, considering the fact that they do not have the intelligence of the human brain. They are all feeble, insignificant creatures. The rock badger has almost no way to defend itself, except by hiding in the rocks. Colonies of these rodents will set sentries to watch for predators, and upon the appointed signal, these little guys scurry back into the clefts of the rocks. Because of their uncanny ability to hide, they are practically impossible for any predator to capture. Equipped with the wisdom God has provided these animals, they all survive and thrive, and populate the earth!

Somehow we are led to think that wisdom always accompanies powerful institutions and corporations. But God can give an insignificant little family economy special insight into the design or manufacture of an amazing product that thousands of people will find helpful. Very often, it is the poor, wise man that saves the city (Eccl. 9:14–16). However, nobody remembers this poor man whose wisdom saved the city, and great monuments are built for a few fools who take the credit for saving the city. While great empires collapse and the glory of Rome, Spain, France, England, and America fades away, there are pockets of wisdom to be found in the corners of these kingdoms. Quietly, the kingdom of God works here and there, like yeast in a loaf of bread. While the pseudo-wisdom of this world ignores, despises, or even persecutes those who embrace the foolishness of the cross, in the end God brings to nothing this worldly wisdom (1 Cor. 1:19–21). Perhaps you thought that there would be wisdom in the universities or in the great palaces. But sometimes you will find it where you least expect it—in some obscure corner of the empire with the spider, and a humble Christian family.

As men attempt to escape reality and ignore God, it is not long before they lose that sense of wide-eyed wonder. Sadly, many schoolchildren find the science class boring, especially if it is delivered in a cold, academic setting. If you find yourself unimpressed by the most complex, the most intelligent, and the grandest elements of God's creation, sometimes it is better to go back to the simple things. Take a few hours, and observe what God has done in the creation of the amazing little ant and the locust. Study the simpler creation, and nurture a little wonder there, first. Then you will learn to marvel at the grandest works of God in creation and providence.

Family Discussion Questions:

1. Why is it easy to miss the little things that retain so much wisdom? Why do we have a hard time being impressed by God's creation?

2. What are the four insignificant little aspects of God's creation that are endowed with a good amount of wisdom?

3. Who was the man who saved the city in Ecclesiastes 9, and how does that tie into this passage?

4. Is the wisdom of God's Word, the church of Jesus Christ, and the cross of Christ given much recognition in the most powerful courts, the most powerful board rooms, and the most powerful legislatures in nations today? Why or why not?

PART 321 ~ FOUR SMOOTH OPERATORS
Proverbs 30:29–31

There be three things which go well, yea, four are comely in going; a lion which is strongest among beasts, and turns not away for any; a greyhound; an he goat also; and a king, against whom there is no rising up.

In this little one-page collection of wisdom, Agur has dealt with the nature of reality, the nature of truth, salvation, the good life, economic relationships, familial relationships, culture, science, and human psychology. Now he turns to the subject of political leadership. Granted, it is placed in another list of four remarkable and impressive things. In this case, they are the things that are well-coordinated in action. This is in contrast with those things that don't function very well. Take for example the man with the broken leg who tries to run a marathon. He drags his twisted leg for a couple hundred yards, and all those watching wince with every step he takes. Obviously, the marathon is not going well for him!

There are those who, by God's creation and providence, are well able to operate under the conditions in which they find themselves. The lion has no predator in the field and he rules the jungle. The greyhound can run effortlessly for miles. The male goat can navigate the cliffs well. But what does all this have to do with kingly leadership ("against whom there is no rising up") that is able to avert civil uprisings, strikes, and the like? Whether it be church, business, or civil body, wise leadership is key to the stability of the community. When leaders lose the faith of their followers, they will experience church splits, strikes, or political revolutions. But how does the leader keep a unified group? The text does not specify how this is done, but we can assume it is the same way that the he-goat navigates the cliffs. God equips the amazing Rocky Mountain goat with excellent balance and a rubbery cloven hoof that clings to small crevices on cliffs that have an almost vertical incline.

Ultimately, God does the same thing for the leader. Managing social groups can be more difficult than navigating a mountain cliff. There are just too many variables and too many things that can go wrong. On the one hand, excessive control over the group can lead to rebellion, while too little control can result in anarchy and chaos. Good leadership calls for a tremendous amount of wisdom on the part of the leader. When you see a leader who can lead well, motivate a group, maintain the unity of the cause, and keep everybody reasonably happy, you have to conclude that this fellow must have an amazing gift. And, of course, that gift can only have come from God.

Family Discussion Questions:

1. What are the four things that operate well under the conditions in which they find themselves?

2. Why is leadership so difficult? Have you ever seen churches, businesses, or nations come apart? Give several examples.

3. What qualities are found in a leader who can keep it all together?

PART 322 ~ BRIDLE THE TONGUE
Proverbs 30:32

If you have done foolishly in lifting up yourself, or if you have thought evil, lay your hand upon your mouth.

In the middle of all these considerations of the big things of life, Agur throws this one little practical lesson into the mix. But in truth, this is not an insignificant matter. In fact, of all the practical lessons in the book of Proverbs, this one is the most frequently mentioned. The control of the tongue may be the most difficult challenge in the development of the character of a person. Therefore, the Bible returns to this important lesson repeatedly in both Old and New Testaments (Jam. 3:2–10; Matt. 12:36–37).

But here, Agur offers additional guidance for this important subject. In one sense, we ought always to guard the tongue; but there are times in which we should add additional sentries. For example, in the modern world, there are times when airports and other public transit departments heighten the security levels. When terrorist activity picks up, the authorities encourage commuters to be on their guard, ready to react if they see any suspicious activity. In a similar manner, we must call our sentries to their post to guard the tongue carefully under certain conditions and times (as delineated by this verse). In the first place, if you sense pride in your own heart, a tendency to compare your own performance with others, or a spiteful attitude toward others, you should immediately sound off all the warning signals and above all, *shut your mouth*. Do not say anything at all. Also, when you sense an uncharitable or envious attitude towards others rising up within your own heart, do not proceed any further. Instead of acting on these thoughts by resorting to gossip or slander, it would be better to drop to your knees and repent of those arrogant and malicious thoughts.

The potential of the human heart to think the worst of a brother or sister is not to be underestimated! Therefore, the sanctified mind is always scanning and re-scanning the inclinations of the heart and the intentions of the mind for signs of human depravity. As the old catechism puts it, "Some sins are of themselves and by reason of several aggravations more heinous in the sight of God than others." By refusing to add sinful words to sinful thoughts and intentions, you can nip the sin in the bud and prevent more damage to relationships. This is all part of the sanctification process for the believer.

Proverbs 30:33

Surely the churning of milk brings forth butter, and the wringing of the nose brings forth blood; so the forcing of wrath brings forth strife.

To understand the picture given here, you need to grab your nose and ring it hard for about ten minutes. Now that is a good way to start a nosebleed. There are potentially hundreds of ways in which you might provoke someone to wrath. Some children are always teasing. They delight in any kind of negative reaction they can get out of another child. This then serves as a prelude for a quarrel or perhaps even a fist fight. But the Bible calls us to peacefulness, and those who provoke strife will disrupt the peace in our homes and create miserable lives for everybody.

In most quarrels, there is someone responsible for initiating the fight. Of course, at the end of the altercation, you will almost always find that others have committed sin as well. But the one who does the nose wringing is more culpable and should be held to account for this. The source of all the wars and the altercations in the world is the very same thing we find in homes and playgrounds where pride and quarrelsomeness operate. Until parents train their children in the ways of peace by the power of the Spirit of peace, the wars of the nations will never cease.

Likewise, husbands and wives must be careful not to provoke by their language in the home. Oftentimes, the use of sarcasm towards family members can be hurtful and provoking. When a husband implies that his wife made an error because of her stupidity, his words bear the impress of unloving spite towards her. Or when a wife enjoys pointing out her husband's failures, she fails to render him the honor and love that God requires of her. Usually, this kind of language sparks a contention that can lead to shouting, cursing, and even physical abuse. The best time to quell a potential argument is at the very beginning, when sharp words would likely incite anger on the part of the other. As the argument continues to escalate, it becomes increasingly difficult to diffuse it.

Family Discussion Questions:

1. What is one of the best ways in which you can prevent the sins of the tongue? According to Agur, what are the two warning signs that indicate that you had better keep your mouth shut?

2. How well do you monitor your own attitude? Are you well aware when your heart is turning sour and negative towards another?

3. Do you have any problems with teasing in your home? What form does it usually take? What kinds of words do you find most provoking in your home?

PART 323 ～ A MOTHER DISCIPLES HER SON
Proverbs 31:1–3

The words of king Lemuel, the prophecy that his mother taught him.
What, my son? and what, the son of my womb? and what, the son of
*   my vows?*
Give not your strength unto women, nor your ways to that which
*   destroys kings.*

Following thirty chapters of a father teaching his son, a
mother now enters the picture to give her admonitions. Most
commentators hold that "Lemuel" is a nickname for Solomon,
and this chapter contains the wisdom his mother passed on
to him. The influence a woman has upon her children is
undeniable and important. When mention is made of a king
in the Old Testament, whether good or evil, almost without
exception, the name of his mother is included. When the
accomplishments of men are chronicled in the great books
of history, rarely do mothers receive the credit they deserve.
The influence of mothers upon men like Augustine, St. John
Chrysostom, George Whitefield, and George Washington
is nothing short of legendary. All of these great men were
effectively raised by their mothers, receiving great spiritual
and practical instruction from them. They would never have
achieved a high status in history had it not been for direction
of their mothers. Chrysostom's father died when he was two
years old, and Augustine's was an unbeliever. Both George
Whitefield and George Washington's mothers were widowed
early in their sons' lives.

When a mother loves her son, she will see to it that she
communicates the most important things to him. Others
may teach the lesser principles, but a mother whose heart is
wrapped around her son will be sure he has the most important
lessons down. From the outset, she will remind her son where
he came from—her womb. This is something no son should
ever forget, even if he does command the greatest empire
in the world! For nine long months, his mother carried and
nurtured him in the tender chambers of her womb. Only the

foulest ingrate would forget this fact and refuse this woman her due honor.

She warns her son from the outset concerning inappropriate relationships with women. There is an honorable course with women, and there is a dishonorable way. Unfortunately, men of power and influence often fall into the "womanizing" trap, and they always pay dearly for it. They think they can have any woman they want by way of fornication and prostitution, or more honorably, by polygamy. But either way, they will pay for it. Solomon took the direction of polygamy, and he compromised his leadership as a result of it. Also, a man with multiple wives becomes overwhelmed with providing for the financial, emotional, and physical needs of his wives if he is attempting to show them any honor. This warning is probably more appropriate for the adulterer who is virtually addicted to pornography, prostitution, adultery, and other illicit forms of fornication. When a man serves his flesh in an idolatrous fashion, the service to his gods consumes him. Thus, his womanizing drains him of the masculine energy he would ordinarily employ in leadership. On the other hand, the man who lives his life according to God's rules will maintain a proper balance. He will find his relationship with his wife empowering and consummately fulfilling.

This mother's sage advice is proven again and again with every generation and every century that goes by. We frequently hear of yet another senator or congressman who is embroiled in sexual scandal of some kind. Without exception, these men weaken their position in leadership and undermine the integrity of the office in which they serve. Just over the last few years, a Republican governor from South Carolina lost his position when he was found cavorting with a woman in South America who was not his wife. Another Governor from New York was caught using state funds for his high-priced paramours. One of the greatest golfers in the history of the sport recently watched his internationally-acclaimed reputation shrivel when the news uncovered a string of illicit affairs. Even the president of the United States was impeached when the nation learned of his incessant philandering ways. These anecdotal cases are just a smattering of the stories covered in the last few years in this country. Whether or not a nation has accepted these sins as normative, men will always pay for their misdeeds with women. You would think that men would learn this lesson after thousands of years and millions of examples of failure.

Family Discussion Questions:

1. Give examples of mothers who had a profound influence upon their sons for good or for evil (use biblical records as well as secular sources).

2. What advice has your mother given to you over the years? Give several examples of important lessons that still stick in your mind. Have you taken this advice to heart and applied it to life?

3. What does it mean to "give your strength to women?" How do men give their strength to women? Why are leaders especially vulnerable to this sin?

PART 324 ~ LEADERSHIP AND ALCOHOL
Proverbs 31:4–7

It is not for kings, O Lemuel, it is not for kings to drink wine; nor for princes strong drink;
lest they drink, and forget the law, and pervert the judgment of any of the afflicted.
Give strong drink unto him that is ready to perish, and wine unto those that be of heavy hearts.
Let him drink, and forget his poverty, and remember his misery no more.

When it comes to the matter of wine and strong drink, we must be careful to stick to what the Bible says. There is some debate over the consumption of alcoholic beverages among many Christian groups today. Actually, the widespread prohibition of alcoholic beverages is a relatively new phenomenon in the history of the Christian religion. Over the last 150 years, a number of Christian denominations have taken a strong stand against all use of alcohol. As they turned against God's law as the standard for ethical behavior, Christians also enthusiastically endorsed their own legalistic traditions. Some who would argue vehemently against the biblical requirement of the death penalty for the drunkard son who curses his father and mother (Prov. 21:18–21; Matt. 15:5–8) would imprison Christ for making wine at Cana at His mother's bidding (John 2:1–11). In every generation, men are inclined towards replacing God's laws with their own. They manufacture an ethical standard they believe to be better than God's, hoping that this will improve things. Because we all tend towards this form of autonomy, it is important that we continually return to the Word of God as our standard to correct our thinking by it. God's Book of Wisdom does provide plenty of cautionary warnings related to the consumption of alcohol: a fool had better not touch the bottle unless he understands the wise use of God's good gifts. From these words spoken through the mouth of a wise mother, we obtain four plain statements concerning alcohol.

#1: It is not for kings to drink wine.

#2: It is not for princes to drink strong drink.

#3: Strong drink is for those who are ready to perish.

#4: And wine is helpful to cheer up the heavy heart.

First of all, a king is not a prince, a plumber, or a pastor. A king is a powerful ruler who is ultimately and solely responsible for the civil realm. In the modern world we are not familiar with monarchical forms of government, where power is somewhat distributed between several branches of government. But in the case of a king, the "buck" stop with him. Where he takes on ultimate responsibility for life and death decisions, he had better not drink wine or cloud his mind in any way with opiates. He must be "on his game" as long as he is in the position of ruling.

Could this principle apply to anybody else who sits in a position of judgment? Occasionally, jurors do make life and death judgments, particularly in death penalty related trials. Within the church, an elder makes judgments that may impact a man's status in the body of Christ (Matt. 18:17). It is possible that the work of an elder may, at points, be as important as the work of a king. Nevertheless, to apply this first rule to any and every person carte blanche is to go well beyond the intent of this verse.

Taking up the second statement in reference to the use of alcohol, who are these princes that should stay away from strong drink? From other references to "princes" in the book of Proverbs and elsewhere, it seems that they are either underlings to the king or his potential successors. During the reign of King David, the young prince Absalom adjudicated certain cases at the gates of Jerusalem. While the king is ultimately responsible for what happens in the kingdom, these men serve as advisors and appointees of the king.

Because of the risks involved with heavy alcohol consumption, princes would do well to stay away from strong drink. For example, the risks of addiction and dependence are very high, and leaders that rely on these crutches often give way to drunkenness. Also, heavy use of alcohol reduces one's capacity for making wise judgments. Scientists have observed the reduced brain size and capability in those who drink heavily when compared with those who are moderate in their consumption. In other words, an extensive use of alcohol over a long period of time can shrivel the brain.[41] For those who carry heavy responsibilities in society, advanced age should carry the benefit of added wisdom and improved judgment. Therefore, it is counterproductive for a leader to diminish his capacity in the position God has placed him by heavy use of alcohol.

16http://articles.cnn.com/2008-10-14/health/healthmag.alcohol.brain.shrinkage_1_brain-volume-moderate-drinkers-light-drinkers?_s=PM:HEALTH

"Strong drink" connotes high alcoholic content such as whiskey, vodka, or gin. Let's be careful not to look upon these things as "evil," anymore than we would consider guns, knives, or watermelons as evil. Everything has a use, and to use things wrongly can land a man or a woman in a sinful lifestyle. According to Lemuel's mom, heavy drink is for those who are approaching death. There is a right use of whiskey and pain-killing drugs that disconnect the mind from the reality of pain and suffering, but these intoxicants are primarily intended for those who are on what is known as the "death trajectory." Mercifully, God has provided means to alleviate pain for those who suffer from chronic illnesses. However, in a death-oriented culture millions of people escape into the drug world of methamphetamines, cocaine, marijuana, whiskey, and prescription drugs. Most people who are addicted to drugs were not dying when they began to use these heavy, mind-altering drugs, but they placed themselves into the death trajectory because they loved death more than life (Prov. 8:36).

For all that, the Bible still does not forbid the moderate use of wine. A few sips of wine will affect the moods, more than a glass of water, for example. Food can provide the same effect. After a hard day at work where a man struggles through sixteen hours of difficulty and discouragement, he is usually greatly refreshed after a good meal or a few sips of wine. His entire outlook on life will change shape, but there is another cautionary note here. Sometimes people will begin to rely on coffee, food, and drink to "cheer them up" on a regular basis. A man turns to his six-pack of beer every evening for his escape from the tedium of life, while his wife reverts to her comfort foods and the sin of gluttony. While we should not deny the reality that every meal provides an opportunity for rejoicing, and every sip of wine may give a little good cheer, these things cannot of themselves give us what our souls cry out for. Our chief delight must come from God, and if we cannot rejoice before God in our meals and our drinks with sincere gratitude to Him, then we will spiral into vain idolatry. If God fades away, then joy will fade too, and food and drink become another escape from reality. Joy in eating and drinking is fine, but we must do so in sincere gratitude to God.

Family Discussion Questions:

1. What are the four principles relating to alcohol provided in this passage?

2. Why is it a risk for leaders to drink wine or strong drink?

3. What is the purpose of "strong drink" and drugs, according to these verses? Is it legitimate for a Christian to use drugs "recreationally?" At what point may Christians take drugs (whether morphine or marijuana?)

4. Is it legitimate to drink wine for its heartening capacity (or eat food for the same reason)? Is it ALWAYS legitimate to eat and drink for this reason?

PART 325 ~ THE BUSINESS OF
TRUE STATESMEN
Proverbs 31:8–9

Open your mouth for the dumb in the cause of all such as are appointed to destruction.
Open your mouth, judge righteously, and plead the cause of the poor and needy.

Now for the crowning piece of advice from a mother to her son who will become king. In a nutshell, this is the business of a king or anybody who rules in the civil magistrate. Righteous leaders should save the lives of the poor innocents who are persecuted to death by tyrants. But who are these tyrants? Usually, they are men who will persecute God-fearing, humble believers. They also tend towards advocating the murder of babies and the elderly.

The righteous leader's basic priority in government is to protect the life of God's people, as in the cases of Joseph and Esther in the Old Testament. He protects their freedom to bear children, to raise them in the fear of the Lord, and to meet together as a church body. He defends their responsibility and freedom to exhort one another daily in the Word (Heb. 3:13). Secondly, the righteous civil leader will do his utmost to keep petty tyrants or doctors from killing their patients. This duty is neglected regularly today in many countries where abortion and euthanasia are legalized. A recent survey of Belgian nurses found that about half of them administer toxic drugs to their patients without their victims' knowledge or consent.[42] If there was a righteous leader left in that country, he would fight this sort of thing for the sake of the silent ones who are "appointed to destruction." Every age has its problems with tyranny and injustice. In the pagan lands before the Gospel penetrated, infanticide, euthanasia of the elderly, or widows being burned on the funeral pyres of their husbands were common practices. In the present day, such practices are sanitized under the cloak of "good intentions," "morning-after pills," "clinical abortions to excise fetal tissue," and "mercy killing." But truly righteous leaders should be able to see through these thin facades of hypocrisy. There isn't much one can do when a person wants to commit suicide, but it is important that the civil magistrate prevent wholesale murder at the hands of trusted doctors.

Righteous leaders do not lead by opinion polls. For those who lead in the fear of God (Ex. 18:21; 2 Sam. 23:1–2), it doesn't matter what the majority wants. What matters is righteous judgment according to God's standards. They look out for the rights of the minority who have no mouthpiece, and they will defend the most vulnerable from those who take undue advantage of them. When an American chemical plant in India killed thousands of people (after being warned multiple times of their failure to take necessary precautionary measures to protect human life), the trial for the directors who were involved lasted almost twenty years. In the end, they were fined a pittance.[43] In cases of gross negligence, biblical law

42 http://www.dailymail.co.uk/news/article-1285423/Half-Belgiums-euthanasia-nurses-admit-killing-consent.html
43 http://news.bbc.co.uk/2/hi/south_asia/8725140.stm

requires the death penalty for those who allowed the "bull to push its horn." (Ex. 21:28–30). Because civil governments work in collusion with large corporations to such an extent, it becomes almost impossible for justice to prevail in such important trials. While governments are busy regulating and fining the corporations to fill their own coffers, there is very little actual restitution to the true victims in cases of corporate negligence. Any righteous man interested in true justice will not play this game. His business is to defend the victims and seek restitution for them.

Questions:

1. What is the business of righteous leaders in the civil magistrate? What is their focus in that office?

2. What have righteous leaders done in the past to bring justice to the widow and orphan?

3. What could righteous leaders do today to bring about justice for the persecuted minority (or weak and helpless)?

PART 326 ~ THE VIRTUOUS WOMAN
Proverbs 31:10–12

Who can find a virtuous woman? For her price is far above rubies.
The heart of her husband safely trusts in her, so that he shall have no need of spoil.
She will do him good and not evil all the days of her life.

The remainder of the chapter is taken up with the description of the "virtuous woman." Continuing to advise her son, the wise mother lists the qualities of a good wife. Is there anything more important for a young man's success than his choice of spouse? Every young man and woman should memorize these verses and meditate often on the qualities listed.

Importantly, the word for "virtuous" is taken from the Hebrew *Chayil*. It is better translated "valiant" or "highly effective." From creation, God intended for the woman to be a helper appropriate for the man in his dominion work. As an ax head on an ax handle, the woman and the man unite to form an economic force that gets things done. Without the woman, the man is generally not fit either emotionally or physically to take on the dominion work he has to do. But together, they form a team that gets the job done. Therefore, the Proverbs 31 woman is better pictured by Vermeer's *Milk Maid* than by some anorexic model on the cover of Cosmopolitan magazine. She is courageous, productive, active, strong, and faithful in her role as wife and mother. The word is a military word used for an army that usually wins its battles. This woman knows how to get the job done as she acts upon the vision of the household. She is a doer.

The thrust of this chapter deals mainly with the economic role of the wife in the home. All of this assumes that the family still serves as the basic economic unit in society. Since our word "economics" comes from the Greek word *oikonomia*, which is translated "the vision of the family," the basic economic unit is the family. For thousands of years, families saw themselves as working for a common economic interest. In the Scriptures, Joseph, David, Rachel, and Rebekah would tend to their father's sheep. Aquila and Priscilla worked together as tentmakers (Acts 18:2–3). Most companies today do not contract with families for a job; they hire individuals and segregate families into institutions and corporations. That is why this passage makes little sense to the modern mind. Notice that the virtuous wife has her *husband's* best interests at heart in her economic endeavors. Is she beholden to her corporate board or to her own husband? Does the heart of her corporate boss safely trust in her that he shall have no need of spoil? This speaks to how a woman sees herself. Does she see herself belonging, in an economic sense, to her own family or to a corporation or a government entity? Increasingly, the modern woman separates herself from her family and finds herself plugged into the large fascist-corporate economic infrastructure. The feminists tell her that this is ultimate freedom, but over time she finds herself more enslaved to corporations, banks, and government-instituted social programs. The family fragments, more children are raised outside the context of the family, socialism advances, and the biblical vision fades.

Paul speaks of the godly wife in 1 Timothy 5:14 as the *oikodespoteo,* meaning that she manages the home. According to Titus 2:4, the godly wife is the *oikouros,* which means she works in the home. Offensive though this may be to the egalitarian feminists today, the wife works for her husband's interests. She manages his estate. She spends his money and she facilitates income for the household economy. When her economic loyalty moves away from her husband's household, she has already disintegrated the marriage in some measure, at least in the economic sense. The marriage will only prosper as she works to gain her husband's trust, and as her husband learns to trust in her. Rather than micro-managing her every expenditure, he should be convinced in his own mind that she is always after the best interests of the household. To doubt her is to undermine her effectiveness in her work. If, however, she has failed to earn his trust and she is a self-consumed shopaholic, then she forfeits his trust and the marriage will suffer for it.

Nevertheless, the virtuous woman's price is far above rubies because she is trustworthy, hard-working, industrious, and frugal. The Bible does not ignore the economic well-being of the home, because the economy of the home includes the expenditure of time, money, and resources. A wise and careful use of these assets is what makes up a highly functional household that accomplishes a great deal in ministry, service, hospitality, charity, and dominion work.

Her task in life is to support her husband, that she should do him good and not evil all the days of her life. She delights in pleasing her husband. She seeks his spiritual, physical, and financial well-being. Sadly, there are few biblical examples that bear out this vision. Remember that Eve tempted her husband to the first sin. Jezebel inspired her husband to act wickedly. King Herod's wife facilitated the murder of John the

Baptist. Job's wife was less than helpful when she encouraged her husband to "curse God and die." Michal despised David as he danced before the Lord, while Solomon's wives drew his heart away from the Lord.

If these verses give us a vision for a good wife, how might we best prepare our daughters to this end? That question is foremost in the minds of godly parents who want the best for their daughters who hope to marry. We ought to raise our daughters with good financial sense, wise frugality, delegation skills, an understanding of economic value, and a love for hard work.

But as families raise their daughters with the "independent" mindset, they prepare their daughters for fragmented economies and divorce. The hearts of their husbands will not safely trust in them, because there is little unity in their household economy. They set their future families up for quarrels over finances. If a daughter learns dishonor, discontentment, and disloyalty in her father's home economy, how can we be sure that she will not exhibit the same things in her husband's household? Could this be one significant cause for the dysfunctional conditions that define the Christian households in the West today? What is the best way for our daughters to learn godly submission, honor, contentment, and loyalty? Some say that the sooner a daughter is emancipated from her father's home and lives on her own, the better she will learn these things. It is hard to believe this to be the case. For the last generation or two, independence became the rule for most daughters. But this also coincided with the greatest systemic breakdown of the family ever seen in the history of the Western world. Where there are broken relationships between fathers and daughters, the sad event of emancipation is almost inevitable. This is not always the case. Thank God, there are exceptional cases here and there where we find the precious rubies emerging from their fathers' homes with a spirit of godly submission, honor, contentment, loyalty, and industry!

Also reference comments on Proverbs 27:25–27.

Family Discussion Questions:

1. What does the word "virtuous" mean?

2. Whose heart safely trusts in this virtuous woman? Why is that important?

3. Provide examples of good wives in the Bible. Give a few examples of those who were not helpful to their husbands.

4. How might we prepare our daughters to be the kind of wives that are envisioned in these verses?

PART 327 ~ ECONOMIC PRODUCTIVITY
Proverbs 31:13–16

She seeks wool, and flax, and works willingly with her hands.
She is like the merchants' ships; she brings her food from afar.
She rises also while it is yet night, and gives meat to her household, and
   a portion to her maidens.
She considers a field, and buys it; with the fruit of her hands she plants
   a vineyard.

These verses speak of the virtuous woman's productivity in the home. This woman fills her time with fruitful endeavors. How much of modern life is consumed with the trivial and unproductive? Even on a Monday morning, when the average worker sits down to do her work, she spends much of her time with meaningless tasks that produce little real income for her employers. How much time is spent updating blogs, checking e-mail, surfing the Internet, chatting on the telephone, gossiping with neighbors, and watching television? The virtuous woman resists wasting her time with such fruitless activities. She has a keen sense of what produces and what doesn't.

On the other hand, she doesn't mind spending money if she can get quality food and other necessities for her family. Indeed, this woman is no miser. She might even spend extra time and money on food with higher nutritional value. But what she wants is a healthy, productive home economy. She doesn't consume for the sake of consuming. And she doesn't look at shopping as some kind of a therapeutic balm for her materialistic, idolatrous soul. When an entire society is committed to consuming and under-producing, the national debt will exceed trillions of dollars. But this woman rejects and Epicurean view of life in favor of a productive vision.

She also has an eye for good investment property and she seeks out lawful means whereby she may increase the net worth of the household. While her commitment is to the household economy, she certainly is not confined to the home. But under normal circumstances, her husband would not indenture her as a slave or a hired servant to some master, householder, or business. "Where the Spirit of the Lord works, there is liberty" (2 Cor. 3:17). Therefore, true believers will seek freedom from the unnecessary servitude of men (1 Cor. 7:21–23). A woman will find far more freedom in the warm, loving home of a husband who loves his wife as Christ loved the church than she would in a large corporation with eight levels of management above her.

From verse 15, it is evident that the woman of the house is a mentor for her "maidens." As older men should mentor the younger men, it is incumbent upon the wiser, older women to mentor the younger women too (Tit. 2:4–5). This was normative in biblical times, although it is a practice long neglected due to the imposition of an institutional form of schooling upon our young ladies. One of the qualities required of a true Proverbs 31 woman who manages a substantial household economy is that she be able to delegate and subcontract work. It takes a certain maturity to direct and motivate others to do the work.

Another important element constituting the economic vision of her home is *diversification*. The family is the most versatile, loyal, and diverse economic force. Economic downturns are inevitable. Markets come and go, and corporate security is an oxymoron. So this woman will manage multiple income streams representing a variety of products and services.

It is important to note that this lady isn't consumed with carving out "me time" because her highest fulfillment comes in serving others. She is happy to be a wife and a mother. She sees her position in the household and she fits into it with grace and peaceful contentment.

At this point, some women begin to look at the vision laid out here is overwhelming or even unachievable. But this is to misunderstand God's wisdom. The vision provides a map for a road that is not quickly traversed, nor is intended to be a short journey. Vision does provide direction, and by faith, we move in the direction of the vision, one step at a time. Therefore, our young daughters should prepare for womanhood with this God-ordained pattern in mind.

Family Discussion Questions:

1. Do we have a productive mentality or a consuming mentality? What is the difference between these two perspectives?

2. How productive is your average day? What did you get accomplished yesterday?

3. Does our household economy include any assets? Who manages the assets of the household?

4. Is there any way that we can obtain more freedom from corporate structures, to enable a little more opportunity for building a household economy?

5. How much mentoring of young maidens goes on in our households and church community?

PART 328 ~ CHARITABLE ENDEAVORS
Proverbs 31:17–20

She girds her loins with strength, and strengthens her arms.
She perceives that her merchandise is good; her candle goes not out by
*   night.*
She lays her hands to the spindle, and her hands hold the distaff.
She stretches out her hand to the poor; yes, she reaches forth her hands
*   to the needy.*

The ideal figure recommended for a woman in many cultures is the wispy, anorexic shape that is represented by the models that are splashed over the covers of women's magazines. This is not the picture we get here. While the Bible forbids the sins of gluttony and drunkenness, there are no specific biblical guidelines for a woman's body mass index, weight, and body shape. But that is not to say that the Proverbs 31 woman is some lazy slob. And she certainly isn't some delicate wall flower absent of the motivation to do productive work. She understands that she needs a healthy body in order to do the physical work that must be done in the home. If she is overwhelmed by physical exhaustion, or if her muscles atrophy from inactivity, she will not have the strength to produce in the household economy. She also pays attention to her diet. Anybody who tries to subsist on sugary doughnuts and soft drinks will usually find these things counter productive to good physical and emotional health. Some women have a naturally strong constitution, some are weaker. But whatever this woman's genetic makeup happens to be, she has the willpower to employ it to its fullest capacity in the home.

This woman also has an eye for "quality." Some judge the output of a person merely on the basis of the quantity of work produced. Yet quality is just as important! Without a conscientious eye for detail, a manufacturer will produce shoddy products that require constant maintenance or even replacement. Companies that cannot produce good quality products will eventually go out of business. Therefore, the best companies will strive for higher levels of quality, less variation that yields malfunction or dissatisfaction in the eye of the consumer. This requires the ability to measure quality both in a subjective sense and an objective sense. In other words, she must perceive that her merchandise is good before she sends it out to the market.

Every household should maintain what we call a "charitable department" in the home. In fact, God's law requires that godly families provide at least 3.33% of their income to the poor (or 10% distributed every three years, Deut. 14:28–29). If families would do this sort of thing faithfully, there would be no need for governments to tax the people as much as 50–70% of their income to cover welfare and education programs for the poor. Abigail Adams, before leaving to join her husband in Paris during the war, gave final instructions to those managing the family farm: "In November you will be so good as to give on my account the sum of two dollars to widow Abigail Field, two dollars to the widow Sarah Owen, who lives in the same house with her sister Field, one dollar to Mrs. Fuller, and one dollar to the widow Mary Howard, and one dollar to the wife of John Hayden, who is an aged woman and one of my pensioners—one dollar to the widow Mary Green."[44] The Proverbs 31 woman then administers the charitable department in the home. She looks out for the poor and needy in the church or the community surrounding her home.

Family Discussion Questions:

1. What is the ideal figure for a woman?

2. How might a woman take care of herself, so as to be in her best condition for the work she has to do?

---

44 David McCullough, *John Adams,* (Simon and Schuster: New York, NY, 2001), p. 292. Abigail Adams was a prime example of this woman, maintaining the home economy while her husband John served with the Continental Congress. According to David McCullough, "She managed the farm—scrimped, saved, wove her own wool, made the family's clothes—determined not only to stay free of debt, but to make improvements. She would do her part in her way. . . because it was expected of her in his absence." (Ibid, p. 171)

3. How important is "quality" in the food we cook, the yard work we do, and the work we produce in this home? Do we produce a high level of quality, or is most of our work pretty haphazard and shabby?

4. From a biblical perspective, what institutions are supposed to be looking out for the poor—the family, the church, or the state? How does the family look out for the poor? Does our family have an active "charitable department" operating?

PART 329 ~ OVERSEEING THE NEEDS OF HER HOUSEHOLD
Proverbs 31:21–23

She is not afraid of the snow for her household; for all her household are clothed with scarlet.
She makes herself coverings of tapestry; her clothing is silk and purple.
Her husband is known in the gates, when he sits among the elders of the land.

This woman is primarily concerned for her husband and children—not herself. It is a self-oriented narcissistic society that has killed eighty million children by abortion and the abortifacient birth control pill during the last fifty years. But this self-orientation doesn't stop with abortion. Since the industrial revolution, parents increasingly remanded their children to orphanages and part time orphanages (known as "day care centers"). Millions of parents turned their children over to governments to feed through school lunch programs and public welfare. In nations like South Korea, the birth rate fell from 6.0 to 1.1 within about forty years! Whereas China mandated a one child per family policy by forced abortions and infanticide, barely achieving a birth rate of 1.6, South Korea didn't need to avail itself of such Draconian measures at all! They simply adopted the self-centered feminism and existentialism of the West. A publication called *The Japanese Journal of Population* explains the imploding birth rates in South Korea: "Young women wish to have their own roles in life other than spouse and mother... these young women no longer comply with family arrangements that mothers and grandmothers took for granted; they have invested a lot in education and have their own personal expectations and ambitions... they are looking for financial autonomy and they cannot tolerate subordination to male authority." So the modern woman is concerned with herself, her autonomy, her own roles in life, and her own personal expectations and ambitions. She is mainly concerned with herself. But not so for the Proverbs 31 woman! She makes sure that her household is well taken care of with clothing, proper medical care, food, and nutrition.

Beyond this, she is vitally concerned with the spiritual, moral, and academic condition of her household as well. While the spiritual well-being of the household is ultimately the responsibility of the husband (Eph. 6:4; 1 Thess. 2:11), he may delegate some of it to his wife. The prime example of this is found with Lemuel's mother who is providing some spiritual training for her son in this final chapter of Proverbs. Of course, there is no hard and fast separation between the academic and the character lessons a child needs to learn. God's Book of Wisdom carefully intertwines what a child needs to know about human relationships, government, leadership, business, science, epistemology, metaphysics, and ethics, with the character of the child himself. Thus, the Proverbs 31 woman looks well to provide both the material and spiritual clothing for attiring her household.

However, she does not ignore herself entirely. From verse 22 we learn that she decorates herself beautifully with fine clothing. The apostles encourage modesty in dress, employing the Greek word *Kosmio* (1 Tim. 2:9; 1 Pet. 3:3–4). This word means "an appropriateness in dress, that is suitable to the person and the situation in which she finds herself." That is, one would not wear a wedding dress to church worship or a bathing suit to a wedding. Also, a woman whose family income stands at $40,000 per year should not be wearing dresses that cost $1,000. These might be more appropriate for a woman whose household income approaches $1,000,000 per year. Moreover, a woman whose husband is a respected leader in the community should dress appropriately to render her husband due honor. If she presents herself in public as a careless slob, she fails to support him in his calling.

From verse 23, we receive a little insight into the particular household to which this woman belongs. Evidently, her husband is a respected leader in the community. Whether church elder or city councilman, it doesn't matter. He is a pillar in the community. He takes the time to lead, because his household is in order and he has a wife who effectively manages the estate (1 Tim. 3:4–5). The social order cracks when women lead in the state; and this sort of thing happens when families disintegrate and fathers abdicate (Is. 3:12). Everything turns on its head. Without men to lead and women to manage the household economies, both churches and civil governments will hardly bear the strains. Unrest, instability, and constant dissension ensue. What God gives us in this passage is a well-balanced social system that really functions well.

Family Discussion Questions:

1. Who is responsible for providing the spiritual training in the home? Who is primarily responsible? Who is responsible for providing the clothing for the household?

2. What does the Greek word *Kosmio* mean in reference to clothing?

3. Is it wrong for women to lead in the gates? What is happening to a society where women must lead in the church and in the state?

PART 330 ~ A HOPEFUL OUTLOOK ON LIFE
Proverbs 31:24–25

*She makes fine linen, and sells it; and delivers girdles unto the
merchant.
Strength and honor are her clothing; and she shall rejoice in time to
come.*

The world is filled with investors, government officials,
marketers, and middle men; but the people who are most
important in the economy are the producers! Too often, these
folks do not receive the commendation they deserve. These are
the farmers, fishermen, builders, and manufacturers. Because
of government subsidies, debt-based corporate economies,
and price controls in the present economy, it has become
exceedingly difficult for the small household economy as
described here to survive. But these productive household
economies always constitute the backbone of a healthy
economy. They may not take front page billing in the business
section of the newspapers, but without them, there would be
no food, no clothing, and no homes for the marketers, the
investors, and the government officials to purchase.

Some people will command respect because of their position,
and some because of their character. The woman described
here commands respect by her character and her works. In the
perceptions of the community around her, she stands forty feet
tall! Every year, she steadily grows in faith, patience, wisdom,
love, and joy. She has the strength to withstand a hundred
difficult spiritual, emotional, or financial trials without giving
in to bitterness and depression.

Moreover, this woman looks forward to the future with hopeful
and joyful expectation. Without an optimistic outlook towards
the future, very little may be accomplished in the present. If
our physical and spiritual efforts for the kingdom of God were
of no value whatsoever, how motivated would we be to pursue
anything at all? Today, men are moving from materialism to
escapism because they are realizing they have so little to live for.

Earthly economies rely on hopeful expectations, as does every effort expended for God's kingdom. So this woman—above all women—must have an eternal hope in the resurrection of Christ and the final perfecting of all things. The works of her hands are not wasted because she invests in people who will live to the glory of God in eternity!

During the decline of humanist empires, men always lose hope in the future. The materials they worshiped fail to save them from economic collapse and political disintegration. But this is not the case for those whose hope is in the resurrection of Christ (1 Cor. 15:19–20). Where there is solid hope for the future, there is faith to build economies, have children, and pass a faith on to those children.

Family Discussion Questions:

1. What are the traits used to describe this woman's character?

2. How might we remain optimistic in the work that we do in this world? What gives you the motivation to get to work on a Monday morning? Do we slip into the traps of materialism and escapism?

PART 331 ~ THE USE OF HER TONGUE
Proverbs 31:26

She opens her mouth with wisdom; and in her tongue is the law of kindness.

There is no more important area of life to master than the use of the tongue, and it is no less important in the home. This woman has learned the incredibly difficult skill of using her tongue with wisdom, being careful not to talk endlessly over the phone or in person about unimportant things. When she does open her mouth to speak, it is a well-constructed idea intended for the edification of others. She understands that in the multitude of words there is no lack of sin (Prov. 10:19), so her words are not laced with worry, faithlessness, pride, and contentiousness. When she sins in the home, she is quick to use her tongue to humbly confess her transgressions and restore her relationships with her husband and children.

Seeing this woman is governed by the law of kindness, how is it that Rudyard Kipling would take the position that "The female of the species is more deadly than the male"?[45] In this famous poem, he writes of the woman, "Unprovoked and awful charges—even so the she-bear fights, speech that drips, corrodes, and poisons—even so the cobra bites." Will this be the natural pattern observed in the life of every woman? Obviously, it is not the case of the woman described in this chapter of whom we read, "In her tongue is the law of kindness." By nature, a woman is geared to defend her children and her home. But in the proper social context, it is the primary responsibility of men to defend the home and speak with the enemies in the gates (Neh. 4:14; Ps. 127:4–5). Only in the exceptional case will Jael drive a tent peg through the temple of an enemy general (Judg. 4:21). The normative principle by which this woman operates in the home is kindness—she does not excel in her feminine gifts when she is driving tent pegs through the temples of enemy generals. This is not what beautifies the woman. It is her habitual, daily kindness that warms the home and the hearts of those that reside there. Her default setting is kindness. When guests leave the home after enjoying this woman's hospitality they remark, "I have never met a kinder woman! She was so considerate of our every need."

But for many women it is most difficult to maintain this demeanor with their own children. The little ones may try her patience with disobedience, slothfulness, bickering, and an ungrateful spirit. Of course, all these things amount to sin in the lives of her children. By faith, she must address that sin over and over again. It is faith that enables her to retain a spirit of kindness even in the discipline. She must lace her corrections with kindness. Never forgetting to administer grace in the correction, she will point out that there is a Savior who saves children from these dreadful sins. As with most

45 Rudyard Kipling, "The Female of the Species"

mothers, she will face the temptation to strike the rock as Moses did in the wilderness. But anger and impatience will accomplish nothing fruitful.

Affirmation and kindness should make up the general atmosphere in which we relate to our children. If our only interaction with our children involves correction and rebuke, there is little encouragement there. Throughout the day, mothers especially should affirm their children hundreds of times with kind words, grateful pronouncements, prayer blessings, and sweet commendations. If the environment is affirming, then the stage is well set for moments of correction that will follow here and there throughout the day.

Parents must inculcate this character trait into their daughters from a very early age. By nature, our daughters will want to use their tongues to hurt others. Whereas boys try to dominate by physical force, girls will often resort to emotional manipulation and domination by the wrong use of the tongue. Ungodly social systems arrange human relationships according to the wrong principles, and we see this everywhere today. Thus, the competitive, egalitarian view of men and women drives these sinful patterns in the home. This is no way to arrange a Christian household; therefore, we must train our daughters every day to speak graciously, and to be careful not to hurt others by the words they say. If we hope to have beautiful daughters who will manage their homes by the law of kindness in years to come, we must invest hundreds and thousands of hours training them in this vital area.

Family Discussion Questions:

1. What does it mean to speak with wisdom?

2. How does a mother speak kindly to her children?

3. How might the women in our household improve the use of the tongue? Can you detect any worry, faithlessness, contentiousness, and emotional manipulation in the words that you use?

PART 332 ~ A COMPETENT HOUSEHOLD MANAGER
Proverbs 31:27

She looks well to the ways of her household, and eats not the bread of idleness.

The twenty-seventh verse contains a summary statement of everything said about the virtuous woman to this point. She is a terrific *oikos-despoteo* or household manager. She is the most loyal, the most competent, and the most committed steward of a household economy you could find anywhere on planet earth.

How might our daughters prepare now to "look well to the ways of the household?" Unfortunately, most colleges and universities are not interested in producing young ladies who are committed to this economic outlook. This is not to say that they cannot provide some valuable knowledge and skills. But the preparation we seek for our daughters must actually yield the successful launch of godly, productive households. If your daughter had a very good education, by the time she was twenty-six years old, she might know the derivative of a cosine. She might have learned how Freudian psychology differs from Skinner's, and who Rome fought in the Punic Wars. No doubt she would understand that Plato asserts ideal forms as an absolute and eternal reality of which the phenomena of the world are a transitory reflection. She would have some understanding of how pinocytic vesicles function in an amoeba. And, of course, she could parse just about any Latin verb. But more often than not, the average girl will not know how to manage a staff of seven in a home or how to handle a budget of $150,000 per year without running the household into the ground. She won't have a clue how to cook a meal, hire a contractor, and develop and maintain assets; or how to raise children, how to change diapers, how to calm a baby, how to nurture a two-year-old, or how to exercise authority, how to create a budget, how to cut food costs by 40% without increasing her shopping time, or how to train a five-year-old in social skills. She doesn't know the best way to maintain vehicles. She doesn't know how to assess value in products and services. She doesn't know how to decorate a house. She doesn't know how to engage in hospitality with skill, wisdom, and grace. She doesn't know how to look after the ways of her household. But she sure can parse Latin verbs!

Without negating the importance of academic instruction, it is important to remember that education must prepare a woman for life, family relationships and discipleship, and some useful form of work. Biblically speaking, an education must lead to practical dominion work and kingdom building, which includes the cultivation of fruitful relationships in family and church (Tit. 2:3–5; Jam. 1:22–23).

This is not the picture of a young daughter sitting around eating bon-bons, either. That is, she does not eat the "bread of idleness." She is engaged in the household economy as early as four or five years of age, even if she is mopping the floors and feeding the chickens. Of course, the problem with many household economies is that there is very little going on. Therefore, it is incumbent upon fathers and mothers to include more projects under the purview of their household. If some of the projects require college-level training, a father might encourage that with his daughters (without capitulating to ungodly worldviews and social-views upheld by most colleges.) But keep in mind, the goal is to prepare a daughter who will "look well to the ways of her household."

Family Discussion Questions:

1. How might we prepare our daughters to "look well to the ways of their households?" Will colleges and universities help in accomplishing this for us? What part will college play in preparing our daughters for life?

2. Do our daughters eat the "bread of idleness?" As a household, do we have enough worthwhile enterprises going on to keep the household busy? ?

PART 333 ~ COMMENDATIONS FOR A VIRTUOUS WIFE AND MOTHER

Proverbs 31:28

Her children rise up, and call her blessed; her husband also, and he praises her.

Her relationship with her husband and children is a testimony to her character. Her children dearly love her, and her husband provides her with encouraging commendations. This also helps her to be the woman that she is. Typically, it is difficult for a wife to strive to meet the Proverbs 31 vision without a husband who is encouraging her along the way. This is part and parcel of the vision of the godly home.

Children may not understand the full value of their mother's service and love for them until later in their lives. At some point in their lives, they should carefully assess the value of this woman and all she has poured into the household. Then, they will call her blessed, and be a blessing to her. When a grandmother carefully arranges the photographs of her children and grandchildren on her living room wall, she basks in the blessings that God has given to her. These are her blessings. Her life is full and fulfilled because she is a mother and a grandmother. But mostly she is blessed because her children are godly. They fear God and honor their mother when they bless her

Family Discussion Question:

1. Do our children commend their mother as they ought to? Does she receive encouragement from her husband? How might we better show our appreciation for a godly mother and wife in the home?

PART 334 ~ THE FUNDAMENTAL THING
Proverbs 31:29–31

Many daughters have done virtuously, but you excel them all.
Favor is deceitful, and beauty is vain; but a woman that fears the
*   LORD, she shall be praised.*
Give her of the fruit of her hands; and let her own works praise her in
*   the gates.*

Once again, the passage reminds us that what is presented here is a high standard to which all women should aspire. Some women will be stronger in one area and others will excel in another. Thankfully, God's Word provides a standard to which we ought to continually assess ourselves. Comparing ourselves to others or our wives to other women is not helpful. We must always return to Scripture and compare ourselves to the vision of womanhood and manhood that "excels them all!" We run the race and we strive to excel. We may not achieve perfection, but the question that is of essence is, "What is our direction?"

The thirtieth verse is the hundred-carat diamond set in a garland of rubies. It stands out sharply from the rest of the passage. First, however, it is important to remember that King Lemuel's mother is describing the ideal wife for her son. Too many young men are drawn to external beauty and favor when seeking a wife. Charm speaks to graceful mannerisms and beauty describes the woman's facial features and body shape. There is no question that God has created women with a special beauty and the eyes of men such that they will appreciate it. To deny this is to deny reality. Nevertheless, when young men prioritize the externals over the internal, they will marry badly and terrible consequences may ensue. Indeed, the precursor to all the horror of the pre-flood wickedness and violence involved this very thing. It was when the sons of God saw the daughters of men as "beautiful" and attractive (Gen. 6:2) that an ungodly synthesis formed and the wicked Nephilim appeared. This intermarriage with ungodliness was socially devastating and brought about the destruction of the whole world! But many young men from godly homes continue to make this fatal mistake to this day. These young men prioritize the charm, the beauty, the high manners, and apparent intellectual class of unbelieving women, as they choose their spouses. They find them exciting and fun. But they are only looking at the externals. Sadly, they are but superficial men and they will live to pay for it. As this wise mother put it, beauty is fleeting and charm is deceitful. A charming, beautiful woman can turn into an ungrateful, unfaithful, manipulating witch over the years. What will happen when she faces emotional and financial trials? How does she deal with conflict in the home and in the community? When she faces the trials of life, all her charm begins to fade away and she turns into a sour, discontented dripping faucet. Also, it would be well if our young people would keep in mind that age brings with it the cares and concerns of life, and physical deterioration inevitably comes with the years. Simply compare a hundred pictures of men and women at twenty years of age, forty years of age, sixty years of age, and eighty years of age, and you will see the physical changes in stark contrast. Some women age gracefully and retain some beauty in the face because of internal joy and peace. But there are also some beautiful young women, whose beauty will fade in their later years as their faces fold up into ugly lines of anger, bitterness, and disappointment.

What matters most in the choice of a spouse then, is the fear of Yahweh. This is where the book began and this is where it will end (Prov. 1:7). The ever-present and ever-significant reality in the cognition of this excellent woman is God Himself. To fear God is to believe in His existence as the most important reality. It is to believe in His power, wisdom, and sovereignty as He reveals Himself in the Word and to respond with the only appropriate response—awe-inspired reverence. According to the metaphysic of the God-fearing woman, God is the ultimate "elephant in the room." This being the case, that virtuous woman will live in the constant awareness of the reality of God. Every other consideration is dwarfed in reference to the significance of God. Everything else takes second and third place.

Both the Old and New Testaments bear out the universal truth of the proposition that the fear of the Lord is the everlasting Gospel of Christ (Rev. 14:6–7) and it is basic to human relationships. Where there is no fear of God, there will be no significant honor for fathers and mothers, husbands and wives, or elders and magistrates (Eph. 5:21–22; 1 Pet. 2:17, 5:5–7). Where there is no reverent fear of God, there can be no faith and certainly no love for Him (1 Pet. 1:17–22). The fear of God is basic to our relationship with God and with others.

This woman is a true believer. All others who consider the existence of God, who are not in right relationship with Him, will seek to suppress the truth of God in unrighteousness (Rom. 1:18). Whatever fear they experience is quickly replaced by rebellion and willful, blind ignorance. But the woman who fears God is happy to live in the fear of God because she is in right relationship with Him through Christ (Rom. 8:1–2).

The woman depicted in this chapter is no great statesman or military captain. She will never score very high in the estimation of those who chronicle the rise and fall of the great empires of men. She weaves cloth and makes linen. She is not interested in tooting her own horn and she isn't particularly keen on seeing her name in the papers. But the strength of her reputation is undeniable to anybody who knows her. Within communities where people live together for thirty or forty years at a time, and where they manage to avoid the transience of the modern city life, people will come to know each other. After awhile, the true character of those who reside in the community is known by all, including the "Proverbs 31 woman." "Now there is a woman who is honest, industrious, nurturing, and kind," they will say. "There is a woman who fears God and has lived it for forty years in this community." As her name is mentioned among the elders in the church, a silent awe falls upon the men. They consider her contributions, her care for the poor, her faithful children, and the wise counsel she provides for the younger women in the congregation, and they know that their community would be terribly impoverished without her. For a moment, they bow their heads and thank God for the ministry of this woman. The value of a person in a community has little to do with political position, financial wealth, and popular fame, but has a great deal to do with the fear of God, wise speech, kind words, industrious work, charitable offerings, and careful management of a home. May God help us as we cultivate these things in our own lives and the lives of our children!

Family Discussion Questions:

1. What is the fundamental lesson of the book of Proverbs?

2. Why did the sons of God marry the daughters of men in the book of Genesis?

3. Why are young men given to looking on the outward appearance instead of on the heart?

4. How would you know if a woman feared God?

5. How is a person's reputation and value established in a community? Is it merely a matter of political influence and fame?

INDEXES

~

SUBJECT INDEX   277

SCRIPTURE INDEX   291

TOPICAL INDEX   301

SUBJECT INDEX

A

abomination
    I: 32, 57, 71, 107, 116, 147, 176,
        234, 236, 256
    II: 10, 16, 17, 123, 124, 139, 179,
        180
    III: 15, 141, 148, 213

abortion
    I: 8, 32, 58, 79, 171, 224, 232
    II: 17, 27, 47, 121, 216
    III: 32, 33, 50, 64, 104, 114, 137,
        199, 251, 261

Absalom
    II: 52
    III: 248

Adam (first man)
    I: 17, 46, 90
    II: 10, 157, 243, 245
    III: 71, 193

Adams, Abigail
    I: 90, 116
    III: 260

adultery
    I: 13, 19, 62, 64, 105, 224, 228
    II: 17, 191, 203
    III: 14, 149, 181, 198, 199, 210,
        225, 234, 245, 289

advice. *See also councel*
    I: 100, 169, 207, 210
    II: 69, 132, 133, 145, 172, 223
    III: 73, 170, 203, 204, 224, 245,
        246, 250, 289

advisor. *See also councelor*
    I: 138
    II: 132, 133
    III: 159, 248

Africa
    I: 180, 216
    II: 93, 209, 243
    III: 25, 139, 160, 179

agenda
    I: 11, 33, 40, 58, 244
    II: 87, 162, 176, 184, 195, 196,
        211
    III: 7, 15, 181, 182, 277

Ahab (King)
    I: 93
    II: 149, 214, 216, 224
    III: 13

AIDS
    II: 169, 196, 238

alcohol:
    I: 143, 168, 172
    II: 12, 94, 113, 114, 115, 169,
        232, 233, 243, 244, 245, 246
    III: 80, 119, 148, 247, 248, 250

American Presidents
  Adams, John
    I: 90, 116, 129
    III: 88, 152, 260

  Bush, George W.
    II: 54
    III: 112

  Clinton, Bill
    II: 90

  Johnson, Lyndon B.
    I: 254
    II: 62, 188

  Monroe, James
    III: 88

  Obama, Barack
    II: 54
    III: 25, 133

Roosevelt, Franklin Delano
  II: 188
  III: 206
Washington, George
  I: 93, 109
  II: 54, 104
  III: 88, 244
anarchy
  II: 17, 19, 45, 85, 146
  III: 138
anger, angry
  II: 5, 6, 11, 12, 30, 31, 32, 37, 43,
    47, 51, 57, 84, 91, 92, 93, 101,
    102, 104, 114, 119, 138, 139,
    144, 163, 165, 166, 170, 171,
    172, 175, 176, 180, 186, 196,
    197, 211, 213, 223, 226
  III: 50, 89, 103, 104, 119, 124,
    183, 192, 208, 209, 214, 243,
    267, 272
anxious, anxiety
  I: 244
  II: 139, 193
  III: 7, 156, 222
application
  I: 5, 23, 83, 118, 226
  III: 5, 10, 18, 26, 53, 72, 108, 118,
    128, 140, 143, 202, 219, 220
apostasy, apostasies
  II: 3, 82, 121, 130, 168, 189, 222,
    237
  III: 146
Aquinas, St. Thomas
  II: 201, 231
Aristotle
  I: 264
  II: 190, 191, 231
atone, atonement
  I: 8, 52
  II: 59, 158, 246
  III: 31, 154

B
bitter, bitterness
  I: 46, 47, 95, 139, 164, 172, 185,
    195, 243, 256
  II: 26, 30, 31, 43, 56, 75, 132,
    139, 170, 180
  III: 31, 35, 60, 89, 105, 106, 107,
    207, 230, 236, 264, 272
Bonhoeffer, Dietrich
  I: 38
British Isles
  England
    I: 74, 162, 180
    II: 68, 174, 223
    III: 51, 88, 174, 177, 178, 238
  Ireland
    I: 93, 162
  Scotland
    I: 74, 196
    III: 22
Bush, George W. *See American Presidents*

C
Cain
  I: 95, 234
  II: 52, 58
  III: 19, 108, 189
Canada. *See North American Countries*
cancer
  II: 115, 118
  III: 39, 40
capital punishment
  II: 161
  III: 18, 28, 55, 169
Castro, Fidel
  I: 12
  III: 8, 84, 139, 225
character
  I: 2, 3, 7, 49, 61, 63, 74, 82, 90,
    91, 100, 105, 109, 114, 119,
    120, 124, 125, 127, 133, 134,
    138, 141, 153, 162, 171, 177,

179, 180, 181, 182, 189, 192,
193, 206, 209, 216, 219, 220,
221, 222, 224, 225, 226, 262
II: 2, 17, 36, 37, 39, 40, 41, 53,
60, 65, 76, 79, 81, 84, 88, 90,
91, 96, 97, 108, 113, 116, 125,
127, 129, 132, 137, 154, 156,
159, 185, 192, 194, 204, 205,
216, 220, 221, 222, 229, 237,
239, 242, 246
III: 2, 11, 14, 30, 38, 42, 44, 56,
69, 76, 79, 80, 94, 102, 114,
123, 124, 127, 131, 134, 138,
139, 147, 150, 153, 165, 166,
177, 179, 192, 193, 199, 203,
217, 227, 235, 236, 241, 262,
264, 265, 267, 270, 273
charity
I: 93, 112, 121, 208, 223
II: 84, 99, 164, 187, 197, 198, 199
III: 150, 172, 173, 254
church
I: 4, 5, 7, 14, 16, 19, 32, 44, 46,
53, 54, 55, 56, 57, 59, 62, 66,
73, 82, 83, 86, 87, 95, 101,
113, 115, 124, 127, 132, 151,
164, 174, 188, 206, 207, 217,
218, 229, 231, 234, 237, 238,
240, 241, 247, 248, 252, 257,
261, 262
II: 4, 13, 24, 26, 29, 30, 31, 42,
43, 45, 48, 49, 57, 73, 75, 76,
78, 79, 80, 84, 85, 86, 104,
116, 119, 120, 121, 149, 150,
152, 154, 164, 166, 167, 168,
175, 177, 179, 180, 183, 185,
187, 188, 189, 193, 194, 197,
211, 213, 234, 240, 242. See
also deacon, elder, pastor
III:4, 8, 9, 14, 22, 31, 35, 49, 53,
54, 57, 59, 62, 77, 83, 84, 89,
93, 94, 104, 105, 110, 111,
112, 113, 115, 119, 121, 124,
132, 140, 150, 169, 170, 174,
178, 184, 187, 190, 194, 213,

219, 223, 235, 236, 237, 239,
240, 248, 251, 257, 258, 260,
261, 262, 263, 269, 273
Clinton, Bill. *See American Presidents*
commandment
I: 10, 60, 62, 77, 94, 168, 231
II: 97, 98, 136, 137, 151, 170,
182, 191, 213, 245
III: 10, 14, 35, 196, 219, 220, 224,
226
communism. *See also Marxism*
I: 224
III: 51
communist
I: 97, 224, 232
II: 186, 200
III: 8, 30, 85, 139, 159
corporation
II: 78
III: 55, 133, 134, 193, 253, 257
counsel. *See also advice*
I: 14, 57, 84, 113, 115, 140, 141,
150, 238, 240, 251, 253
II: 7, 13, 19, 36, 57, 69, 70, 102,
103, 116, 117, 121, 125, 132,
133, 134, 183, 211, 223, 227,
238
III: 11, 13, 14, 42, 90, 103, 109,
111, 144, 274
counselor. *See also advisors*
I: 172
II: 69, 72, 145, 207, 223
III: 236
courtship
I: 246
II: 23, 24
III: 234
covenant
I: 19, 260
II: 103
III: 89, 108, 128, 129, 175, 176,
194, 198

D

Daniel
  I: 93
  II: 170
  III: 13, 71
Darwin, Charles. *See also evolution*
  I: *129, 177*
  II: 110. *See also* evolution
  III: 40, 41, 68, 81, 82, 83, 128,
    129, 157
David (King)
  I: 3, 7, 116, 128, 182
  II: 3, 39
  III: 3, 16, 19, 79, 103, 128, 152,
    178, 195, 199, 221, 248, 253,
    255, 260
deacon
  III: 14
debt
  I: 31, 53, 115, 125, 134, 136, 138,
    149, 169, 208
  II: 50, 65, 80, 95, 97, 124, 131,
    132, 155, 185, 190, 194, 195,
    197, 212, 213
  III: 10, 34, 37, 38, 114, 146, 147,
    148, 159, 199, 257, 260, 264
depravity
  I: 107
  II: 8, 20, 157, 160, 201
  III: 116, 124, 242
destruction
  I: 3, 14, 68, 72, 75, 94, 97, 98, 99,
    101, 104, 106, 109, 110, 111,
    122, 123, 135, 156, 159, 160,
    215, 216, 226, 232, 238
  II: 3, 12, 14, 20, 21, 27, 29, 30,
    31, 47, 48, 51, 63, 65, 67, 83,
    93, 111, 115, 131, 136, 157,
    160, 166, 184, 189, 213
  III: 3, 7, 11, 67, 84, 99, 104, 124,
    125, 138, 183, 199, 210, 225,
    250, 251, 272

devotions. *See also worship, family
    worship*
  I: 7, 14, 15, 16
  II: 53, 61, 154, 231
  III: 128
Dewey, John
  I: 4, 169
  II: 3
  III: 3, 40, 153
discipleship
  I: 3, 4, 39, 90, 257, 262
  II: 3, 4, 21, 77, 174, 198, 208,
    234, 235, 240, 241
  III: 3, 4, 108, 112, 165, 269
discipline
  I: 51, 133, 182, 217, 246, 263
  II: 46, 63, 64, 100, 116, 207, 218,
    225, 226, 227
  III: 27, 93, 123, 128, 194, 197,
    266, 289
discretion
  I: 3, 7, 18, 29, 30, 46, 119
  II: 3, 91, 92
  III: 3, 224
divorce
  I: 19, 63, 102, 105, 115, 124, 125,
    139, 144, 206, 211, 250, 258
  II: 95, 120, 121, 135, 159, 192,
    196, 214, 237
  III: 9, 94, 108, 137, 142, 149, 164,
    181, 198, 199, 214, 225, 255
doctrine
  I: 35, 82, 159, 201
  II: 173, 213
  III: 11, 157, 208, 213, 229
Dostoyevski, Fyodor
  II: 111

E

economics
  I: 2, 112, 113, 138, 169, 179, 264
  II: 2, 18, 36, 51, 120, 187, 195,
    200, 234
  III: 2, 43, 132, 202, 253

economy
    I: 107, 108, 109, 112, 124, 138,
        158, 210, 224, 262
    II: 35, 36, 54, 55, 65, 78, 127,
        129, 155, 156, 157, 184, 206,
        212, 213, 215, 233, 236
    III: 8, 9, 32, 33, 34, 55, 56, 111,
        131, 168, 169, 180, 223, 238,
        254, 255, 256, 257, 258, 259,
        260, 264, 268, 269
egalitarian, egalitarianism
    I: 73
    II: 67, 90
    III: 142, 254, 267
elder
    I: 114, 240
    III: 113, 190, 202, 235, 236, 248,
        263
England. *See British Isles*
epistemology
    I: 2
    II: 2, 234
    III: 2, 262
Esther
    I: 93, 205
    II: 176
    III: 13, 190, 250, 296
ethical, ethics
    I: 2, 17, 97, 98, 131, 161, 204,
        243, 244, 245
    II: 2, 8, 85, 94, 135, 156, 185,
        217, 234
    III: 2, 7, 58, 75, 82, 83, 136, 140,
        141, 177, 202, 210, 213, 234,
        247, 262
Europe
    I: 127, 152, 180, 215, 216, 257
    II: 97, 110, 122, 162, 233
    III: 73, 88, 114, 146, 174, 179
European Countries
  France
    I: 74, 116, 216
    II: 68
    III: 88, 238

Germany
    I: 41, 162, 180, 216, 223
    III: 29, 30, 150, 153
  Switzerland
    I: 74, 162
    III: 173
evolution. *See also Darwin, Charles*
    II: 237
    III: 51, 82, 150, 174, 227
exhort, exhortation
    I: 196
    II: 14, 152, 183, 193, 206, 207
    III: 46, 251

F

faith
    I: 2, 3, 17, 20, 26, 36, 39, 44, 74,
        83, 86, 87, 91, 98, 153, 159,
        162, 163, 170, 171, 177, 187,
        192, 197, 201, 202, 207, 209,
        213, 214, 215, 216, 229, 232,
        248, 253, 255
    II: 2, 3, 12, 13, 15, 20, 24, 37, 38,
        67, 71, 82, 110, 121, 139, 163,
        165, 171, 179, 181, 185, 193,
        194, 200, 207, 208, 222, 227,
        237, 240
    III: 2, 3, 17, 22, 23, 41, 43, 46,
        48, 51, 53, 93, 94, 104, 106,
        107, 112, 113, 121, 122, 131,
        132, 133, 134, 140, 146, 147,
        162, 163, 168, 169, 170, 171,
        172, 174, 178, 183, 184, 193,
        194, 199, 202, 204, 211, 219,
        223, 225, 240, 258, 264, 265,
        266, 273
faithful, faithfulness
    I: 21, 25, 36, 74, 83, 84, 113, 133,
        149, 166, 173, 174, 180, 182,
        183, 189, 191, 212
    II: 57, 77, 78, 96, 108, 119, 120,
        121, 194, 196
    III: 31, 44, 46, 48, 49, 50, 56, 57,
        107, 123, 130, 131, 132, 165,
        194, 195, 253, 274

family worship. *See also devotions*
  I: 16, 37, 38, 171, 196, 225, 264
  II: 21, 104, 154, 227
  III: 146
fear:
  I: 2, 3, 8, 9, 14, 15, 16, 24, 25, 29,
    30, 37, 39, 40, 41, 61, 63, 65,
    73, 74, 80, 82, 85, 86, 87, 91,
    102, 103, 104, 105, 108, 110,
    112, 113, 118, 131, 138, 140,
    152, 155, 161, 169, 171, 177,
    180, 185, 191, 202, 209, 213,
    214, 215, 217, 222, 227, 228,
    229, 232, 238, 244, 246, 248,
    255, 261, 264, 265
  II: 2, 3, 10, 11, 12, 13, 14, 20, 28,
    68, 83, 93, 98, 105, 108, 109,
    110, 111, 113, 114, 122, 130,
    132, 133, 136, 139, 142, 153,
    163, 175, 189, 190, 191, 194,
    196, 216, 225, 226, 227, 229,
    230, 232, 239
  III: 2, 3, 7, 10, 25, 26, 62, 73, 115,
    120, 134, 135, 136, 152, 153,
    155, 156, 174, 175, 187, 188,
    194, 198, 211, 212, 213, 234,
    251, 270, 272, 273, 274, 289
fear of God
  I: 2, 3, 8, 9, 41, 61, 63, 65, 74, 82,
    85, 86, 87, 105, 108, 112, 113,
    118, 140, 155, 161, 169, 180,
    185, 202, 209, 214, 215, 222,
    227, 229, 232, 238, 244, 246,
    248, 264, 265
  II: 2, 3, 10, 13, 20, 98, 110, 142,
    153, 190, 191, 230, 232, 239
  III: 2, 3, 120, 136, 153, 155, 156,
    187, 188, 194, 211, 213, 234,
    251, 273, 274, 289
fear of the LORD
  II: 11, 105, 190, 229, 230
fool
  I: 13, 15, 35, 67, 75, 92, 93, 94,
    96, 99, 102, 103, 119, 123,
    124, 140, 141, 172, 173, 186,

    191, 192, 193, 202, 204, 227,
    230, 242, 249, 251, 253
  II: 41, 44, 45, 46, 48, 52, 53, 55,
    57, 59, 63, 64, 81, 90, 115,
    116, 222, 223
  III: 12, 13, 14, 16, 67, 68, 69,
    72, 73, 74, 75, 76, 77, 78, 79,
    81, 83, 84, 85, 103, 104, 128,
    129, 140, 170, 188, 189, 191,
    204, 235, 236, 247
foolish, foolishness
  I: 26, 33, 39, 67, 70, 76, 80, 82,
    87, 88, 89, 90, 94, 96, 101,
    103, 106, 114, 127, 137, 148,
    164, 173, 177, 178, 184, 186,
    191, 210, 211, 220, 222, 227,
    230, 233, 242, 249, 250, 253,
    262, 263
  II: 32, 35, 36, 44, 46, 53, 56, 57,
    63, 64, 69, 83, 90, 91, 94, 101,
    130, 134, 142, 171, 204, 206,
    238
  III: 14, 15, 16, 36, 68, 72, 74, 76,
    77, 79, 81, 83, 84, 96, 112,
    128, 129, 150, 162, 188, 189,
    191, 192, 234, 238
fornication
  I: 19, 46, 62, 64, 66, 90, 172, 193
  II: 17, 62, 94, 163, 196, 203, 229
  III: 33, 34, 124, 141, 142, 148,
    158, 164, 171, 179, 194, 202,
    225, 245
foundation
  I: 2, 3, 8, 77, 102, 105, 213, 214,
    230, 232, 233
  II: 2, 3, 20, 195
  III: 2, 3, 54, 65, 73, 178, 181, 199
France. *See European Countries*
French Revolution. *See also Robespi-
  erre, Maximilien*
  I: 160
  III: 25, 26
friend
  I: 38, 53, 54, 100, 114, 143, 150,
    158, 191

II: 43, 49, 50, 51, 64, 69, 80, 86,
120, 160, 161, 199, 203, 228
III: 19, 32, 50, 57, 66, 91, 105,
107, 109, 110, 116, 118, 121,
122, 161

friendship
I: 53, 54, 117
II: 42, 49, 50, 51, 64, 80, 81, 120,
160, 211
III: 31, 32, 56, 57, 105, 107, 110,
111, 118, 120, 121, 168, 171,
183

G

generation
I: 25, 35, 61, 76, 86, 105, 162,
187, 196, 210, 215, 216, 246,
254, 255, 262
II: 15, 31, 36, 37, 49, 65, 82, 95,
96, 97, 99, 103, 107, 110, 114,
133, 147, 156, 168, 185, 189,
190, 200, 204, 213, 215, 235,
238, 243, 246
III: 9, 25, 26, 38, 64, 67, 88, 112,
113, 114, 119, 129, 130, 131,
132, 137, 140, 150, 152, 157,
158, 164, 171, 175, 176, 199,
201, 207, 224, 225, 226, 227,
245, 247, 255

Germany. *See European Countries*
Golding, William
II: 204
Gospel
I: 6, 5, 33, 83, 124, 125, 163, 171,
191, 193, 194, 197, 212, 260
II: 4, 11, 12, 24, 28, 55, 77, 82,
88, 93, 114, 115, 122, 126,
168, 180
III: 4, 62, 63, 73, 78, 140, 147,
151, 194, 211, 219, 230, 251,
273

government
I: 2, 12, 33, 112, 118, 123, 124,
125, 136, 138, 144, 145, 149,
169, 171, 179, 185, 205, 207,
208, 210, 232, 255

II: 2, 11, 14, 19, 36, 47, 52, 54,
55, 56, 57, 61, 62, 65, 67, 68,
72, 78, 79, 81, 103, 104, 112,
114, 115, 123, 124, 129, 131,
140, 143, 147, 148, 153, 155,
174, 183, 188, 192, 194, 195,
198, 199, 205, 206, 213, 214,
215, 216, 224, 225, 234
III: 2, 11, 12, 18, 19, 26, 39, 42,
51, 55, 71, 77, 110, 111, 132,
133, 134, 137, 138, 139, 147,
149, 157, 158, 159, 166, 178,
179, 180, 181, 182, 185, 192,
193, 195, 212, 213, 227, 237,
247, 250, 252, 253, 260, 261,
262, 263, 264

Greek
I: 75, 264
II: 36, 190
III: 69, 71, 253, 262, 263
guilt
I: 47, 52, 90, 131
II: 11, 31, 59, 144, 157, 158, 182,
207, 245, 246
III: 90, 97, 115, 136, 148, 161

H

habit
I: 33, 98, 160
II: 69, 91, 101, 131, 164, 237
III: 38
hate
I: 12, 35, 57, 59, 73, 74, 78, 79,
83, 95, 128, 176, 183, 206,
219, 258
II: 8, 25, 48, 87, 89, 90, 116, 133
III: 28, 31, 53, 90, 95, 99, 160,
177, 187, 189, 193, 290
Hebrew
I: 85, 98, 128, 151, 171, 173
II: 7, 27, 180
III: 60, 252
Hemingway, Ernest
I: 70, 190
II: 245

Henry, Patrick
  I: 93, 129
  III: 137, 152
heretic
  III: 136
 Arius
  II: 201
 Pelagius
  II: 201
Herod
  I: 93
  II: 149, 216
  III: 136, 157, 254
Hirsch, E.D.
  I: 169
Hitler, Adolf
  I: 12, 38, 93, 129, 203, 206
  III: 13, 22, 30, 79, 80
homosexual
  I: 105, 222
  II: 47, 143, 157, 170, 179, 180
  III: 63, 112, 137, 140, 141, 142,
    150, 213, 214, 234
homosexuality
  I: 90, 193, 224
  II: 17, 27, 47, 48, 87, 169, 179,
    180
  III: 63, 94, 141, 142, 149, 150,
    173, 214, 225, 226
honor
  I: 10, 28, 43, 80, 116, 134, 136,
    154, 173, 174, 187, 206, 207,
    230, 231, 250, 264, 265
  II: 12, 19, 32, 33, 36, 40, 42, 45,
    67, 86, 109, 111, 112, 113,
    135, 137, 150, 156, 173, 174,
    186, 190, 235
  III: 26, 67, 68, 69, 79, 80, 96, 157,
    168, 196, 199, 206, 208, 219,
    227, 230, 243, 245, 255, 263,
    264, 270, 273
humanism
  I: 17, 82, 129
  II: 68, 103
  III: 208, 215, 217

humanist
  I: 9, 75, 79, 96, 113, 135, 152,
    171, 182, 218, 265
  II: 15, 41, 62, 68, 110, 111, 153,
    174, 175, 187, 201
  III: 150, 170, 172, 199, 206, 219,
    225, 226, 265
humility
  I: 43, 69, 74, 127, 130, 134, 164,
    175, 185, 186, 201, 209, 231,
    264
  II: 22, 24, 35, 60, 67, 73, 102,
    104, 130, 132, 133, 174, 187,
    190, 191, 211
  III: 40, 127, 156, 162, 163, 170,
    187, 204, 214, 215, 231, 232,
    237, 290
husband
  I: 19, 23, 24, 51, 64, 67, 116, 130,
    131, 133, 184, 185, 188, 257
  II: 69, 78, 94, 151, 159, 165, 166
  III: 9, 30, 33, 49, 61, 103, 109,
    119, 120, 173, 179, 236, 237,
    243, 252, 253, 254, 255, 257,
    260, 261, 262, 263, 266, 270

I

India
  I: 162
  II: 122
  III: 251
innocent
  I: 11, 57, 58, 62, 132, 232
  II: 14, 31, 85, 152, 157, 224, 226
  III: 12, 18, 21, 160, 165, 173, 189,
    190, 191, 202, 217
Ireland. *See British Isles*

J

Johnson, Lyndon B. *See American
  Presidents*
Joseph
  I: 219
  II: 150
  III: 13, 19, 21, 28, 44, 48, 250,
    253

judge
   I: 29, 84, 86, 141, 142, 189, 235
   II: 17, 18, 72, 74, 166, 167, 220,
      223, 230, 246
   III: 28, 29, 69, 72, 73, 74, 95, 149,
      166, 167, 214, 250, 259

K

Kennedy (family)
   I: 254
   II: 162
Keynes, John Maynard
   I: 72, 108, 169
   II: 195, 200
  Keyensian
   II: 195
kingdom
   I: 8, 33, 101, 149, 154, 161, 216,
      221, 228, 234, 262
   II: 32, 35, 66, 115, 123, 146, 150,
      172, 183, 193, 199, 208, 229,
      235
   III: 15, 22, 31, 47, 78, 108, 113,
      150, 180, 238, 248, 264, 265,
      269
knowledge
   I: 5, 1, 8, 13, 15, 30, 222, 227
   II: 1, 20
   III: 1

L

law
   I: 8, 9, 10, 17, 21, 35, 44, 58, 60,
      62, 64, 72, 73, 74, 76, 84, 88,
      93, 97, 106, 138, 147, 148,
      149, 153, 170, 173, 193, 194,
      223, 225, 228, 239, 254
   II: 8, 17, 18, 19, 32, 45, 47, 56,
      66, 85, 88, 93, 95, 100, 101,
      112, 122, 124, 128, 135, 138,
      146, 150, 157, 162, 182, 190,
      205, 206, 208, 217, 227, 230
   III: 14, 18, 21, 23, 25, 26, 27, 28,
      37, 48, 49, 55, 66, 72, 122,
      123, 140, 141, 142, 145, 146,
      148, 149, 150, 161, 174, 177,

      181, 201, 202, 207, 210, 211,
      212, 218, 230, 246, 247, 251,
      260, 265, 266, 267
liberal
   I: 121
   II: 27, 161, 195, 198, 200
   III: 64, 72, 104, 142
loan
   I: 53, 134
   II: 99, 131, 194
   III: 146, 147, 206

M

marry, marriage
   I: 8, 19, 51, 52, 96, 105, 113, 115,
      172, 185, 192, 211, 251, 257,
      258
   II: 29, 35, 61, 95, 96, 135, 142,
      157, 159, 166, 185, 214, 237
   III: 17, 33, 34, 61, 63, 66, 98, 112,
      140, 179, 183, 198, 199, 200,
      202, 230, 234, 254, 255, 271,
      274, 291
Marxism. *See also communism*
   I: 40, 145, 149, 243
   II: 67, 79, 90, 213, 216
   III: 25, 26, 43
Marx, Karl. *See also communism*
   I: 129, 169
   II: 110, 186, 200
   III: 84
materialism
   I: 90, 98, 110, 192, 258, 260
   II: 49
   III: 150, 225, 264, 265
materialist, materialistic
   I: 82, 129, 196, 218, 257
   II: 35, 57, 71, 171, 185, 200
   III: 43, 221, 227, 257
metaphysics
   I: 2
   II: 2, 234
   III: 2, 70, 262
Monroe, James. *See American Presidents*

Montessori, Dr. Maria
I: 169
Mordecai
I: 205
II: 176
III: 97
murder
I: 12, 45, 58, 79, 130
II: 17, 85, 112, 121, 122, 135,
136, 146, 243
III: 14, 18, 19, 28, 55, 66, 67, 69,
84, 124, 158, 161, 202, 250,
251, 254
music
I: 18, 41, 79, 80, 165, 214
II: 120, 135, 136, 194, 233, 240
III: 27, 56, 68, 94, 150, 164, 184,
226
Muslim
I: 216, 224
II: 128
III: 7, 150, 171

N
Nietzsche, Friedrich
I: 177
II: 42, 79
North American Countries
America
I: 4, 3, 74, 112, 127, 144, 145,
149, 152, 179, 180, 181, 205,
208, 216, 255, 257
II: 4, 3, 62, 63, 65, 96, 97, 110,
113, 124, 132, 209, 212, 215,
217, 219, 244
III: 4, 3, 63, 79, 88, 101, 106, 133,
139, 146, 153, 154, 160, 174,
178, 179, 181, 198, 206, 238,
245
United States
I: 4, 102, 162, 213, 216, 254, 257
II: 4, 41, 62, 93, 155, 162, 205,
212, 224
III: 4, 112, 150, 172, 173, 245

Canada
I: 4, 180, 208, 215, 224
III: 173, 174

O
Obama, Barack. *See American Presidents*

P
pastor
I: 3, 82, 172, 173, 177, 187, 188,
238
II: 2, 17, 61, 79, 80, 180, 223
III: 2, 63, 80, 112, 151, 154, 213,
247
Paton, John
I: 196, 197
II: 106, 121
Paul (Apostle)
I: 11, 55, 110, 128, 159, 162, 170,
200, 203, 212, 223, 228, 236,
245, 248, 262, 263
II: 19, 55, 58, 77, 105, 114, 120,
142, 144, 162, 172, 177, 194,
195, 220, 235
III: 8, 43, 48, 58, 59, 62, 78, 81,
84, 89, 99, 101, 132, 144, 156,
171, 222, 254
peace
I: 21, 27, 28, 45, 65, 93, 98, 113,
145, 146, 184, 185, 187, 212,
214, 222, 226, 227, 241, 245,
247, 250, 253
II: 13, 14, 24, 29, 35, 37, 47, 57,
63, 93, 95, 105, 106, 114, 171,
175, 188, 198
III: 9, 12, 20, 43, 61, 62, 70, 113,
135, 187, 235, 237, 242, 243,
272, 291
philosophy
I: 1
II: 1, 46, 201
III: 1, 99, 202

Plato
  I: 4, 9
  II: 3
  III: 3, 268
pleasure
  I: 68, 105, 137, 168, 179, 204,
    233, 251
  II: 39, 142, 152, 168, 169, 170,
    171, 172, 225
  III: 7, 64, 65, 66, 180, 208, 209,
    222
police
  I: 156
  II: 12, 15, 18, 43, 45, 85, 101,
    109, 112, 122, 198
  III: 134, 161, 181, 182, 212
poor
  I: 25, 31, 61, 72, 78, 89, 97, 112,
    116, 120, 156, 160, 161, 162,
    163, 180, 193, 197, 206, 207,
    208, 219, 220, 221, 223, 233,
    243, 244, 245, 246, 255, 257
  II: 38, 39, 40, 42, 53, 62, 67, 79,
    81, 84, 87, 88, 99, 101, 104,
    107, 114, 128, 131, 159, 163,
    164, 166, 168, 186, 187, 188,
    194, 195, 197, 198, 205, 206,
    209, 210, 211, 224, 225, 230,
    244
  III: 21, 22, 56, 66, 70, 139, 143,
    144, 145, 146, 147, 148, 150,
    151, 157, 158, 172, 173, 174,
    185, 186, 190, 193, 194, 195,
    196, 204, 220, 224, 226, 227,
    228, 234, 238, 250, 259, 260,
    261, 274
poverty
  I: 54, 55, 63, 91, 97, 117, 120,
    121, 123, 208
  II: 39, 67, 84, 86, 88, 103, 127,
    169, 177, 185, 187, 188, 206,
    232, 233, 234
  III: 37, 38, 163, 166, 167, 194,
    219, 220, 223, 246, 292

R
relationship
  I: 12, 19, 34, 53, 63, 71, 72, 86,
    96, 100, 114, 117, 118, 139,
    177, 186, 195, 235, 236, 259,
    260
  II: 11, 13, 23, 29, 37, 40, 46, 58,
    69, 74, 75, 84, 106, 109, 115,
    116, 150, 157, 170, 186, 203,
    221, 228, 234, 235, 239, 240
  III: 19, 28, 34, 45, 47, 49, 54, 57,
    91, 92, 96, 105, 106, 135, 143,
    156, 189, 198, 204, 211, 223,
    234, 245, 270, 273
repentance
  I: 20, 22, 34, 49, 58, 59, 83, 84,
    95, 96, 99, 100, 108, 125, 147,
    153, 157, 159, 160, 176, 183,
    188, 207, 229, 254, 256, 258,
    260
  II: 29, 43, 60, 90, 97, 100, 107,
    143, 163, 168, 178, 180, 181,
    182, 189, 192, 193, 211, 213,
    221, 222, 234, 240
  III: 24, 31, 59, 96, 98, 99, 135,
    152, 154, 161, 162, 163, 175,
    183, 184, 190, 198, 204, 214,
    230, 242
rhetoric
  I: 74, 264, 265
  II: 88, 104, 190, 191
  III: 61, 132, 135, 187, 188, 189
riches
  I: 11, 27, 28, 75, 91, 104, 116,
    117, 122, 123, 160, 161, 162,
    210, 211, 233, 244
  II: 25, 81, 91, 95, 96, 156, 163,
    172, 185, 186, 187, 190, 205,
    219
  III: 8, 129, 144, 151, 165, 220,
    292
Robespierre, Maximilien . *See
    also French Revolution*
  III: 26, 97

Roman Catholic
I: 224
II: 128
III: 162

Roosevelt, Franklin Delano.
See American Presidents

Rousseau, Jen-Jacques
I: 4, 9, 169
II: 3, 204
III: 3

Russell, Bertrand
I: 70

Russia
II: 113, 122
III: 30, 104, 158

S

sacrifice
I: 99, 215, 234, 246, 249
II: 9, 35, 123, 151, 152, 179, 180,
185, 186, 244
III: 49, 89, 189, 213

Sanger, Margaret
II: 209, 210

Sartre, Jean-Paul
I: 228, 229
II: 58
III: 156

science, filds of
anthropology
I: 2, 77
II: 2, 234
III: 2
astronomy
I: 77
III: 39, 232
biology
I: 77, 129
II: 190, 230
III: 39, 232
chemistry
I: 3, 41, 77, 152, 245, 264, 265
II: 3, 110, 153, 239
III: 3, 39, 216, 232

genetics
I: 129
physics
I: 77, 191
IIII: 39, 216, 232

Scotland. *See British Isles*

seduce
I: 154
II: 242
III: 179

slave, slavery
I: 33, 124, 125, 127, 130, 149,
219, 255
II: 112, 113, 124, 150, 155, 169,
195, 208, 214, 218
III: 51, 147, 149, 196, 203, 236,
257

slothful, slothfulness
I: 148, 149, 152, 222, 225, 248,
249
II: 6, 65, 96, 107, 108, 112, 154,
155, 177, 178, 179, 201, 202
III: 37, 38, 85, 86, 87, 118, 165

Solomon (King)
I: 1, 3, 7, 83, 89, 110, 225
II: 1, 3, 52, 142, 157
III: 1, 3, 37, 39, 65, 79, 215, 244,
245, 255

sovereign, sovereignty
I: 5, 44, 97, 118, 126, 159, 160,
186, 220, 227, 236, 239, 254,
255
II: 10, 15, 53, 73, 74, 76, 87, 103,
140, 141, 149, 150, 184, 196,
205, 208, 211
III: 36, 82, 97, 120, 135, 137, 141,
152, 162, 170, 177, 193, 201,
207, 209, 231, 232, 272, 290

Stalin, Joseph
I: 12, 129
III: 29, 30, 139, 158, 178

Stanley, Dr. Thomas
I: 144, 145
II: 96
III: 130, 131

suicide
I: 44, 70, 79, 157, 190, 226
II: 245, 246
III: 97, 161, 202, 251
Switzerland. *See European Countries*

T

temptation
I: 11, 46, 48, 49, 50, 52, 63, 64,
66, 68, 69, 74, 87, 89, 115,
136, 144, 159, 175, 248
II: 10, 21, 65, 69, 86, 99, 203,
217, 221, 244
III: 7, 10, 15, 16, 38, 74, 89, 94,
107, 191, 222, 267
theology
I: 2, 152
II: 2, 120, 200, 201
III: 2, 26, 27, 40, 41, 219
tongue
I: 44, 45, 57, 62, 96, 99, 100, 101,
104, 119, 131, 132, 139, 140,
142, 143, 144, 186, 227, 230
II: 7, 29, 38, 43, 52, 63, 64, 76,
78, 95, 134, 152, 155, 175,
177, 233
III: 50, 60, 61, 77, 98, 119, 167,
198, 241, 243, 265, 266, 267
training
I: 6, 91, 181, 183
II: 6, 191, 193
tyranny
I: 3, 44, 75, 76, 97, 112, 123, 208
II: 3, 17, 85
III: 3, 108, 138, 140, 153, 180,
181, 191, 212, 251
tyrant
I: 97, 113, 204, 224
II: 146, 174, 176, 204, 211, 216,
224
III: 22, 24, 30, 134, 137, 139, 152,
155, 157, 158, 159, 160, 177,
250, 251

U

understanding
I: 1, 7, 8, 15, 16, 17, 18, 21, 23,
24, 27, 28, 35, 37, 41, 46, 60,
62, 64, 69, 70, 72, 73, 80, 85,
86, 87, 94, 102, 113, 127, 136,
165, 171, 172, 214, 217, 222,
237, 242, 250, 258, 263
II: 1, 19, 25, 50, 55, 56, 57, 59,
82, 88, 92, 107, 108, 118, 119,
122, 167, 168, 181, 183, 236
III: 1, 8, 9, 10, 37, 40, 74, 78, 118,
137, 143, 151, 158, 184, 201,
210, 215, 217, 255, 268
United Nations
II: 103, 189

V

vagabond
II: 58
III: 108
values
I: 27, 53, 134, 137, 161, 163, 173,
176, 192, 198, 233, 250
II: 15, 35, 121, 185, 244
III: 36, 95

W

Washington, George. *See American
Presidents*
wealth
I: 25, 27, 48, 49, 69, 72, 91, 93,
97, 99, 105, 117, 120, 121,
125, 134, 136, 137, 145, 149,
155, 160, 161, 163, 165, 166,
179, 180, 210, 213, 220, 233,
244, 254, 255
II: 20, 27, 35, 36, 37, 38, 55, 56,
57, 65, 66, 67, 68, 79, 80, 85,
90, 105, 106, 137, 155, 162,
163, 172, 185, 186, 187, 212,
213, 219, 232
III: 96, 104, 131, 144, 147, 148,
151, 152, 164, 172, 178, 195,
236, 274

wealthy
   I: 134, 165, 246
   II: 22, 36, 39, 67, 79, 85, 155,
      190, 191, 195, 205, 217, 219
   III: 151
Whitefield, George
   I: 93
   III: 244
wife
   I: 1, 13, 19, 50, 51, 52, 62, 64, 72,
      102, 105, 116, 117, 130, 131,
      133, 228, 255, 257
   II: 1, 69, 70, 72, 78, 94, 95, 96,
      98, 121, 151, 166, 196, 211,
      213, 221, 237
   III: 1, 9, 30, 33, 34, 49, 56, 61, 72,
      103, 109, 111, 119, 120, 132,
      133, 155, 180, 212, 222, 237,
      243, 245, 249, 252, 253, 254,
      255, 257, 258, 260, 262, 263,
      270, 271
wine
   I: 24, 25, 40, 80
   II: 168, 217, 232, 243, 244
   III: 20, 65, 95, 222, 246, 247, 249,
      250
worldviews
   I: 171
   II: 9, 65, 66, 79, 110, 162, 226
   III: 39, 40, 69, 71, 75, 85, 163,
      219, 228
worship
   I: 4, 9, 13, 16, 37, 38, 66, 86, 100,
      152, 161, 171, 196, 209, 214,
      225, 232, 234, 236, 246, 264,
      265
   II: 4, 21, 68, 83, 94, 104, 121,
      122, 152, 153, 154, 163, 172,
      179, 181, 187, 193, 227, 232
   III: 4, 7, 80, 101, 115, 146, 149,
      154, 212, 213, 262
Wurmbrand, Richard
   II: 162
   III: 30

Y
youth
   I: 19, 50, 51, 52, 56, 61, 66, 231
   II: 77, 127, 135, 148, 196, 234,
      241
   III: 16, 26, 164, 165, 219, 225,
      227

SCRIPTURE INDEX

Genesis

2:16	I: 24
3:5	III: 193
6:2	I: 63
	III: 271
6:13	III: 18
9:6	II: 158
	III: 18, 161
18:20	II:180
19:5	II:180
26:8	III: 90
50:20	II: 150

Exodus

1:15–22	III: 157
18:21	II: 133
	III: 160, 251
20:1	III: 196
20:5	I: 35
20:6	I: 128
20:9	III: 163
21:12: 14	III: 18, 161
21:18–21	II: 176
21:24	II: 226
21:28: 30	III: 252
21:29	III: 28
22:1–4	II: 145, 158
22:2	II: 167
22:22–24	II: 210
22:22: 27	III: 146
30:15	II: 62

Leviticus

5:1	III: 210
18:22	II: 180
18:27	II: 180
20:13	II: 180
23:22	III: 172
24:17: 21	III: 161
25:35: 37	III: 146

Numbers

35:31	III: 18

Deuteronomy

4:21	III: 143
5	II: 246
5:19	II: 128
5:32	I: 44
6:7	I: 179, 210,
	II: 231, 235
	III: 112, 196, 219
6:7–9	III: 174
7:10	I: 239
14:28: 29	III: 172, 260
15	II: 194
15:4–7	III: 146
17:8–13	III: 72
19:9–13	III: 18
19:11–13	II: 167
19:16–18	II: 85
21:18–21	II: 45
22:10–11	III: 68

22:17–20	III: 49
22:25	II: 167
23:19–20	III: 146
24:19	I: 221
25:1–3	II: 226
25:3	III: 72
26:12	I: 221
27	I: 127
27–28	II: 194
28	I: 127
28:14	I: 44
28:64	III: 108
32:4	III: 196
32:15	III: 196
32:35	II: 138

Joshua

1:7	I: 44
23:6	I: 44

Judges

4:21	III: 266
16:27	III: 90
19:22	II: 180

1 Samuel

3:11–14	III: 176
8:10–18	I: 179
8:11: 18	III: 173
15:22	II: 152
16:7	III: 94
23	III: 103

2 Samuel

1:17–27	II: 39
23:1–2	III: 251
24	I: 24

1 Kings

3:1–10	III: 215
2:11	II: 146
12:14	III: 159
21:1: 13	III: 157

Nehemiah

4:14	I: 24
	III: 266
5:15	I: 3
	II: 3
	III: 3

Esther

7:1–6	III: 190

Job

1:21	II: 187

Psalms

14	I: 128
14:1	I: 140
	III: 68
15:5	III: 146
19:8	III: 194
19:10	III: 145
27:13	I: 13, 127
33:9	III: 82
33:10–11	II: 103
34:8	III: 222
34:11	II: 230
34:18	I: 260
36:8	I: 81
37	I: 127, 221, 162
	III: 174
37:21	I: 31
44:18	I: 200

51:5	III: 196	5:22	III: 198
51:3–5	II: 123	6	I: 53–64
72	III: 195	6:1	II: 131
72:12–14	III: 195	6:1–5	I: 115
89:4	III: 195	6:5	II: 51
89:29	III: 195	6:19	I: 190
89:36	III: 195	7	I: 65–69
90	III: 209	7:27	I: 254
94:6–7	III: 24	8	I: 69–80
95:8: 11	III: 106	8:36	III: 249
111:10	I: 210	9	I: 80–89
112:1–2	I: 128, 197	9:8	I: 240
112:1	I: 236	9:10	I: 85
127:4: 5	III: 266	10	I: 89–106
127:5	III: 136	10:1	III: 215
128:1–2	I: 128	10:2	I: 110
133	I: 59	10:8	III: 77
139:21	I: 59	10:11	I: 231
139:23–24	I: 230		III: 198
		10:19	III: 265
Proverbs		10:23	III: 90
1	I: 7–14	10:24	I: 110, 120, 222
1:1	III: 215		III: 198
1:1–4	I: 3	10:25	I: 106, 222
	II: 3	10:28	I: 222
	III: 3	10:30	I: 222
1:7	I: 2, 3, 140, 210,	11	I: 107–127
	II: 2, 3, 216	11:1	II: 18
	III: 2, 3, 272	11:2	III: 162
2	I: 15–21	11:5	II: 131
2:16	I: 46	11:15	II: 51
3	I: 21–35	11:17	I: 125
3:5–6	III: 162	11:18	III: 198
3:7	I: 215	11:23	I: 222
3:33	I: 197	11:30	II: 222
4	I: 35–45	12	I: 127–154
4:19	III: 198	12:6	III: 198
5	I: 47–52	12:7	I: 190, 197, 222

12:10	III: 207	19	II: 81–113
12:14	II: 76	19:3	II: 204
12:15	III: 77	19:5	II: 90
12:23	III: 77	19–12	II: 115
12:25	III: 168	19:25	II: 161
13	I: 154–183	20	II: 113–149
13:1	I: 34, 240	20:2	II: 93
13:8	I: 211	20:10	II: 139
13:10	I: 96	20	II: 149–184
	III: 208	21:1	II: 73
13:14	II: 25	21:9	II: 171
13:16	III: 77	21:15	II: 144
13:18	I: 232	21:18–21	III: 247
14	I: 184–226	21:24	I: 34, 240
14:6	I: 240	22	II: 185–216
14:9	I: 194	22:15	II: 227
14:12	II: 27	23	II: 217–247
14:17	I: 218	23:14	I: 254
14:26	I: 245	23:17	I: 3,
15	I: 227–266		II: 3
15:5	III: 77		III: 3
15:12	I: 34, 240, 241	24:3	I: 78
15:15	I: 243	25:1	III: 215
15:28–29	III: 198	26:12	III: 204
16	II: 7–35	26:13	II: 107
16:2	II: 151	26:20	II: 116
16:7	II: 105	26:22	I: 242
16:14	II: 115	28:2	I: 3
16:17–18	III: 127		II: 3
16:18	III: 162		III: 3
16:33	II: 73	28:26	III: 77, 208
17	II: 35–57	29:2	I: 232
17:10	III: 77	30:11–14	II: 108
17:12	III: 77	31:30	I: 63
17:13	II: 48		
17–21	II: 56	*Ecclesiastes*	
18	II: 58–81	3:4	I: 242
18:7	III: 77	5:2	III: 204

5:4–5	II: 142
9:7	III: 184
9:14–16	III: 238
9:15	I: 78
12:4	III: 83

Song of Songs

2:7	III: 234
8:4	III: 234

Isaiah

3:12	III: 263
8:19–20	III: 218
9:7	III: 195
11:4	III: 195
25:6	I: 81
28:28–29	II: 144
45:7	III: 70
46:11	III: 100
52:7	III: 62
55:8–9	III: 43
57:20	III: 222
66:5	I: 170

Jeremiah

13:23	III: 129
17:9	II: 231
	III: 171
22:13–17	I: 31

Lamentations

5:19	III: 195

Ezekiel

18:21–22	III: 162
18:32	III: 162
31:16	III: 162

Micah

2:8	II: 166

Malachi

2:14	II: 142
2:16	III: 198

Matthew

2:11–18	III: 157
3:12	III: 125
4:17	I: 128
5	III: 15
5:6	II: 99
5:9	III: 187
5:12	I: 244
5:17–19	III: 141
5:23–24	II: 75
5:30	II: 218
6:2	III: 65
6:30–33	II: 173
6:33	II: 172
	II: 199
7:1–3	III: 210
7:6	II: 143
7:7–8	I: 122
7:21–23	I: 235
7:27	III: 162
10:14	III: 188
10:28	III: 136, 211
10:29	III: 82
12:36	III: 83
12:36–37	III: 241
13:28–29	II: 144
15	III: 143, 219
15:4	II: 45
	III: 149, 169, 227
15:5–8	III: 247

15:8	II: 135	18:7–8	II: 139
15:5–6	I: 179	18:10–11	I: 193
16:26	I: 264	19:1–10	III: 98
18:8	III: 125	22:25–26	II: 36
18:15	I: 100, 142	22:30	I: 81
18:15–17	II: 92		
18:17	III: 248	*John*	
19:12	III: 142	1:3	III: 217
23	III: 51, 186	2:1–11	III: 247
23:27	III: 162	3:18	I: 129
25:41	III: 125	6	I: 237
25:46	III: 125	6:44	II: 141
26:11	I: 221	6:53	I: 81
26:52	II: 45	7:45	III: 190
28:18–20	I: 213	8:1–11	III: 210
	II: 172	8:36	I: 125
	III: 176		III: 147
28:20	I: 225	10:27	I: 236
		15	I: 238
Mark		5:1–15	II: 87
2:15	I: 81	15:13	III: 105
3:14	I: 81		
3:29	III: 125	*Acts*	
7:21–23	III: 162	2:23	II: 7
9:43–48	III: 125		III: 217
		2:42	I: 80
Luke		2:46: 47	III: 53
3:17	III: 125	5:1–5	II: 120
5:30	I: 81	5:35	III: 190
6:3	II: 82	9:2	I: 153
7:47	I: 193	15:20	I: 135
10:25–37	III: 190	16:17	I: 153
10:33ff	I: 221		III: 162
12:19–20	I: 123	16:31	III: 219
14:8–10	III: 42	17:30	II: 163
14:31	III: 12		II: 189
16:25	I: 244	17:31	II: 143
16:29–31	III: 74	18:2–3	III: 253

18:25–26	III: 162
18:26	I: 18, 153
19:9	III: 163
19:23	I: 153
	III: 163
20:21	III: 163
22:4	I: 153
24:14	I: 153
24:22	I: 153
26:20	III: 163

Romans

1:9	III: 78
1:17	III: 163
1:18	III: 273
1:19–21	III: 156
1:21	I: 225
2:25	III: 58
3	I: 237
3:4	III: 171
3:10	I: 128
3:10–18	III: 116
3:11	III: 234
3:22	I: 91
4:12	III: 163
5:12	III: 71
6:23	III: 165
7:12	I: 170, 224
	III: 177
8:1–2	III: 273
8:18	I: 244
8:28	I: 146
9:10ff	II: 53, 141
9:13	III: 176
10	II: 181
10:6–10	I: 69
10:14	I: 212
	III: 78

10:14ff	II: 204
10:15	I: 212
	II: 77
	III: 62
11:36	III: 209
12:1–2	III: 162
12:2	II: 82, 181
12:19	II: 138
13	II: 46
13:1–4	III: 18
13:1–8	II: 112
13:4	II: 144
13:4–6	I: 31
13:4–7	III: 28
13:8	I: 31
13:15	I: 95
14:17	II: 35
14:19	III: 187

1 Corinthians

1:19–21	III: 238
1:26	III: 144
1:26–31	II: 145
2:14	III: 78, 81, 129, 189
2:9–14	II: 55
3:12	I: 75
3:17	I: 59
5	I: 238
5:11	I: 242
6:9–10	II: 229
7	III: 219
7:15	III: 187
7:21–23	II: 194
	III: 257
7:36	III: 132
9:5	III: 132
9:18	III: 78

10:16–17	I: 81
10:16–20	I: 80
11:5ff	II: 40
11:18ff	I: 81
13:1: 2	II: 105
13:13	I: 245
14:24–25	III: 80
14:34	III: 235
15:14	III: 78
15:19–20	III: 265
15:26	III: 229

2 Corinthians

3:17	III: 257
4:3–4	II: 126
4:4	I: 202
4:4: 6	III: 129, 189
4:16	I: 242
5:7	III: 163, 171
6:14	I: 11
7:11	I: 203
9	II: 179

Galatians

2:7	III: 78
3:11	III: 163
3:28	II: 88
5:21–24	III: 177
5:24	I: 147
6:1	I: 100, 142
	III: 89
6:2	I: 31, 195
6:5	I: 195
6:7	III: 122
6:7–8	II: 196
6:8	I: 201
6:10	I: 31
	II: 179

Ephesians

2:1–2	III: 81
2:8–9	III: 162
2:8–10	I: 179
4:1	II: 120
4:1–4	I: 59
4:28	II: 178
4:32	III: 207
5:11	III: 124
5:15	III: 171
5:19–20	II: 179
5:21: 22	III: 273
5:23	I: 24
5:25	I: 24
5:28	I: 24
6:1–2	III: 196
6:4	I: 2, 24, 36, 210, II: 2, 192, 226, 231
6:4	III: 2, 112, 207, 219, 262
6:5: 6	III: 48
6:14	I: 159

Philippians

2:8–9	II: 152
2:11–12	I: 179
2:12–13	II: 225
	III: 209
4:5–7	II: 193
4:8	I: 228

Colossians

1:30	I: 73
3:23–25	III: 48

1 Thessalonians

2:11	I: 36
	III: 262

2 Thessalonians

2:10	II: 87
3:6ff	II: 177
3:7–10	I: 249
3:10	II: 28

1 Timothy

1:8	I: 170
2:8	I: 24
2:9	I: 88
	III: 262
2:9–15	I: 24
2:11–12	III: 43
3	III: 219
3:1–5	III: 112
3:4–5	III: 263
3:6	III: 78
3:9	III: 78
3:10	III: 9
3:16	III: 78
4:13	III: 78
5:6–8	II: 235
5:8	I: 24, 55, 249
	III: 132, 164
5:8ff	II: 87
5:9ff	I: 221
5:14	III: 254
5:17	III: 78
6:1–2	III: 48
6:6	II: 219
6:6	III: 222
6:23	II: 220

2 Timothy

2:22	I: 33
3:7	I: 243
3:16–17	II: 181

4:2	III: 78
4:3–4	III: 99

Titus

1:11	III: 99
2:1–10	I: 263
2:3–5	I: 24
	III: 269
2:4	III: 254
2:4–5	III: 257
2:4–6	III: 90
3:10	I: 248, II: 116

Hebrews

1:3	III: 82
1:8	III: 196
3:7–10	III: 106
3:13	I: 196
	III: 251
6:4	II: 237
6:4–6	II: 238
6:1–6	III: 163
10:30	II: 138
10:31	III: 135, 156
11:6	II: 227
11:33	III: 17
12:6–8	III: 207
12:28	I: 215
13:2	II: 88
13:15–16	II: 152, 179

James

1:5	I: 76
1:19	II: 92, 119
	III: 204
1:19–20	I: 204
1:22	I: 210
1:22–23	III: 269

1:27	I: 208
	III: 172
1:29	II: 152
2:1–6	I: 207
2:5	I: 207
	III: 185
3:2–10	III: 241
3:6	II: 29, 76, 175
3:17	II: 23
4:1–3	II: 197
4:15	II: 15
5:4	I: 31
4:13–15	III: 100
5:14–16	I: 219
5:20	I: 85

1 Peter

1:6	III: 184
1:12	III: 78
1:17–22	III: 273
1:25	III: 78
2:7	III: 273
3:1–2	III: 120
3:3	I: 88
3:3–4	III: 262
3:4	III: 43
3:15	I: 74, 210, 265
	II: 190
4:6	III: 78
5:5	III: 162
5:5–7	II: 273
5:6	I: 164

2 Peter

2:10	III: 186
2:19–20	III: 83
2:22	I: 242

1 John

1:9	III: 155
2:9–11	III: 198
2:14–16	III: 126
2:19	I: 238
3:4	I: 224
3:11	I: 95
3:16	III: 105
3:17	III: 111
4:19	I: 237
4:20	I: 236
5:4	III: 211

2 John

1:4	I: 153

3 John

1:4	I: 153

Jude

6	III: 125
13	III: 125
21–23	I: 218

Revelation

2	I: 238
2:3	I: 86, 255
2:1–8	III: 187
6:10	II: 138
12:11	III: 136
13:7	III: 190
14:6	II: 12
14:6–7	III: 273
21:4	I: 199
21:8	II: 89
	III: 162
22:15	II: 89

Topical Index

A

abominations to God: 3:32, 11:1–2, 12:22, 15:9, 15:26, 16:5, 17:15, 20:1, 20:23, 21:27, 28:9

adultery: 5:1, 6:25, 7:1, 22:14, 23:27, 27:8, 29:3, 30:20

advice: 11:14, 12:15, 13:10, 15:22, 19:20, 20:18, 24:6

C

calmness: 12:16, 13:11, 13:16, 14:15, 14:30, 15:28, 16:17, 17:27, 18:17, 19:2, 19:18, 20:18, 20:25, 21:29, 22:3, 23:1, 24:6, 25:16

correction: 9:8, 12:1, 13:18, 15:5, 15:10, 15:12, 17:10, 19:20, 19:25, 23:9, 25:12, 27:5–6, 27:17, 28:23, 29:1, 29:15

corruption: 15:27, 17:8, 17:23, 18:16, 28:16

D

diligence: 10:4–5, 11:16, 12:11, 12:24, 12:27, 13:4, 13:11, 14:23, 20:13, 21:5, 22:29, 24:27, 28:19, 31:13

discipline (receiving): 3:11, 10:17, 13:18, 13:24, 15:5, 19:18, 19:25, 20:30, 22:15, 23:13, 27:6, 29:15, 29:17

discipline for children: 13:24, 22:6, 22:15, 23:13, 29:15, 29:17, 29:21

double standard: 11:1, 17:15, 18:5, 20:10, 20:23, 24:24, 28:6, 28:21, 29:7

E

envy: 3:31, 14:30, 24:1, 24:19

evil desires: 10:3, 13:2, 18:1, 21:25, 21:26, 23:29, 24:1

excess: 12:11, 20:1, 21:17, 23:2, 23:29, 28:7, 28:19, 31:4

F

falsehood: 6:12, 10:18, 11:3, 11:20, 13:7, 15:4, 16:28, 16:30, 17:20, 18:19, 20:14, 22:5, 26:24, 28:13, 28:23, 29:5

fear of God: 1:7, 8:13, 9:10, 10:27, 14:2, 14:16, 14:26, 14:27, 15:16, 15:33, 16:6, 19:23, 22:4, 23:17, 24:21, 28:14, 29:25, 31:30

folly: 10:23, 12:23, 14:1, 14:7, 17:12, 18:2, 18:6, 26:1, 27:22, 29:9

forgiveness: 10:12, 16:6, 16:7, 17:9, 17:14, 19:11, 20:3

friends: 17:17, 18:24, 27:9, 27:10

G

generosity: 11:24–25, 11:26, 14:21, 19:6, 19:17, 19:22, 21:26, 22:9, 28:27, 31:20

gloating: 17:5, 24:17

God's authority: 10:22, 16:1–2, 16:9, 17:3, 19:21, 20:24, 21:2, 21:31, 26:2, 29:26, 30:6

God´s sovereignty: 10:22, 15:3, 15:11, 16:1, 16:4, 16:9, 16:33, 17:3, 19:21, 20:12, 20:24, 20:27, 21:1, 21:2, 21:30, 21:31, 22:2, 24:12, 29:13, 30:4

godlessness: 10:23, 10:28, 11:5, 11:20, 12:6, 12:10, 12:12, 12:20, 13:19, 14:11, 15:12, 15:26, 17:4, 17:11, 17:23, 19:3, 19:27, 21:4, 21:1, 28:1

good/bad company: 1:10, 13:20, 15:12, 15:31, 16:19 ,16:29, 22:5, 22:24, 24:1, 24:21, 28:7, 29:16, 29:24

goodness: 11:17, 14:22, 31:12

gossip: 10:18, 11:13, 16:28, 18:8, 20:19, 25:9, 25:23, 26:20, 30:10

greed: 10:3, 11:6, 11:24, 11:26, 13:4, 15:27, 23:4, 23:6, 27:20, 28:8, 28:22, 28:25, 28:27, 29:24, 30:15

H

haste: 12:16, 14:15, 15:18, 18:13, 19:2, 20:25, 21:5, 22:24, 25:8, 28:20, 28:22, 29:11, 29:20, 29:22

hate: 10:12, 15:17

heart: 4:23, 12:5, 12:25, 13:12, 14:10, 14:13, 14:30, 15:11, 15:13, 15:15, 15:3, 17:22, 18:14, 20:5, 21:8, 22:11, 27:19, 28:14

honesty: 10:29, 11:1, 11:3, 11:11, 14:2, 14:9, 14:11, 16:11, 16:13, 19:1, 20:7, 21:8, 21:29, 28:6, 28:16, 28:18, 29:10

hot-tempered man: 12:16, 14:16, 14:17, 14:29, 15:18, 19:3, 19:19, 22:24, 23:17, 24:19, 29:11, 29:22, 30:33

household: 11:29, 12:10, 14:1, 15:6, 24:3, 24:27, 27:23, 27:25, 28:19, 31:15, 31:27

humility: 11:2, 12:23, 15:31, 15:33, 18:12, 22:4, 25:7, 29:23

J

judgement: 11:4, 11:7, 11:21, 11:31, 12:2, 13:9, 15:10, 15:25, 16:4–5, 17:11, 19:29, 20:20, 21:13, 21:16, 22:22, 23:18, 24:12, 24:22, 26:26

L

language: 10:11, 10:19, 10:31, 10:32, 11:9, 12:14, 12:18, 12:23, 12:25, 13:3, 14:3, 15:1–2, 15:4, 15:23, 15:26, 15:28, 16:22, 16:24, 17:7, 17:20, 17:27–28, 18:7, 18:13, 18:21, 20:19, 21:23, 24:26, 25:11, 25:20, 25:27, 27:14, 29:20, 30:32, 31:26

lazyness: 6:6, 10:4–5, 10:26, 11:16, 12:24, 12:27, 13:4, 15:19, 18:9, 19:15, 19:24, 20:4, 20:13, 21:25, 22:13, 24:10, 24:30, 26:13, 31:27

leadership: 11:14, 16:10, 16:12, 20:26, 20:28, 22:10, 25:5, 28:3, 28:15–16, 29:4, 29:12, 29:14

lies: 3:28, 12:17, 12:19, 12:22, 13:5, 14:5, 14:25, 17:4, 17:7, 19:5, 19:9, 20:17, 21:6, 21:28, 25:18, 26:18, 29:12, 30:7

love: 10:12, 15:17, 16:6, 17:9, 17:17, 18:24, 27:6

lust: 29:3, 30:19, 31:3

M

marriage: 5:15, 12:4, 18:22, 21:9, 21:19, 25:24, 31:11, 31:23, 31:28

mercilessness: 18:23, 21:10, 21:13, 24:29, 28:3, 30:14

mercy: 14:31, 19:17, 19:22, 22:9, 24:11, 25:21, 28:8, 31:8

mocking: 14:6, 17:5, 24:9, 30:17

N

neighbor: 3:27, 3:29, 11:9, 11:12, 14:21, 25:17, 25:20, 27:14, 31:8

O

obedience: 1:8, 13:13, 16:20, 19:16, 19:27, 23:22, 28:7, 29:18, 29:19, 30:17

P

parents: 1:8, 10:1, 13:1, 15:5, 15:20, 17:6, 19:26, 20:20, 23:22, 28:24, 30:11, 30:17, 31:1

partnerships and securities: 6:1, 11:15, 17:18, 20:16, 22:26, 27:13

patience: 10:28, 14:29, 15:18, 16:32, 19:11, 20:22, 21:28, 24:16, 25:15

peace: 12:20, 15:16, 17:1

planning: 15:22, 15:26, 16:1, 16:3, 16:9

poverty: 14:20, 14:31, 16:26, 17:5, 19:1, 19:22, 22:2, 22:22, 23:21, 28:27, 29:7, 29:13, 30:8, 31:8, 31:20

prayer: 15:8, 15:29, 28:9

pride: 10:17, 11:2, 12:1, 13:1, 13:10, 13:13, 13:18, 15:1, 15:25, 15:32, 16:5, 16:18, 16:19, 17:19, 18:12, 19:16, 21:4, 21:24, 25:6, 27:1, 27:2, 28:9, 28:26, 29:1, 29:23, 30:6, 30:13

prudence: 10:5, 14:4, 15:6, 20:4, 30:25, 31:21

Q

quarrels: 13:10, 15:1, 15:18, 17:1, 17:11, 17:14, 17:19, 18:6, 18:19, 19:13, 20:3, 21:9, 21:19, 26:17, 26:20, 26:21, 27:15, 29:22, 30:33

R

reaction of others: 10:7, 11:10, 28:12, 28:28, 29:2, 29:27

reliability: 11:13, 13:17, 17:2, 20:6, 22:29, 24:27, 25:13, 27:18, 27:23, 28:20

restraint: 15:16, 15:17, 16:8, 16:19, 17:1, 23:2–4, 25:16, 25:27, 28:25, 30:7, 31:4

revenge: 12:28, 20:22, 24:29

righteousness: 2:9, 11:19, 13:5, 13:6,
15:8, 15:9, 16:7, 16:8, 16:13,
16:17, 21:3, 21:21, 24:16

reward: 10:3, 11:8, 11:17, 11:18,
11:21, 11:25, 11:27, 11:31,
12:14, 12:21, 12:26, 13:21,
14:14, 14:22, 15:24, 16:7, 16:18,
17:11, 17:13, 19:17, 19:23,
20:17, 20:21, 21:21, 22:8–9,
24:20, 25:22, 26:27

riches: 10:2, 10:16, 11:4, 11:16,
11:28, 13:11, 14:20, 15:16,
15:27, 16:8, 16:19, 18:11, 19:4,
20:21, 21:6, 22:2, 23:4–5, 28:6,
28:11, 28:16, 28:20, 28:22, 30:8

S

seduction: 1:11, 28:10

seeking after righteousness: 10:14,
10:28, 11:23, 11:27, 14:8, 14:16,
15:9, 15:14, 16:17, 17:24, 18:10,
18:15, 18:17, 19:8, 21:21, 21:29,
22:11, 23:19, 24:6, 24:14, 28:5

self-assessment: 3:7, 12:15, 14:12,
16:2, 16:25, 18:11, 19:21, 20:6,
20:9, 21:2, 21:23, 25:6, 26:12,
26:16, 27:2, 28:11, 30:12, 30:20

self-control: 10:19, 11:12, 13:3,
16:32, 17:28, 23:2, 25:28, 30:32

son: 10:1, 13:1, 15:20, 17:6, 17:21,
17:25, 19:13, 19:26–27, 23:24,
29:3, 29:15, 29:17, 31:28

T

teachability: 3:11, 9:9, 10:8, 10:17,
12:1, 13:1, 13:10, 13:18, 15:5,
15:31, 15:32, 16:20, 17:10,
21:11, 23:12, 28:9, 29:1, 29:9

transitoriness: 23:5

trusting God: 3:5, 10:29, 11:28,
14:26, 16:3, 16:20, 18:10, 28:25,
28:26, 29:25, 30:5

truth: 12:17, 12:19, 14:5, 14:25

V

violence: 10:11, 12:6, 14:31, 16:29,
18:23, 21:7, 22:16, 22:22, 28:3,
29:10, 29:13, 29:22, 30:14

W

wisdom: 1:1, 3:13, 8:1, 10:8, 12:15,
16:16, 16:21, 19:20, 21:11, 28:5,
28:26, 30:26

women: 5:15, 11:16, 11:22, 12:4,
14:1, 18:22, 19:13–14, 21:9,
21:19, 22:14, 25:24, 27:15,
30:20, 31:10, 31:3

To order other Family Bible Study Guides,

go to GenerationswithVision.com, call 1-888-839-6132,

or send an e-mail to mail@generationswithvision.com

The Bible is the Core Curriculum in the education of a child.
If we provide our children excellent academic instruction
in mathematics, science, and grammar, but neglect to teach
them Genesis, Psalms, Proverbs, and the Gospels, we have
failed in the education of our children.